ROBERT E. SIBSON

Since 1960, the author has been president of Sibson & Co., Inc., a management consulting firm with headquarters in Princeton, N.J. His organization focuses its consulting services in the areas of employee relations, strategic business planning, and general management for professional services enterprises. Prior to that, Mr. Sibson was personnel manager of the Raytheon Company's Government Equipment Division; personnel director of Schick Inc.; assistant to the director of industrial relations of the Otis Elevator Co.; and associate labor relations consultant with Simpson and Curtin of Philadelphia.

D1060918

COMPENSATION

COMPENSATION

Robert E. Sibson

A complete revision of
WAGES and SALARIES

amacom
A division of American Management Associations

571753

Harriet Irving Library
JUL 6 1978
University of New Brunswick

Library of Congress Cataloging in Publication Data

Sibson, Robert Earl, 1925-
Compensation; a complete revision of Wages and salaries;

1. Wages. 2. Job evaluation. I. Title.
HD4909.S52 1974 658.32'2 73-91604
ISBN 0-8144-5358-9

© 1960, 1967, 1974 AMACOM
A Division of American Management Associations, New York.
Compensation is a second revision of *Wages and Salaries,* originally published in 1960 and revised in 1967.

All rights reserved. Printed in the United States of America.

This publication may not be reproduced, stored in a retrieval system, or transmitted in whole or in part, in any form or by any means, electronic, mechanical, photocopying, recording, or otherwise, without the prior written permission of AMACOM.

International standard book number: 0–8144–5358–9
Library of Congress catalog card number: 73–91604

Fifth printing

To SALLY W. SIBSON

first partner in Sibson & Company, Inc.
first collaborator on this book, and
first everything else since 1950.

INTRODUCTION

a Friend of
Shar
IRTeap
m

THE COMPLEXITIES of pay administration in the modern business firm, and the problems it poses to management, have been well recognized. A periodic survey of senior line and staff executives, for instance, conducted by Sibson & Company (now covering over 400 executives and 237 companies) clearly shows that an overwhelming number of executives consider compensation the second most difficult personnel problem, both for their companies and for themselves.*

There is every indication that the complexities and therefore the time and cost involved in pay administration will continue to increase. These increasing complexities are due to the increasing number and diversity of positions which typically exist in enterprises. The greater technology and diversity of activities inherent in these proliferating positions further complicate the matter. Still other factors that contribute to the complexity of pay administration include the phenomenon of steadily rising incomes, the continued complexity of and change in tax laws, Internal Revenue Service regulations, and Accounting Principles Board regulations. New factors include the growing pressures for change arising from the changing expectations and attitudes of

* The first order of priority in employee relations identified by nine in ten general management executives is, simply, how to increase the productivity of employees at every level of the organization.

younger members of the work force. Some form of government control or guidance in pay matters may also be a regular part of pay administration.

It must be recognized that some form of compensation program cannot be avoided, for wherever the employee-employer relationship exists, there must be some system of pay administration to determine the "right price" for the employee's services. In this sense, pay administration is a part of every enterprise's activities. The question is, therefore, not whether a company should have a compensation program but exactly what type of program is appropriate for that enterprise. It also means that some form of compensation program must be regarded as one of the costs of doing business.

Significant resources, of both time and money, must be allocated to a compensation program. The goal is to expend these resources judiciously, to get a business return from these expenditures, and to develop a program which is equitable to employees. To accomplish such a goal, the compensation program should, generally speaking, meet the following objectives:

- It should be structured so as to help attract and retain the numbers and kinds of employees required to operate the business. Both the levels and forms of compensation for each group of employees must be reasonably competitive with pay levels and practices that prevail in the various labor markets in which the enterprise competes.
- The program should help to maintain the company in a reasonably competitive position in its product market. The resulting level of compensation must not place the company in a noncompetitive cost situation.
- The nature of the program and the associated administrative time costs must be reasonable and must be in proportion to the other priorities and time demands on the company's financial resources and available management time.
- The program must gain employee acceptance. This does not necessarily mean that employees must "approve" pay actions, or that compensation policies and practices are somehow subject to popular referendum. It does mean that employees must understand the policies and practices and accept both their concepts and specific actions as being reasonable and impartially administered.
- The compensation program must play a positive role in motivating employees to perform their duties to the best of their abilities and in a manner which supports the achievement of enterprise goals.

- The program must gain acceptance by the firm's "public"—which includes owners and, increasingly, the government and to some extent customers, investors, and the general public.
- The compensation program must provide opportunity for employees at every level to achieve their reasonable aspirations in a framework of equity, impartiality, and reasonableness.

These objectives are fairly common to almost all enterprises. Additional goals could, of course, be identified in specific company situations. Much could be said about each of these objectives. At first look, they may seem self-evident. But to be meaningful to the enterprise they must be further articulated and translated from general statements to concrete guidelines for the development, administration, and audit of a compensation program.

These objectives for compensation administration programs involve not only problems in terms of articulation, use, and implementation but, in fact, potential contradictions. For example, compensation levels could be set high enough to facilitate the attraction of suitable employees at every level of the organization. In a growing company which must recruit significant numbers of employees from outside sources, this might require compensation levels 20 to 30 percent higher than average levels in the marketplace. The setting of this objective might well be contradictory to maintaining the company in a reasonably competitive position in its product markets.

A major task for any company—which requires relatively small amounts of time but has very significant impact on the successful development and administration of a compensation program—involves a realistic look at compensation objectives in the context of a company's own situation and its own business objectives. Specifically, this exercise—seldom employed—involves the articulation of concrete compensation objectives and strategies at a given period in a company's history that are sufficiently detailed to establish guidelines for staff specialists and line managers alike. In terms of the development of compensation programs, such statements of objectives are one of the essential inputs or design specifications for program development. The identification of objectives, tailored to the company's needs and situation, can also be a useful tool in day-to-day administration and decision making by staff executives and line managers.

The development of *objectives* can then be a major input to the creation of company compensation *policies*. These policies must clearly be more than a set of statements of intent, more than platitudinous and generalized statements of company conscience. They must genuinely serve the purpose of providing guidelines for program development, for day-to-day decision making, and for review and audit of the compensation program.

Without such compensation objectives and policies, the company and its individual managers are likely to be involved repeatedly in crises over pay questions. Even when management's actions are correct in terms of the practicalities of the moment, these crises usually involve excessive costs and, over a period of time, result in confusion, inequities, and trouble.

A third requirement for effective compensation administration is the use of appropriate pay methods and techniques. The goal here is not technical excellence per se but the use of those methods and techniques which are best tailored to the company's situation and best designed to implement the policies and meet the objectives of the enterprise. Some wage and salary specialists tend to be preoccupied with technical excellence and the cleverness of procedures. Technique itself, however, should not be the goal. Rather, methods must be designed to effectuate compensation policies, to assist managers in solving pay problems, and, in general, to facilitate the achievement of company objectives and employee expectations.

Because each company is unique in terms of its products, its organization, its policies and objectives, the background of its managers, its management style, its economic and operating characteristics, and many other factors, *there is no one best compensation program.* In general, people with canned answers—be they job evaluation plans or merit increase systems—are offering solutions that meet *their* needs. They are looking for questions that match *their* answers. They assume that all businesses are essentially alike, something every business manager knows is simply not the case. To fashion the most appropriate program for a given company, the staff expert must choose from among many sound and workable alternatives that set of techniques which is best tailored to his particular enterprise.

Finally, sound compensation administration involves excellence of execution. Execution includes planning, deciding, administering, and explaining pay action. The ideal for any enterprise is, of course, excellence of plan design plus excellence of execution. But in terms of accomplishing results, if there must be imperfections, let them be in the area of plan design, not in plan execution.

Essentially, line managers are responsible for execution. Staff specialists help by providing information, doing various mechanical jobs, and, most important, providing sound advice and counsel. But the keystone of excellent compensation administration is effective execution. It is for this reason that line managers must be well informed about the essentials of compensation administration and must be given the time to do the job. In part, their effectiveness as managers should be judged by how well they carry out their personnel responsibilities, including the execution of the compensation administration program.

The essential purpose of this book is to provide information about compensation administration which line managers need in order to meet their responsibilities. Obviously, a very large section of this book is designed to provide basic knowledge of compensation policies, practices, and techniques. Advanced technology, details of administration, methods of program design, and the specifics of legal requirements are omitted. It is presumed that line managers have available to them staff specialists who can provide these pieces of information and insight when required.

In addition, the book contains material designed to guide supervisors and managers in solving daily problems, and it presents some ideas and suggestions for improving their performance in compensation administration.

Concentration on the management aspects of applying a compensation program should not lead managers to think that the technical aspects are unimportant. Sound wage and salary administration requires sound policy guidance, sound conception of techniques, and comprehensive and accurate data and information input. As compensation administration continues to grow, the techniques will become increasingly complex and the input of the staff specialists will become more necessary than ever to the overall effectiveness of the program. However, with the assistance of qualified specialists, either from inside the company or from outside consulting firms, the line manager's primary concern is to use effectively the techniques he has. Stop.

The original edition of this book was based largely on a comprehensive study of wage and salary administration practices in fifteen leading companies; discussions with employees and line managers in Raytheon Company, Otis Elevator Company, Schick Incorporated, Armstrong Cork Company, and the Lancaster plant of RCA; and the extensive research information at American Management Associations. The present volume is a very considerable extension and thorough revision of that original work. Although almost nothing in this version contradicts information contained in the original volume published fourteen years ago, it reflects two important changes: first, the growth of knowledge and experience in compensation administration in the business community during the past fifteen years and, second, significantly greater experience by the author in helping more than 400 firms —in a consulting capacity—to design, administer, and review their compensation programs.

My primary indebtedness is to the clients of Sibson & Company, Inc. I am also indebted to my associates at Sibson & Company, because the information and knowledge contained in this book represent not only my personal experience but also the accumulated knowledge and experience of the firm.

Finally, behind every book is a worker—the one who types the manuscript, does the editing, and generally suffers a lot. The "hero's medal" for this work goes to Gail Van Aken, who would never have predicted two years ago, just after her graduation from Rider College, that she would be taking shorthand notes for the book while going down the runway in a 727 at Newark Airport.

Robert E. Sibson

CONTENTS

1 OBJECTIVES OF COMPENSATION ADMINISTRATION 1

2 ELEMENTS OF COMPENSATION 13

3 JOB INFORMATION 26

4 JOB EVALUATION 36

5 PRICING JOB VALUE 53

6 INDIVIDUAL PAY ACTIONS 66

7 APPRAISING PERFORMANCE 86

8 PLANNING, CONTROL, AND ADMINISTRATION 108

9 WAGE INCENTIVE PLANS 127

10 SALESMEN'S COMPENSATION 139

11 COMPENSATION OF PROFESSIONAL PERSONNEL 155

12 SUPERVISORY, TECHNICAL, AND ADMINISTRATIVE PERSONNEL 174

13 MANAGEMENT COMPENSATION 190

14 FRINGE BENEFITS 212

15 MANAGEMENT RESPONSIBILITY 226

INDEX 231

1

OBJECTIVES OF COMPENSATION ADMINISTRATION

COMPENSATION ADMINISTRATION is a management method which can be valuable to owners of the business, helpful to managers, and of importance to employees. Furthermore, compensation has received increasing attention from government agencies, not only in such traditional areas as administration of the Fair Labor Standards Act but in new areas of interest such as pay stabilization. Finally, the importance of employee pay to the economic health of the country makes compensation practices of increasing concern to the general public.

This book is primarily directed toward the interests of three of these principals: owners of the company, managers, and employees. These three groups are the direct participants in the enterprise. Collectively, they represent the company.

For the owners of the company, employee compensation represents a substantial part of the total costs of doing business. How well the company controls these costs, and how much employee productivity it obtains in return, can have an important effect on the success of the enterprise. In a company whose wage costs are a large percentage of total costs and whose products are services, wage costs and productivity are especially crucial elements of business success.

Similarly, the success of the individual manager in doing his job depends in part on wage costs and employee productivity in his department. Supervisors are frequently in the unique position of representing all three business groups: owners, managers, and employees. In addition to being managers, they often acquire stock—through stock options, stock purchase plans, thrift programs, or profit-sharing plans—and are therefore part of the owner group as well. Moreover, they are paid employees whose welfare is affected by the firm's pay program. This personal involvement should serve as a constant reminder, even to the most business-oriented manager, that the price of employee services represents income to employees as well as part of the cost of doing business.

Thus managers play a crucial and sometimes difficult role in compensation administration. Not only do managers' actions and decisions have a major impact on the success of the pay program, but the individual supervisor is often the focal point of conflicting interests of owners, managers, and employees.

For the individual employee, salary establishes a standard or style of living. It also represents an evaluation of his experience and ability. These two factors make pay levels—and pay progress—of paramount concern to employees.

The company's wage and salary program is therefore important to owners, managers, and employees alike. When the objectives of the three tend to be in conflict, the program may be an effective means of balancing the interests of these groups.

COMPANY OBJECTIVES

Within the limits established by government regulations and general labor market conditions, the company designs and administers the pay program. If nothing else, therefore, the pay program should meet the company's needs and objectives. Company objectives with respect to a compensation program may be viewed in terms of three levels of achievement: solving the pay problems of the enterprise, making a strategic contribution to the achievement of enterprise goals, and contributing to the development of the organization.

Solving the Pay Problems of the Business

Although pay problems vary considerably among different companies, and even among different departments in the same company, certain basic problem areas are common to most operations. Management recognition of the real problems of the business is the first step toward their solution.

One problem which exists in every enterprise is the question of pay relationships within the company. It is quite natural for employees to compare their pay with that received by fellow workers—indeed, this is the easiest income comparison for them to make. When they believe that inequities exist, they will tend to feel that they are underpaid or to suspect favoritism, and they will generally lose confidence in the company pay program.

Employees are also sensitive about pay levels for comparable work in other companies. Their knowledge of pay elsewhere is generally imperfect, but if they get the impression that their pay is lower, serious employee unrest will result. This problem not only influences employee attitudes but also affects the company's ability to attract and retain the number and kinds of employees it needs to operate efficiently. Moreover, since relative pay levels affect relative costs, they have a bearing on the company's ability to compete effectively in the product market.

Reward for outstanding work constitutes another important pay problem for employees and managers. People who perform more competently than others generally expect more money in return. Unless they get it, their desire to do more efficient work will very likely be diminished or destroyed altogether.

Finally, in most enterprises there is a broad range of pay problems that are essentially administrative in nature. These include:

- Establishment of policies, procedures, and practices which help managers to solve their daily pay problems and get rapid answers to problems outside their authority.
- Communication of pay information to supervisors and employees to promote understanding and gain reasonable acceptance of the company pay program.
- Maintenance of a proper balance among base pay, premium payments, fringe benefits, pay for time not worked, and various forms of indirect payments to employees.
- Maintenance of proper records and other data which managers need in order to make intelligent pay decisions.
- Compliance with various legal requirements.

Unless the company meets these problems realistically, it faces constant grievances and employee discontent which may lead to lowered productivity, greater turnover, and a decline in employee morale. Lowered productivity, particularly among management and professional employees, may be difficult to measure since it often manifests itself in subtle ways—indifference, indolence, politicking, or just plain loafing. If these problems become serious, it is likely to be the company's most effective workers who leave because they are typically more sensitive to inequities in pay and are better able to obtain positions elsewhere.

The effectiveness of compensation administration in terms of managerial performance (like the success of virtually any personnel activity) can be measured by three levels of achievement. The first—an essential criterion—is simply that the compensation program must avoid trouble. To achieve this, the compensation program must deal effectively with the pay problems of the firm. Otherwise the pay program will require unnecessary management time, will give rise to unconstructive discussion and debates, and will result in declining employee morale and lowered productivity. If a company fails to meet this first level of achievement, then the trouble caused by the inadequacies of the pay program represents a real detraction from enterprise success.

Even if the pay program succeeds in avoiding trouble it does not really add anything to the enterprise. It just avoids trouble and makes sure that compensation practices do not detract from enterprise success. Solving pay problems is, therefore, an essential level of achievement and a limited objective. Solutions usually involve spending large amounts of time and money to avoid trouble, correct past mistakes, adjust to changing circumstances, or meet one-time situations. Based on studies and experience, probably two out of every three companies of significant size meet this level of achievement.

Contributing to Business Success

There are, in every enterprise, opportunity situations as well as problem situations in compensation administration. The second objective of pay practices is to exploit such opportunities by developing pay programs that contribute to the goals of the business.

A simple example of how pay practices can exploit opportunities or add a strategic dimension to enterprise success is the handling of pay increases. Particularly in an inflationary economy, annual pay increases are critical to a large percentage of employees. The amounts of these increases must be reasonable, and the manner in which they are distributed must be equitable. Otherwise, the program will not succeed in meeting even the first level of achievement—solving pay problems. If, in addition, the pay program is such that employees

Table 1. **Solving pay problems: the value-cost concept.**

Response to Pay Problem	*Units of Time or Cost* *	*Units of Business Value (+) or Loss (−)* *
Do nothing	0	−100
Do the wrong thing	100	−100 or −200
Solve the problem	100	0
Contribute to business success	110	+100
Develop the organization	115	+200

* Numbers are illustrative only.

who are growing in their capabilities and are becoming more valuable to the company receive significantly greater increases than those who are not growing, then pay practices have added a strategic element of success to the enterprise. They have created a built-in financial incentive-reward system for employees.

As Table 1 shows, only incremental costs are usually involved in a compensation effort which exploits opportunities as well as solves problems. In a sense, these additional costs are an expense of the business, for they avoid detractions from company goals. But they can also be regarded as an investment—an investment which frequently yields extraordinary capital returns.

Developing the Organization

A third level of achievement possible in a pay program is organizational development.* To attain this third level of achievement, the company must make a somewhat greater investment in time and money over that necessary to obtain the second level of achievement. But as suggested in Table 1, the impact on enterprise success can be even greater than the impact of attaining the second level of achievement.

Returning to the example of pay increases, the organizational development dimension of pay administration might involve an examination of performance increases to identify those employees who have been awarded very high increases and those who have

* There are organizational development dimensions in many other facets of personnel administration, including recruiting, job structuring and organization, manpower planning, and, of course, training and manpower development.

received little or no increases. Examination of such cases, which usually represent 10 to 20 percent of total company employment, can provide insights into elements of job success. Communication of these elements to other employees may improve their performance. Quite frequently, such analyses also pinpoint personnel training needs or operational deficiencies which, when dealt with, result in improved employee performance.

Examples of opportunity situations are cited throughout this book. The point here is that, as far as management actions are concerned, it is essential not only to look at the problems of the business but also to be constantly alert to opportunities to make strategic contributions to the achievement of enterprise goals and to use compensation practices to develop people in the organization.

NEED FOR A FORMAL PROGRAM

Because of the complexity of compensation practices, a reasonably formalized wage and salary program is essential in all but the smallest operation. A formal program, though difficult to define, is characterized by the establishment of standards which serve to guide individual pay decisions. Such guides are formalized in the sense that they are predetermined and put in writing. Of course, they do not represent a substitute for human judgment, but they can contribute to more consistent, sounder, and less subjective decisions.

Just how useful a formalized approach is depends both on the correctness of the policies, techniques, practices, and ground rules established to implement the program and on the quality of management decisions within this framework. The major drawback to a formal program is that it can become restrictive and inflexible. This may happen if it becomes an end in itself rather than a means to an end, it is used as a staff technique rather than as a management practice, or if it is taken as a substitute for judgment.

The usefulness of a formal program can be evaluated by comparing it with other possible approaches to pay administration. One alternative may be labeled the "market approach," which rests primarily on the proposition that if managers merely pay the going rate for workers in various categories, market forces will automatically result in equitable pay. This may have been practical at some time in the past, but under current conditions use of a survey as the sole means of setting pay levels is unworkable. Labor markets are not clearly defined, survey methods are imperfect, and many jobs are unique to the individual company. Furthermore, the application of the "natural laws of supply and demand" may be too harsh to be acceptable to employees, the business, or the community.

Another approach to pay administration, individual bargaining, is equally unacceptable as a basic technique. For one thing, the preponderance of bargaining strength almost invariably rests with the employer. For another, the application of brute strength can hardly be counted on to produce realistic solutions to pay problems. Finally, individual bargaining brings chaotic conditions in both the employment market and the company's internal pay relationships.

A third possible approach, collective bargaining, may equalize bargaining strength and eliminate favoritism, but it does not necessarily bring more logical pay decisions. Without standards to guide the thinking, control the prejudices, and restrain the arbitrary decisions of negotiators, the results of collective bargaining are no more inherently correct than the results of individual bargaining. For these reasons, mature negotiators in collective bargaining situations guide their thinking by many of the techniques associated with a formal wage and salary program.

In practice, elements of the market approach, individual bargaining, and collective bargaining are part of even the most formalized pay program. Every company is influenced to some extent by the pay received by employees of other companies. Similarly, individual bargaining plays a part in any pay program, for whenever human judgment is exercised, some personal thinking and values will be reflected in the decisions that are made. Finally, in companies with unionized employees the adoption of any formal pay program is itself subject to collective bargaining.

Line managers need not, of course, acquire a comprehensive knowledge of the design or administration of pay administration programs. But they do need to understand essential aspects of the program in order to approve recommended pay practices (if they are at that level of management) or to implement, administer, and make pay decisions. It is for this reason that essential elements of pay administration are described throughout this book. In this context, a few notes about formal plans are relevant to the line manager.

First of all, a formal plan does not necessarily mean an elaborate plan, though a minimum amount of structure is required in all but the smallest firms. In fact, the more elaborate a formal plan is, the more difficult it is to implement and communicate. Therefore, the design goal of the experienced specialist is to develop the simplest plan necessary to meet company needs and objectives.

Some managers feel that the preset guidelines, practices, and controls of a formal plan restrict their latitude in decision making. In fact, the very purpose of formalizing plans is to establish guidelines and practices for the implementation of company policies in a consistent and equitable manner throughout the organization. For example, a job evaluation plan represents guidelines and practices for determining the relative value of positions in the company. Such a plan establishes the criteria for making decisions and the procedures which must be followed in making these decisions.

A formal plan requires that all managers think the same way and this, of course, does impose certain restrictions on them. However, such restrictions are essential in any organization of real size, not only to gain reasonable consistency and equity in administering the pay program but also to make sure that basic guidelines and policy matters are based on the highest level of personnel knowledge and experience available. Moreover, without the restrictions and guidelines of a formal plan, there would be chaos in pay administration. Even if each manager's decisions were "right," there would be inherent inequities simply because their decisions were different. And in any organization some managers would make unsound decisions or be guided by well-intentioned but ill-advised principles.

Thus one of the most difficult aspects of designing a pay program is to establish sound guidelines and practices without unnecessarily restricting management latitude or forcing decisions without adequate consideration of individual circumstances. When the manager, in his experience, perceives that his company's system is not adequately considering the realities of individual situations; when he feels that it significantly and unnecessarily impedes his efforts to achieve optimum business results; or when he believes that it creates other significant management problems at the operating level, he can take one of three courses of action. He can evade the program to the extent that he can get away with it; he can complain bitterly and loudly; or he can report specific instances and make constructive suggestions. Obviously, the interests of the manager and the company alike are best served when the manager follows the third course of action.

MANAGEMENT APPROACH TO PAY PROBLEMS

As has already been noted, there is no single pay program which properly serves the needs of every enterprise—or, for that matter, any two enterprises. Each company is unique in terms of its business, its goals, its strategies, and its management style. Because its problems are different, its solutions must also be different. There is, however, a general approach to developing a pay program which is appropriate to almost every organization. This basic approach involves identifying needs, determining objectives, developing programs, and planning and executing the programs.

Identifying Needs

The first step in compensation administration is making a realistic appraisal of needs. Too frequently, company needs are assumed to be self-evident. Defining them is seldom this simple, however, and it is easy to be misled by casual observation, preconceived notions, or opinions based on incomplete knowledge of important facts.

Needs can be determined in various ways. Personnel specialists should have sufficient knowledge and experience to predict problems and to recognize potential troublespots. Staff assistants can help by knowing the right questions to ask—an ability which can sometimes be as valuable as knowing alternative answers. In addition, payroll data, grievance records, reports of exit interviews or opinion surveys, and other company material can be useful in identifying needs. A great deal can be learned by talking directly with employees; in this way, management can at least learn what pay problems exist in their minds.

The most valuable single contribution to the design and implementation of the pay program is that of the line manager. The staff survey, the personnel audit, and other inputs can set a framework of general objectives, plans, and programs which are designed to meet the needs of the enterprise. The line manager's inputs, however, identify the real operating problems and operating situations which exist in the company with respect to pay administration. These inputs are critical not only in terms of design details but in terms of priority. What the company needs, in other words, is more than a conceptually correct program. Needs can best be reported by the line manager, who observes and experiences them. Just how the company gets these inputs is a difficult matter, and an art which has been somewhat neglected. One way is for staff people to spend more time with line managers familiarizing themselves with real compensation problems and opportunities.

Determining Objectives

It may not be practical to attempt to solve all the pay problems of the enterprise. Some of them, such as the intrusion of personal judgments in pay decisions, cannot be solved by any known methods.

Others which appear on the surface to be pay problems may actually involve problems of organizational planning, work scheduling, manpower planning, or recruitment. Furthermore, the solution of one pay problem may create other more serious problems, or the time and effort involved may be prohibitive. Because of such considerations, it is important to make a qualitative analysis of needs and then to translate these needs into realistic, specific, and attainable objectives.

Developing Programs

After objectives have been established, various techniques and procedures must be developed for achieving them. The process of determining needs, setting objectives, and then designing programs may seem laborious, but it does not involve more effort in the long run. Rather, it is the only way to insure that the resulting programs are geared to actual problems. Furthermore, pay programs are easier to design and apply when specific needs and objectives have been established.

Planning and Executing the Programs

Once a program has been determined, plans must be developed for implementing it. Unless this is done, important aspects of the program may be overlooked. The planning process involves specifying who is responsible for accomplishing the various objectives of the program. It also involves establishing a timetable to insure that the various operations will be performed on time and in the correct sequence and to set deadlines for those who have responsibilities under the program. Finally, planning should provide for follow-up at various stages to determine both progress and results.

THE EMPLOYEE'S VIEW OF COMPENSATION ADMINISTRATION

The employee's view of a compensation program is generally different in important respects from that of the company. This is one of the key compensation problems in many enterprises. Even when the pay program is sound, well administered, and effectively communicated, difficulties can arise if employee aspirations are out of phase with company objectives or if the employee's concept of a fair and equitable program is different from that of the company.

To some extent, there is always some conflict between employee aspirations and company needs. For instance, employees always want more; but employers need to control wage costs or at least administer the pay program within the restraints of their financial capacity. These criteria, of course, are not totally at odds. As the cost of living rises and as pay levels in the labor market increase in an inflationary economy, the company must increase its employees' pay in order to attract and retain the number and kinds of people necessary to run the business. The conflict of view is one of degree; employee aspirations typically exceed company needs for granting increases.

Probably more important are the employee's criteria of fair pay practices—which are frequently quite different from the employer's criteria. For instance, one employee criterion of fairness involves what a worker thinks he *needs* or what he *wants* in order to maintain the style of life he has established. The employer, of course, should not weigh such things as the size of the worker's family or the income needs of his self-established life style in making individual pay decisions.

The employee's criteria for making pay comparisons are also frequently different from those of the company. The company, of course, thinks primarily in terms of competitive pay in the labor markets where it competes for talent. Employees share this view to some degree, although less perfectly; but they also have other criteria. They may be influenced by the life style and therefore the apparent income of their neighbors. Or they may make comparisons with their peers. For instance, many publishing firms experience difficulties because they have college graduates—some with masters' degrees—doing clerical work. Here workers' pay is geared to the work done; but these employees tend to compare their incomes with those of their college contemporaries—many of whom are doing higher levels of work which call for higher pay.

For the employee, probably the most important single criterion of the appropriateness of a pay program is personal pay progress. Employees are less conscious of labels than employers—they do not, for instance, make the same distinctions between promotional increases, cost-of-living increases, and merit increases. Rather, they tend to compare how much they are making this year with how much they made last year or five years ago.

Because pay history is an important employee criterion, it should be part of the data of the company. In recent years information has been reported with respect to the pay progress of employees in different groups. A summary of this information over an eight-year period is

Table 2. **Average annual percentage pay increases for various employee groups, 1965–1972.**

Employee Group	*1965*	*1966*	*1967*	*1968*	*1969*	*1970*	*1971*	*1972*
General management	7	7	7	9	8	8	8	9
Manufacturing managers	6	7	7	8	8	7	8	8
Marketing managers	6	7	8	8	9	7	8	9
Engineers								
Average	6	6	7	7	8	8	8	8
Fast-track	7	7	8	8	9	9	9	9
Accountants								
Average	8	7	7	7	9	8	9	8
Fast-track	8	8	9	9	10	9	10	9
Office workers								
Average	5	5	6	7	8	7	8	8
Fast-track	7	7	9	10	10	9	10	10
Factory workers								
Average	6	6	6	7	8	7	8	8
Fast-track	7	7	7	7	8	8	9	9

shown in Table 2. The fact of the matter is that many compensation programs make pay progress difficult because their guidelines and procedures do not permit pay increases of the magnitude reported in Table 2—particularly for the fast-track or high-potential employee.

If the company pay program is to be effective—in the sense that it avoids trouble—it must take into consideration the employee's criteria because these are a key part of the real pay problems of the enterprise. The company must collect information with respect to these criteria and must seriously weigh them in developing its programs and in making decisions with respect to amounts available for pay increases and methods of allocating these amounts. Finally, the company must do a reasonably good job of communicating such information. This can best be done by holding meetings between groups of employees and staff specialists.

2

ELEMENTS OF COMPENSATION

COMPENSATION ADMINISTRATION in the modern business world is a complex activity. It involves knowledge of many techniques and technicalities which are difficult to master. The combined techniques of compensation administration do not represent "professional knowledge" as the term is defined in the academic disciplines of law, medicine, economics, psychology, and the physical sciences. Rather, the technology of compensation administration is business technology, diverse and complex information related to enterprise activities. Some of this business technology also requires a layman's knowledge of law, economics, and mathematics.

Only the specialist in compensation administration can be expected to master all the techniques of compensation administration. The personnel generalist need only understand compensation technology well enough to manage the work of the specialist and to interrelate his activities with the work of other personnel specialists to achieve a desired employee relations objective. The line manager, in turn, need only know enough about the technology of compensation administration to implement the program in his own area of responsibility and to make pay decisions. He must understand the program well enough to communicate it to his subordinates, particularly when it is necessary to explain specific decisions and actions. The techniques of compensation administration discussed in this book are intended to outline the knowledge required by the line manager to perform his role and to some extent the knowledge required by the personnel generalist.

One critical area that must be a part of the line manager's and the personnel generalist's understanding is a knowledge of the forms of compensation, the importance of each form, and the role each plays in a sound overall program of remuneration of employees. Another critical area of knowledge relates to different groups of employees and how compensation practices must differ for each.

Employees receive remuneration from both financial and nonfinancial sources. Financial elements of income refer to payments made and costs incurred. They represent the bulk of employees' income and can be measured and analyzed. Furthermore, while many facets of work are important to employee satisfaction and productivity, money is—for most employees during most of their work careers—by far the most important. For all these reasons, financial income—compensation—will be treated in depth in the following section. Some of the principal forms of nonfinancial remuneration will be identified at the end of the chapter.

FINANCIAL ELEMENTS OF INCOME

There are a number of distinct forms of financial income or compensation. These forms of compensation were not established arbitrarily. Rather, they evolved to meet different employee needs and/or different company objectives. Therefore, while financial elements of income may be categorized in various ways, the most useful way is to identify them in terms of employee needs and company objectives. The classification is as follows:

Salaries or wages. The base pay which an employee receives on a periodic basis.

Bonuses. Lump-sum awards, usually on an annual basis.

Long-term income. Lump-sum awards earned over a long period of time, typically five years.

Benefits. Insurance benefits and pay for time not worked.

Estate-building plans. Plans which assist employees in accumulating savings or in managing savings which they are accumulating.

Salaries or Wages

Salaries or wages set the standard of living of the employee. For the average employee, base pay represents the bulk of his income.

It also reflects the company's evaluation of his work. For the employer, base pay represents the fixed employee cost of doing business. It is also a basic element of compensation administration and a determinant of the level of other forms of employee remuneration such as pensions and life insurance.

Bonuses

A bonus award for the employee represents extra income and an opportunity to attain above-average earnings. Moreover, the fact that the bonus is paid in a lump sum enables the employee to buy goods or services which can have a meaningful impact on his way of life—something that would not be possible if the amount were paid in 24 or 52 equal installments. Frequently, a bonus also represents a reward for achievement of short-term goals. To the company, a bonus is a variable cost; it provides an opportunity to motivate employees to achieve short-term goals and can be, under certain circumstances, a valuable tool in attracting and retaining employees.

Long-Term Income

Long-term income plans, such as stock options, are usually provided only to higher-paid employees. These too represent extra income to employees—frequently a considerable amount—and often hold the promise of very high income. Like bonuses, long-term income awards represent rewards for achievement and frequently involve large lump-sum payments which can dramatically change an employee's life style. In addition, some long-term income plans provide for income at lower tax rates. To the employer, long-term income plans are variable costs that frequently have favorable accounting treatment. They also represent a principal method of building "golden handcuffs" into the compensation program. Finally, long-term income plans can motivate employees to achieve long-term goals of the enterprise and can be extremely important in attracting and retaining higher-level personnel.

Benefits

For the employee, insurance benefits represent economic protection against risks, including death, disability, and illness. Company insurance programs offer protection at a lower cost to the employee and in many cases provide benefits which the employee could not obtain as an individual. Another employee benefit, pay for time not worked, offers employees more time for their personal and social lives without loss of income. For the company, insurance benefits represent a method of meeting basic social responsibilities to employees—usually on a tax-sheltered basis. Increasingly, of course, comprehensive insurance benefits have become so widespread that employees have come to expect them in any compensation program. Thus reasonably competitive insurance benefits are essential if the company is to attract and retain employees.

Figure 1. **Company and employee needs and objectives inherent in different forms of compensation.**

FORM OF COMPENSATION	EMPLOYEE	COMPANY
Salary	Sets a standard of living	Fixed cost
	Reflects employer's evaluation	Basis for administering other forms of compensation
Bonuses	Extra current income	Variable cost
	Reward for achievement of short-term goals	Motivation for attainment of short-term goals
	Opportunity for above-average income	Attract key personnel
	Impact of lump-sum income on life style	Favorable short-term cash flow
Long-term income	Reward for achievement	Favorable financial aspects
	Opportunity for high income	Holding power
	Possibly lower net tax	Motivation for attainment of long-term goals
	Key estate-building mechanism	Attracts key personnel
Benefits	Tax-sheltered income	Meet company's social responsibilities to employees
	Low-cost insurance against economic risks	Holding power
	Time off from work	Employee security
Estate-building plans	Leveraged savings	Flexible supplement to insurance programs
	High-level fund management	Build favorable attitudes

Estate-Building Plans

Estate-building mechanisms include stock purchase plans, thrift plans, and some forms of profit-sharing trusts. They also include, for higher-paid employees, special stock purchase plans, estate-counseling services, and leveraged mutual funds. All these plans help an employee accumulate savings and/or better manage savings, frequently on a tax-sheltered basis or at lower cost.

The various company needs and employee objectives associated with financial elements of income are summarized in Figure 1. The extent to which these objectives are actually achieved depends on company circumstances, the firm's compensation policy and strategy, the appropriateness of the plans used, and the income levels of employees. The important point is that there are distinctly different forms of compensation in the pay practices of any firm and that each form serves a different purpose to the employee and the company. Thus financial elements of income cannot be substituted for one another. The emphasis on certain forms may vary for different groups of employees, but each element must be present to some extent in the overall compensation package.

As shown in Table 3, each element of compensation represents a significant part of total remuneration for employees at all salary levels. For the lowest-paid employee, the nonsalary elements of compensation represent 35 percent of salary (and in some firms as much as 50 percent). For the higher-paid executive, nonsalary elements of compensation total far more than salary—typically 170 percent in the case of the manager earning $100,000.

Table 3. **Magnitude of income from different forms of compensation, as percentage of salary.**

	Annual Salary of Employee			
Form of Compensation	*$7,000*	*$15,000*	*$25,000*	*$100,000*
Salary (including overtime)	100	100	100	100
Bonus	0	10	20	60
Capital income	0	0	20	70
Estate building	5	5	5	10
Employee benefits	30	30	30	30
Total	135	145	175	270

The base salary or pay range is, of course, still the key element of compensation at all job levels in the enterprise. It is the key element in lower-paying jobs, if for no other reason than that it is the largest single element of compensation. But even in higher-paying jobs salary is an important element of compensation because it is the basis upon which many other forms of compensation are built. For this reason, the design of the base pay system is critical to the success of the compensation program and to the enterprise in general. It is necessary for managers to understand the base pay system in order to play their proper role in compensation administration.

NONFINANCIAL ELEMENTS OF INCOME

There are a number of forms of employee income which do not involve actual payments of money and which frequently do not involve costs —or at least identifiable costs—to the company. By definition, these are the nonfinancial elements of remuneration. Because nonfinancial forms of income are indirect—not subject to analysis in terms of income, value, or company cost—and because their impact on employees or employers is difficult to measure, they cannot be given the same type of detailed analysis as the financial elements of remuneration. However, it would be a gross error to overlook them, and they are examined briefly below.

It is useful to identify the various nonfinancial elements of compensation in terms of their nature and intent, as was done with the financial elements of remuneration. Here again, these forms of income were not established arbitrarily; rather, they evolved because different kinds of nonfinancial remuneration serve different employee needs and company objectives. Nonfinancial elements of income include:

- Elements of company environment which represent a form of remuneration to employees.
- Elements of work environment which have real value to employees.
- Nontaxable income or values to employees which are tax-sheltered (other than insurance benefits or "qualified" pay plans).
- Items which represent value to employees but which are really designed to support them in their work or make their work more effective.
- Perquisites of the job which, for instance, have value in terms of establishing status.

Company Environment

There are many ways in which company environment can represent a real form of remuneration to employees—remuneration which involves no cost to the company other than a slight cost of communication. The value of company environment can, for instance, relate to the social merits of the enterprise, as in the case of hospitals. It can involve the visibility of the activity—this is true, for instance, in airlines. It can be related to the fact that the company and its employees are "where the action is"—a situation that is true in many news media organizations.

Or the value of company environment can relate to the fact that the company is a pioneer in its field, working on the frontiers of knowledge. A classic example is the work at the Manhattan Project or, more recently, at NASA. Working for a prestige organization, in the sense either that it is extraordinarily well known or that it has been outstandingly successful, can also be an element of value to employees. Examples of prestige companies include the Prudential Insurance Company, General Electric, and AT&T. Success companies include Black and Decker, Xerox, and Polaroid.

Work Environment

Work environment is another meaningful nonfinancial element of income which not only involves no cost to the company but can frequently result in cost savings or added business success. Items of work environment are more difficult to identify and assess than items of company environment; primarily because the characteristics that are a positive element of work environment in one company may not be positive in another.

Certainly, the physical elements of the work environment are of value to the employee and affect his output. These include special equipment conducive to effective work, appropriate work space, cleanliness, attractiveness of layout and decor, availability to shopping centers, transportation facilities, and a variety of other items. Work assignments can also be an important aspect of overall job satisfaction. To the extent that employees do work they enjoy, their job satisfaction and productivity increase. So this item of nonfinancial income also contributes to the company's success.

The management style of the firm is another important element of the work environment. The degree to which employees are treated fairly and with dignity and respect influences the attractiveness of work and therefore represents nonfinancial income. The fairness with which employees' questions and grievances are handled, the type of job security that exists, and company policy regarding layoffs represent other types of nonfinancial income related to work environment. Finally, the levels of expectation which exist in the company can represent a form of nonfinancial income. This is because most employees want to have pride in their work. The degree to which they see themselves making a significant contribution to the company can affect the degree to which their work is satisfying.

Nontaxable Income

There are a variety of ways in which a company can provide income which is not made in cash payments and therefore is not taxable to employees. Company subsidies for meals are one example; another is recreational facilities provided by the company. For higher-level employees there are more exotic forms of nontaxable income such as reimbursements for business meals, travel, and expenses and use of company cars. All these must obviously be work-connected. Nontaxable income represents a limited business expense to the company.

Items of Work Support Income

To many employees, the ways in which the company helps them to perform more efficiently, to work with less strain and stress, and to grow in their careers represent important sources of nonfinancial income—many of which can lead to higher-paying positions. In a sense these items represent, for the employee, building assets rather than income. Training sessions, reimbursements for further education, and similar activities build an employee's knowledge. Here again, there is no cash income, but such activities do enhance an employee's future employment value.

Perquisites

There are many perquisites which can have value to employees. These include the title of the person, the type of office, furniture, or decor—which are really esthetic rather than work-support benefits—and special recognition or awards. All, in one way or another, give status to the individual, and to many employees status represents an important and meaningful nonfinancial reward.

Perquisites do, however, pose some special problems. For one thing, they may only intensify an employee's preoccupation with the symbols of success. They may even motivate the employee to achieve symbols of success rather than specific work goals. Moreover, some of these items, such as titles, can restrict management decision making; for instance, they may prevent a manager from making organizational changes which would contribute to a more effective working group. For these reasons, the subject of perquisites is considered an area of issue and concern, and some leadership companies are giving the subject serious and organized attention.

GROUPS OF EMPLOYEES

The various forms of financial and nonfinancial income have different applicability to different groups of employees. The magnitude of income received from each form varies, as indicated in Table 3. Some forms of income are not appropriate for some employees—overtime is not paid to managers and stock options are not granted to operations workers. In addition, actual compensation techniques vary with different groups of employees. Thus the bonus plans used for factory workers are very different from those used for salesmen. Even basic salary practices must be varied for different categories of work within the firm. Therefore, in addition to identifying the different elements or forms of compensation, management must identify the significant groups of employees within the firm so that compensation programs can be designed to meet their needs.

In the past many firms separated their employees into groups on the basis of whether they were exempt from the Fair Labor Standards Act. Others grouped their employees according to whether they were direct labor or indirect labor—primarily for cost-accounting reasons. Still others simply divided their work force into management and workers. Such simplistic groupings of employees do not fit the modern enterprise.

Of course, employers must obey the Fair Labor Standards Act. They must identify employees who are covered by the act and see to it that they are paid according to the provisions of the law. In practice, most companies have found it necessary to pay overtime to employees who are not, strictly speaking, covered by the law. In any event, legal rules hardly serve as a useful distinction for purposes of compensation administration and other management practices.

Similarly, there may still be sound cost-accounting reasons for keeping track of direct man-hours of work—those which are directly attributable to the unit cost of a product. Modern accounting practices and use of computers, however, make this a relatively easy task. Again, an accounting requirement is hardly a basis for grouping employees to meet management needs.

For management purposes, jobs must be grouped so that work elements and characteristics are similar, the types of training and recruiting methods required are similar, and the backgrounds of those who fill the jobs are similar. When this is done, many personnel practices—such as recruiting, communication, training, and compensation—can be developed to meet the needs of each group.

In most companies there are at least five distinct groups of employees: operations employees; sales employees; supervisory, administrative, and technical employees; professional employees; and management employees. Figure 2 shows the distribution of these groups in the company hierarchy.

Operations workers include both factory and office personnel. Their jobs involve the performance of basically unskilled or semiskilled

Figure 2. **Groups of employees.**

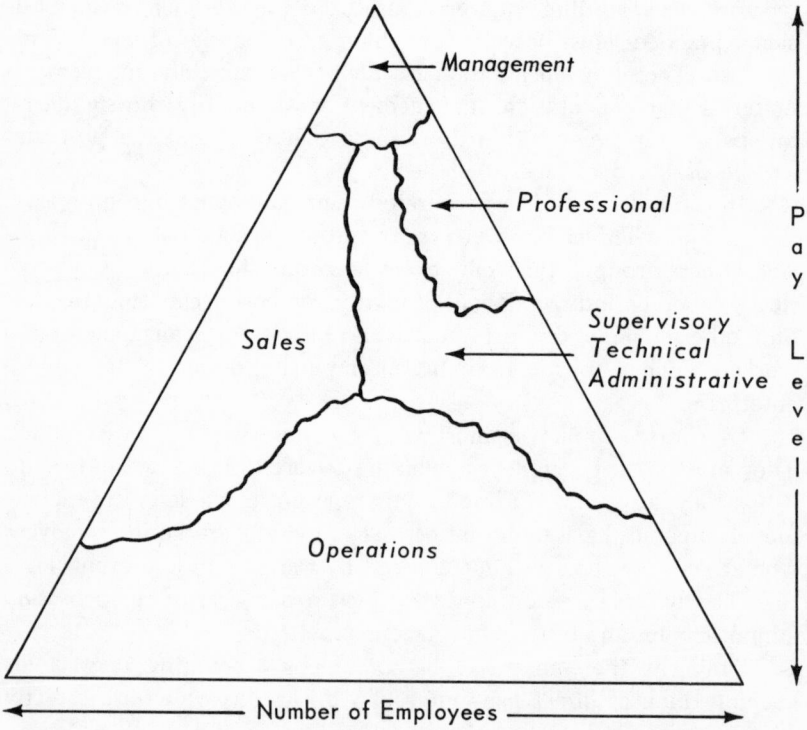

Figure 3. **Pay levels of different employee groups.**

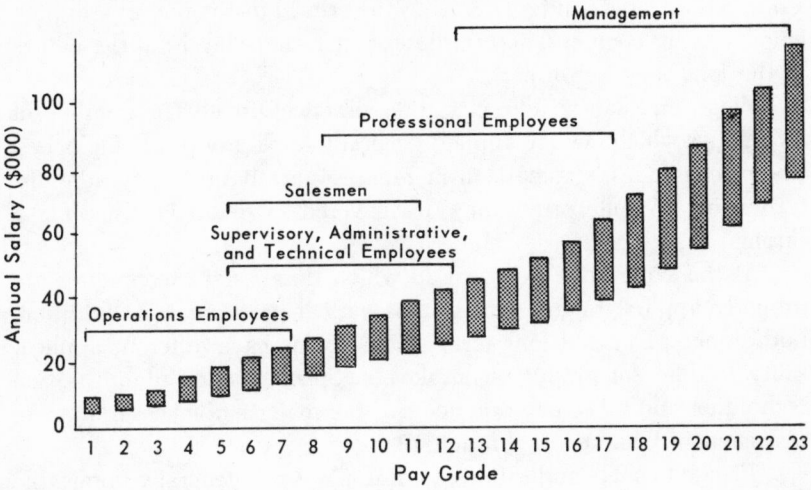

tasks that can be defined and proceduralized. Sometimes, of course, it is useful to subdivide the operations job—for instance, between employees who are represented by unions and those who are nonunion.

Sales employees include field sales personnel—those who are in direct contact with the customers or distributors of the company's products or services. This group generally does not include home office sales personnel in advertising, merchandising, and market research.

At the top of the company hierarchy are management employees—those who make decisions and judgments which affect business results. At the apex of the organization is a small group of higher-level managers who might be defined as executives—those whose decisions and judgments affect the long-term success of the enterprise.

Professional employees are those who apply formal knowledge to the solution of company problems. Included in this group are physicians, lawyers, engineers, and others who apply recognized academic disciplines. Also included are staff personnel—those who apply business disciplines.

Supervisory, administrative, and technical personnel may be defined as employees "not elsewhere classified." They are quite diverse—but all have one thing in common: they hold intermediate-level positions. Supervisors are, of course, intermediate between management and operations workers; technical employees lie between professionals and operations workers; and administrative employees hold positions between high-level staff and operations workers.

Salary levels for these different groups of employees overlap quite a bit, as illustrated in Figure 3. Thus the critical distinction in grouping employees for compensation purposes is not salary level but the nature of the jobs they perform.

Wage and salary administration practices involve a number of techniques which may be applied generally to all groups of employees. These techniques, summarized in Figure 4, are basic to pay administration in any enterprise; they are covered in detail in Chapters 3 through 8.

At the same time, the ways in which these salary techniques are properly applied to different groups vary a great deal. In addition, both bonus plans and long-term income plans have different applicability to different groups of employees. Special salary administration techniques and other pay practices for the major employee groups are discussed in Chapters 9 through 13.

Fringe benefits and estate-building plans are generally applicable to all groups of employees. There are, however, a wide range of bene-

Figure 4. **Aspects of a formal wage and salary program.**

TECHNIQUE	OBJECTIVE
Job information	To determine job facts as a necessary step in job evaluation (as well as in employment, management development, organizational studies, and general supervision). Job facts may be recorded in job questionnaires or job descriptions.
Job evaluation	To determine relative job worth.
Job pricing	To translate relative job worth into money values.
Individual pay increases	To reward employees for higher productivity and better job performance and/or to reflect increases in pay levels in the labor market.
Communications	To give supervisors the information they need to carry out the program and gain its acceptance.
Administrative procedures and practices	To resolve individual problems, keep the program current and operating efficiently, and provide general guidance to managers.
Union participation	To meet the requirements of collective bargaining.
Controls	To insure reasonably consistent and equitable application of the wage and salary program and to maintain control over costs.

fit and estate-building plans, most of which are detailed and complex. These plans are summarized in Chapter 14.

Even this brief summary of the major aspects of compensation administration suggests that it is a diverse and complex subject. Because each of these aspects interacts with at least some of the others, compensation is a systems problem. More specifically, compensation administration is a subsystem of a subsystem: it is an integral part of personnel administration, which is but one important part of management.

3

JOB INFORMATION

JOB INFORMATION is one essential input for an effective salary administration program. Without valid and reliable job information, management would have no basis for making job evaluation decisions. Similarly, survey information would be of little use to management if there were no way of relating the information to jobs in the company. This is not to suggest that job descriptions, job evaluations, surveys, or any other techniques must be part of the salary program of every group of employees. But job information is an essential input to many such programs and to the compensation system overall.

In fact, the two really essential inputs to an effective salary program are job information and people information. Excellence of knowledge in these areas combined with intelligent and sincere administration can result in reasonably effective salary programs using few techniques. For instance, thorough job information can result in reasonably sound job slotting using a very simple job evaluation system. But the opposite is not true. That is, the most excellent and sophisticated job evaluation system will not yield satisfactory results unless there is reasonably complete and sound job information.

NEED FOR JOB INFORMATION

Because job information can serve a variety of management purposes, it is important that the company identify which of its objectives are to be served by the job information system. This should be done before the system is designed because the acquisition, maintenance, and communication of job information must be geared to company purposes.

The most important single objective of obtaining job information is communicating job duties and responsibilities to employees assigned to do the work. Companies spend enormous amounts of money on communication. Most companies do not undercommunicate; they overcommunicate. One study of several companies revealed that between 10 and 20 percent of employee payroll costs involved costs of communication. Yet a majority of the employees in these companies *had an imperfect to inadequate knowledge of their duties and responsibilities.*

It is, of course, hard to think of any information which is more vital to the effective operation of an enterprise than the employees' knowledge of what they are supposed to do. This suggests that one of the best ways to improve communication in most companies is to provide better job information.

Another important objective of obtaining job information is organizational analysis. Job information can be helpful in identifying duplication of work, in pinpointing ways in which work can be reorganized for greater efficiency, and in assessing ways in which work can be better geared to meet the objectives of the enterprise.

Job information can also be crucial to effective staffing. Whether the candidate is within or outside the company, the staffing process must include a knowledge by both parties of the work to be done. It is difficult for a recruiter to select the proper candidate unless he understands the work to be done and therefore the type of experience and training required. Similarly, it is difficult for a candidate to know whether he should accept a job unless he understands the duties it involves.

Job information can also be useful in setting performance standards and establishing job objectives. The former process involves identifying levels of expectations in terms of both quantity and quality of work; the latter process involves identifying specific work objectives to be accomplished. They are key parts of an effective "management by objectives" program.

Job information is the only sound basis for appraising employee performance. Experience has shown that rating employees by personality traits such as attitude and cooperativeness—which are symptoms of performance—is ineffective. It is clearly more relevant and effective to rate performance against specific job duties and responsibilities.

Finally, job information is essential to personnel decisions of all types. These include transfers, promotions, and manpower planning, as well as a variety of compensation decisions such as job evaluation.

JOB ANALYSIS

Job analysis is the process of gathering information about the job and evaluating such information in terms of what is necessary and relevant. Essentially, job analysis involves three questions: What is a job? What should be analyzed? What methods of analysis should be used?

What Is a Job?

In its narrowest sense, a job is what a person does. If this definition were used in compensation administration, each person would have a separate and distinct job that would be reported separately. The result would be as many job analyses as there are employees. This is seldom an appropriate definition for job analysis, except in highly professional organizations.

More typically, a job is a group of essentially similar activities performed by a person or a group of persons. These activities need not be identical. They may, for instance, be performed in different places, with different equipment, in a different sequence, and so forth. Also, some employees may perform certain activities in addition to the main job, activities that are distinctly less valuable and difficult. Or some employees may perform occasional or temporary work—for example, work to fill in for persons absent or on vacation. This is typically the definition of a job which is used in compensation administration and other management practices.

Occasionally, however, a more generic description of a job is used —and frequently this description is identified by "position" rather than "job." A position is a family of jobs in which specific duties vary but some interchangeability of work is possible and the functional nature of the work is similar. Examples include assemblers, clerk-typists, and bookkeepers. The broader the definition of a job, the less likely that job analysis and any resulting job information will accurately reflect the work of each employee. On the other hand, the more precise the job definition, the more costly the process. Very restrictive definitions can result in identifying differences without meaningful distinctions.

Another basic issue involved in determining the job to be analyzed is whether the company should measure work assigned or work actually performed. Some wage and salary experts argue that unless job analysis involves work performed, the company may not give employees credit for what they are actually doing. On the other hand, analyzing work performed may imply that employees should be given latitude to assign work to themselves. It is, of course, the manager's function to assign work. The analyst is essentially an information gatherer and reporter; it is not his place to judge the logic of work assignments or to determine what assignments should be made. He is responsible only for recording those responsibilities that a manager has allowed an employee to assume.

What Should Be Analyzed?

The type and amount of information that should be obtained in job analysis depend upon a number of considerations: whether the analysis is to be used solely for evaluation or for other purposes as well; what job level is being analyzed; what type of evaluation plan will be used; and what job knowledge is held by those who are going to conduct the evaluation. Certain basic areas of information which may be pertinent include:

- Fundamental purpose of the job.
- Work elements assigned. This may require study of specific tasks, areas of responsibility, and examples of work.
- General importance of each job element and its relationship to objectives of the operation.
- Approximate time spent on each duty or area of responsibility.
- Scope of the job and its impact on the operation.
- Inherent authority (not only formal delegation but also latitude of action) and formal or informal audits of work.
- Working relationships, including supervision given and reviewed, committee membership, and special assignments.
- Specific methods, equipment, or techniques which must be used.
- Climate of the job, including objectives and work environment.
- Conditions under which work must be performed: physical effort,

hazards, discomfort, deadlines, travel, pressure, rate of change, innovations required, and so on.

What Methods of Analysis Should Be Used?

Job information can be obtained in various ways, either by a staff analyst or by the individual line manager. One quick and inexpensive method of analysis is the questionnaire, which can be given either to supervisors or to employees who perform the jobs. Because of their importance as a tool of job analysis, job questionnaires are discussed separately below. Direct observation of work performed is another method of job analysis. Some observation is usually essential if the analyst is to gain a real understanding of job duties. Observation is usually the most precise method of analysis, but it is also the most costly.

Valuable information can also be obtained from organization manuals, time-study reports, former job descriptions, and procedure studies. But in the last analysis the individual manager is the basic source of information on the job duties of his subordinates.

Job Questionnaires

A job questionnaire is a special tool for gaining job information. It is a printed or typewritten form which asks essential information about the job and may be completed either by the employee or by his supervisor. The major advantage of the job questionnaire is that it uses the knowledge of those who are closest to the job. In addition, it gives each employee an opportunity to participate in the compensation program. The cost of the questionnaire technique is low, and written job information can be obtained in a very short time.

Another important advantage of job questionnaires is that they can be used as job descriptions, thereby eliminating the high cost associated with writing descriptions. Use of a job questionnaire for this purpose is an effective way of communicating job information to the employee and of keeping job information up to date.

The chief disadvantages associated with job questionnaires are that they depend on the writing ability of individual employees and supervisors, and that inconsistencies can arise when many different people participate. In addition, it is difficult to make sure that employees and supervisors present all the information required or that they do so without exaggeration or embellishments. Use of job questionnaires, in short, involves a problem of quality control.

JOB DESCRIPTIONS

Job information developed through job analysis is most typically recorded in job descriptions. These are written records of job duties and responsibilities that provide a factual basis for making job evaluation decisions. They are usually recorded on a standard form and written in a uniform manner.

Because writing skill is so important in the preparation of job descriptions, many companies assign this task to trained job analysts. To do this, however, the analyst must understand these jobs. The best single guide for writing a job description is any standard guide for clear and concise writing. It is also helpful to develop or use published glossaries of frequently used business terms—such as "responsibility" and "coordinates"—which are not well covered in standard dictionaries. These glossaries help to achieve a consistent use of key words that, in essence, represent a special language of management. Part of a glossary of business terms is shown in Figure 5.

In terms of format, the job description should first name the job, using the title which accurately summarizes duties assigned. It should then outline in a simple form (frequently with short sentences or phrases) a list of duties assigned. Exactly what is included in the listing of job duties and how they are written will depend on the level of the position and the purpose to be served by the description. At the top management level a description of the job is a description of the business. At the operations level job descriptions usually call for a list of specific duties performed, equipment used, and procedures followed. Generally speaking, the broader the use of the description information and the higher the level of work, the longer the job description. Descriptions of operations positions used solely for job evaluation are usually about one page in length. Job descriptions for higher management and professional positions used for a variety of management purposes may run as long as four pages.

Job Specifications

• In addition to giving information about job duty assignments, descriptions frequently outline basic specifications of the job. Examples of specifications include education or experience required to do the job and special knowledge necessary to carry out the work. In addition, specifications might identify the type of relationship skills, analytical ability, or decision-making talent required to perform the duties assigned.

***Figure 5.* Glossary of terms used in position descriptions.**

I. Action Definitions

The following list of verbs includes definitions which have special business meanings not usually found in a standard dictionary. For words not in this list, standard dictionary definitions should be used.

A. *Advise:* To provide, usually on request, information, ideas, or suggestions which aid others in deciding on a course of action or making a decision.

B. *Counsel:* To provide advice, usually on one's own initiative, in which a course of action is suggested or urged and some recourse of follow-up is implied when the advice is not followed.

C. *Control:* To audit or verify, or have audited or verified, and thereby regulate or be informed about to the point of influencing or directing activities.

D. *Coordinate:* To assist or guide interrelated and interdependent activities; to bring about a harmonious combination of activities to the accomplishment of a common goal.

E. *Decide:* To determine a course of action, select an alternative, and so on.

F. *Direct:* To cause activities, decisions, or work to take place.

G. *Establish:* To set up or bring about, on a permanent or temporary basis, with the implied or delegated authority to act.

H. *Influence:* To affect the action, thinking, or conduct of others, whether by word or by example.

I. *Manage:* To plan, direct, and control.

J. *Persuade:* To induce others to believe something or prevail upon them to do something.

K. *Participate:* To take part in; implies joint venture activity or part of a project without ultimate responsibility or authority.

L. *Recommend:* To determine an answer, plan, or course of action and present it to higher-level authority.

One purpose of describing job specifications is to aid in the evaluation of jobs. For this reason, information included in job specifications usually relates directly to the job evaluation plan. For instance, if the analyst has decided that a job requires a college education and the job evaluation plan has a factor relating to education, then the degree of that factor which calls for college graduates would be the factor relevant for that job. This process assumes that the analyst has been correct in his judgment as to job requirements in the first place. In effect, the analyst is evaluating the job when he sets the specifications. The usefulness of these specifications depends upon whether the analyst is qualified to make such judgments.

Should Employees See Their Job Descriptions?

Some managers do not show employees their job descriptions for fear that this will cause controversy or will lead them to resist doing work that is not specifically listed. If job descriptions are well prepared, however, sharing them with employees would seem to be an essential step in using them. Certainly, there can be no harm in showing a person a list of duties he is expected to perform so long as the list is accurate and so long as he recognizes that his superior may ask him to perform other tasks from time to time.

Actually, sharing job descriptions with employees can be important in gaining acceptance of job evaluation results. Unless employees are convinced that their classifications have been determined on the basis of their job duties, it will be difficult for them to accept the results of even the most elaborate evaluation system.

Managers can accomplish a great deal not only by showing employees their job descriptions but by making sure that employees have access to this information on a regular basis. Reviewing description information with employees is one method of assuring proper communication of duties. It can also be a constructive and objective approach to evaluating job performance. Finally, it gives employees an opportunity to make useful suggestions as to how work can be performed more effectively.

Time and Cost of Preparing Job Descriptions

The analysis and reporting of job information can be useful to management in several ways. For example, pay decisions based on actual knowledge of the job are critical to a successful compensation program.

But the values must, of course, be weighed against the costs of preparing job descriptions—which can be extremely high. As a rule of thumb, it costs a company between $100 and $200 to write a management or professional job description, between $75 and $100 to write a middle-level description, and $50 to write an operations-level description. These costs assume that the company has employees who are well qualified to do the job analysis and description writing. This means that a company with 1,000 employees can spend $100,000 the first year in analyzing and describing jobs. For a company whose growth rate is about the same as that of the population, the annual cost of maintaining descriptions is about one-third of the initial price—in this case, an average of $33,000, or $33 per employee.

These general cost figures apply to obtaining and maintaining job information in the form necessary to make compensation decisions. If descriptions are prepared for a broader purpose, such as use as a tool for organizational analysis or organizational development, the cost may be twice as high.

MANAGEMENT USE OF JOB INFORMATION

In its most elementary form, management's job of "getting things done through people" can be said to have six functions:

1. Thinking through what work must be done and organizing it efficiently.
2. Staffing the organization to accomplish objectives.
3. Assigning work to individuals—communicating duties—and setting job standards.
4. Observing and judging how well employees are performing these duties.
5. Improving performance through appraisal of how duties are performed and training employees to work more effectively.
6. Rewarding employees for their performance or taking appropriate corrective action.

Job descriptions play an important role in all these key management activities. Basically, the manager must make certain that all work assigned is essential and that essential tasks are grouped into jobs in the most efficient and economical manner. From the resulting job descriptions he can develop specifications which, in employment, promotion, or transfer decisions, will help to insure that properly qualified employees are selected. The descriptions can also assist the manager in showing employees what is expected of them and in making sure they understand how to do the work assigned.

Moreover, the listing of assigned duties in a job description helps the manager to determine reasonable standards of performance. Many job descriptions, in fact, call for an identification of performance standards for each job responsibility. By reviewing an employee's work in terms of the major duties listed, the manager can judge how well the employee is performing his assignments.

Job descriptions can also be useful in improving manpower utilization. By reviewing the listed duties, the manager can identify time-consuming tasks which are below the overall level of work assigned and can reassign these tasks to lower-paid employees. In addition, the manager can study duties in terms of workloads to determine approximately how many man-hours are required; he can then judge how many employees are really needed for each phase of the work. Management should be concerned with wage costs not only in terms of pay levels but in terms of the number of employees at each level.

Finally, job descriptions can be useful as a basic management tool for improving operating procedures. They may pinpoint duplication of work, indicate a better flow of work, suggest better use of job specialization (or, at the other end, job enrichment), or point out possible bottlenecks. Above all, they enable managers to assess each job duty in terms of its importance to the success of the operation: Is this particular task necessary? What would happen if it were not performed? Is there some way it could be done more efficiently? These are the questions managers should ask about every assigned duty listed in a job description. Much of this analysis can be accomplished by merely studying and comparing descriptions. In addition, some of the more sophisticated techniques of management engineering, such as flowcharts and activity distribution charts, can be applied.

While these are all management responsibilities, much of the work is frequently performed by staff specialists or outside consultants. This is done not only to conserve line managers' time but also to get specialized knowledge and experience and objectivity.

Because job descriptions can be a major aid in organizational development, some companies view job analysis and description writing as a management exercise, with the primary purpose of providing information required for effective management. Descriptions which serve this purpose are more than adequate for sound job evaluation. Better management is the first purpose; job evaluation is a fallout advantage. Such descriptions probably cost more to prepare than descriptions which are designed only for job evaluation purposes. Even the latter, however, require a substantial investment; and a slight additional expenditure can result in job descriptions which not only provide managers with better guides for evaluation but also improve their understanding of the work for which they and their subordinates are responsible.

In summary, job information is essential to sound salary administration, and the cost of getting this information is substantial. Incremental costs can contribute to improved operations—an example of the second level of achievement described earlier. If the job information process also contributes to the development of a more productive work force, then the third level of achievement—developing the organization—has also been met.

4

JOB EVALUATION

SOME FORM OF JOB EVALUATION is essential to every wage and salary program. A company may have many objectives in creating a job evaluation plan, but certainly the basic purpose is to establish equitable internal pay relationships. In order for a plan to achieve this objective, managers not only must be familiar with job evaluation techniques but must be aware of some pitfalls inherent in their use.

THE BASIC APPROACH

In spite of the somewhat bewildering number of plans in effect, there is really only one basic approach to job evaluation. This approach, illustrated in Figure 6, calls for the *measurement of job duties against a predetermined yardstick in order to assess relative job worth.* The quantity measured is job duties. Thus the process is impersonal and has nothing to do with how well the work is performed or the ability, potential, or attitudes of employees. Duties are determined through job analysis and are usually described in writing.

The evaluation plan itself, against which job duties are measured, may be based on any predetermined yardstick that serves to guide managers' judgments. This use of an objective measure is similar to the

Figure 6. **The job evaluation formula.**

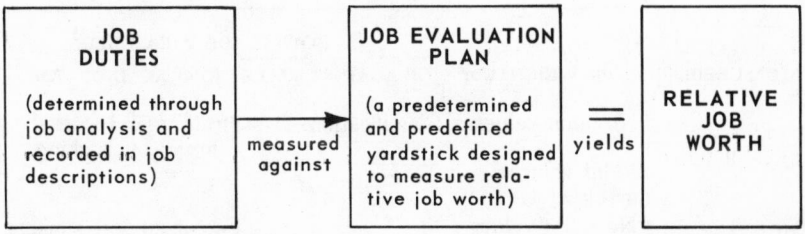

techniques employed by industrial engineers in establishing work standards and to the methods used by quality control engineers in determining inspection standards.

Job evaluation measures job worth in an administrative sense rather than in an economic or social one. Economic worth can be determined only by the natural forces of supply and demand in the marketplace; social worth can be assessed only by the natural forces operating in such activities as individual or collective bargaining. The administrative concept of job worth involves *importance* or *difficulty*. Managers should recognize, however, that market worth, social worth, importance, and difficulty are not identical and may not always correlate perfectly. This is one of the inherent limitations of the job evaluation process.

TRADITIONAL METHODS OF JOB EVALUATION

Evaluation plans which are used to translate job duties into relative job worth may take many different forms. Their technical aspects are of primary concern to staff specialists, who are responsible for recommending a plan. Supervisors, however, need to know the basic aspects of the evaluation system they use. They can also benefit from gaining a general understanding of alternative techniques, which can serve as valuable supplements to their own evaluation methods.

Essentially, the principal measuring techniques for determining relative job worth differ from one another in three areas:

1. What is measured (the whole job or identifiable elements of it).
2. How jobs are weighted (whether or not point values are assigned to establish quantitative measures of job value).
3. How jobs are measured (against other jobs or against a predetermined yardstick).

Figure 7. **Methods of job evaluation.**

1. WHAT IS MEASURED?	2. HOW IS JOB WEIGHTED?	3. HOW IS JOB MEASURED? JOB AGAINST SCALE	JOB AGAINST JOB
Overall job	No point values	Classification	Straight and paired-comparison ranking
	Point values assigned		
Elements or factors of the job	No point values		Factor-guided ranking
	Point values assigned	Point evaluation	Factor comparison

Application of these techniques can result in four basic types of job evaluation plans, as shown in Figure 7: the ranking system, the classification system, point evaluation plans, and factor comparison plans. Combination systems can also be used.

The Ranking System

One widely used method of job evaluation is the ranking system, which ranks one job against another without assigning point values. The evaluator simply compares two jobs and judges which is the more difficult. Once this determination has been made, a third job is compared with the first two and a similar decision is made. The process is repeated until all jobs have been ranked, from the most difficult to the least.

The greatest asset of the ranking system is its simplicity. Little preparation is required, and the evaluation process is quick and inexpensive. Another advantage of the ranking system is that it uses job-against-job comparisons. This is the most accurate method of evaluation because it is far easier to judge which of two jobs is the more difficult than it is to judge the absolute difficulty of either.

Unfortunately, the very simplicity of the ranking method is also its greatest weakness. The system does little to guide the judgment of evaluators; there is a tendency to judge each job on the basis of its dominant characteristic, so that inconsistencies can multiply. In addition, it is extremely difficult to explain or justify the results to employees or managers because there is no record of the judgments of evaluators. Finally, the ranking system can indicate only that one job is more difficult than another, without specifying how much more difficult it is.

Several techniques have been devised to refine the ranking system.

Figure 8. **Paired-comparison rankings.**

(*Italics indicate the higher-ranked job in each pair.*)

Bookkeeper	Clerk-typist A
Clerk-typist A	*Secretary*
Telephone operator	Mail clerk
Clerk-typist A	*Telephone operator*
Telephone operator	*Secretary*
Telephone operator	*Bookkeeper*
Secretary	Mail clerk
Bookkeeper	*Secretary*
Mail clerk	*Bookkeeper*
Mail clerk	*Clerk-typist A*

One of these is paired-comparison ranking, in which evaluators are given a list that pairs every job with every other job and are asked to select which job in each pair ranks higher. In Figure 8, for example, the selection is bookkeeper over clerk-typist A, secretary over clerk-typist A, and so on. The evaluators' rankings are analyzed statistically to produce a master list.

Another refinement of straight ranking is the factor-guided ranking technique. Under this system, evaluators rank jobs not just in terms of overall difficulty but in terms of their difficulty with respect to certain factors—such as knowledge and physical effort required. When the evaluation is completed, a separate ranking is established for each factor.

Factor-ranked jobs can be grouped according to similar levels of difficulty under each factor. When this is done, "degrees" of difficulty are established under each factor. Under a ranking system, these factor groupings serve as an audit or check against overall rankings. The process is, however, a way of building a factor comparison system, in which the degrees that are established are assigned point values.

The Classification System

In the classification system (sometimes called the rating system), each job is measured against a predetermined yardstick whose various categories define overall job value or difficulty. The evaluator compares each job against the yardstick and slots the job into the grade which best describes its characteristics and difficulty. While this system is simple and inexpensive to install and administer, it has several limitations. For one thing, classification has most of the shortcomings of the ranking system. For another, it is very difficult to define levels of overall job worth in any meaningful way. As the number and diversity of jobs have increased, definition of an appropriate yardstick has become especially difficult.

Nonetheless, the classification system does have some applicability, particularly in operations, such as the postal service, which have large numbers of employees who work in relatively few jobs. In addition, in recent years some companies have extended the classification approach to professional positions. Classification systems are used for different levels of professional jobs, defining, in essence, levels of professional attainment and the types of work typically performed at each level. Finally, classification methods are increasingly finding use in the business disciplines such as accounting, personnel, law, industrial engineering, and investment work.

The Point Evaluation System

The point evaluation system is one of the most widely used in business today. Under this system, various factors of a group of jobs are selected and defined. A separate yardstick describing different degrees of each factor is prepared, and a job is then ranked against every yardstick. In essence, this is the same process as the classification system except that the job is evaluated on a separate scale for each factor and point weightings are assigned.

The type of factor yardstick used in point evaluation plans is illustrated in Figure 9. In evaluating jobs, the analyst simply studies the job duties and compares them against the yardstick. He then assigns the job the degree which seems to describe best the extent to which the factor is important. This process is repeated for each factor, and the point values of each factor degree are totaled.

Point evaluation has a number of advantages over the less refined ranking and classification systems. The use of fixed, predetermined factors forces the evaluator to consider the same job elements when rating every job. Furthermore, the assignment of point values indicates not only which job is worth more than another but how much more it is worth. Finally, a record of the judgments of the evaluator is available for explaining the results of the evaluation to supervisors and employees alike.

The major problem with the point evaluation system is the difficulty of selecting relevant factors and assigning appropriate point

Figure 9. **Yardstick in a point evaluation plan.**

FACTOR: Know-how
CONSIDERATIONS: Educational background and amount of experience necessary for satisfactory performance of a given job.

DEGREE	DESCRIPTION	POINTS
1	Requires only average learning ability and good aptitude for factory operations; an average three-week learning period needed for satisfactory performance; ability to follow instructions and perform repetitive operations under periodic check is essential.	28
2	Instructions more varied but still of a routine nature; typical of job with a more diverse work cycle or where minor adjustments to equipment are involved; a basic general shop knowledge gained through previous experience in such jobs as machine operation, methodized assembly, or inspection work is required.	56
3	Requires some specific knowledge, such as blueprint reading and use of adjustable gauges; aptitude for understanding machine operations and shop problems is necessary; calls for systematic training on the job.	84
4	Requires some technical knowledge gained through formal trade school courses and previous shop experience; some advanced technical school training in mathematics and machine shop techniques is required; thorough knowledge of plant operations and equipment and extensive on-the-job training in a variety of phases of shop work are necessary.	112
5	Requires extensive technical knowledge gained through formal training and/or related instruction in advanced technical information (including a high school education and full apprenticeship training); requires ability to perform diverse tasks subject to only occasional check.	140

values to them. In addition, there is the problem of determining the correct number of degrees: ideally, just enough degrees are established to identify minimum measurable differences in the factor. Another special problem of point plans is that of defining each degree clearly enough so that it will serve as a meaningful guide to evaluators and also provide employees with an understandable explanation of the results.

The Factor Comparison System

A fourth evaluation system which has been widely used in business is factor comparison, in which various factors are compared on a job-by-job basis, without definitions for the various degrees. In other words, the evaluator analyzes and ranks all jobs in terms of one factor, then ranks all in relation to a second factor, and so forth, until point rankings have been established for each of the factors used. The evaluator need then only total the points assigned to a job under each of the factors to get the job's overall relative worth.

Factor comparison has two basic advantages. First, it uses the job-by-job comparison technique. Second, it does not involve the semantic problems encountered in building factor yardsticks, since the various degrees do not have to be defined. However, because of the lack of definitions, it is very difficult to explain the results of factor comparison evaluations to employees or supervisors.

As in the point evaluation system, the factors selected, the number of degrees used, and the weighting assigned to each degree are critical. At least three factors must be included in any factor comparison plan. The first essential factor is responsibility, which defines the scope or magnitude of an employee's job and its impact on business results. The second factor is authority (sometimes referred to as latitude of action), which measures the degree of freedom an employee has to exercise responsibility. The third essential factor must measure the knowledge and skill required to perform the duties assigned. In addition, in operations jobs it is sometimes necessary to include a fourth factor which measures the difficulty of circumstances under which work must be performed.

These factors may, of course, be divided. For instance, a plan might measure responsibility in terms of two separate components: responsibility for the use of assets and responsibility for the use of human resources. This is done to inject more precision into the evaluation process. However, the more factors there are included in a plan, the more likely that a given factor will be overweighted or measured twice. Also, the more factors there are, the greater the administrative complications. As a general rule, job evaluation must have three factors and should not have more than six.

Combination Systems

Many companies have combined features of the point evaluation and factor comparison systems to gain the advantages of both. Even when this is not a part of company policy, it is frequently done by individual evaluators or managers in order to gain more accurate results. Combination systems usually involve slotting all jobs by means of a point plan and then auditing the results through a job-by-job comparison within each factor. While the process entails a double evaluation, the results usually justify the extra effort. The major combination systems in use are multiple evaluation and cross evaluation.

In some companies multiple-evaluation plans are a required part of wage and salary administration. One such plan calls for evaluation of each position three times by three different factor comparison techniques. If the results in each case are not identical, the evaluations are reviewed and adjusted. This involves triple work, and the increase in precision must be weighed against the cost.

Cross evaluation is used primarily for auditing the results of job evaluation. In some companies cross-evaluation systems are a formal part of the salary administration program. Usually, however, they are informal and unofficial techniques developed by staff personnel or line managers.

One type of cross-evaluation system involves reviewing the results of all job evaluations in a family of jobs, such as accounting. Comparisons are made of a sampling of the company's accounting jobs, representing a cross section by functional unit, organizational unit, and geographic locations. The results are then checked against the rankings of an evaluator with an understanding of the field to assure that evaluation levels are consistent with normal lines of promotion.

Another cross-evaluation system involves comparing evaluation results with normal career movement patterns. In many large companies there are fairly well-established career patterns: the successive series of jobs a person moves through as he progresses in his field. Cross evaluation tests job evaluation results to make sure that each move is at least a transfer and that most are promotions.

Other methods of cross evaluation include:

- Ranking all jobs by point values assigned and reviewing results by overall judgments.
- Grouping all jobs whose total point values are similar and checking each group to make sure that jobs are worth about the same pay based on survey data and/or company employment experience.
- Examining all positions which have been assigned the same degree of a factor to see if the grouping is logical and reasonable.

MARKET EVALUATION SYSTEMS

The traditional job evaluation systems which have been described up to this point involve judgments on an administrative and, to some extent, artificial basis. The problems with such judgments have been noted. The point here is that under this traditional approach all jobs are valued in dollars *at the end of the evaluation process* by pricing a limited sample of jobs in the labor market.

During the past twenty years, however, an enormous amount of market survey information has become available, making possible a reversal of the traditional job evaluation system. Under the new approach, which may be labeled the market evaluation system, a significant number of jobs are priced at the outset by determining competitive pay levels for similar work in comparable enterprises.

Once these "benchmark" jobs have been priced in the relevant labor markets, the average pay of each establishes the relative pay of one to the other. These relationships become the cornerstone of job evaluation; they are givens which can change only if relative market pay relationships change.

All other positions are evaluated by comparison against the benchmark jobs. This is done most often by straight ranking. However, any of the evaluation systems described or any combination of them may be used to evaluate nonbenchmark jobs (those which cannot be priced directly in the marketplace). The evaluation system cannot change the relative relationships of benchmark positions; the benchmark job relationships, in fact, shape the job evaluation plan.

A market evaluation system is applicable only where a relatively large number of jobs can be priced by available survey information. Generally, a minimum of 10 percent of the jobs, and ideally 20 percent, must be priced in the marketplace in order to apply the market evaluation system. This is usually possible for professional positions, middle-level positions, and management positions.

The major advantage of the market evaluation system is that the market is built into the program from the start, thereby insuring that evaluation results conform to the realities of the marketplace. In addition, the market system is far more manageable than other techniques. Imperfections of pay surveys are great but not as great as the cumulative imperfections of administrative judgments inherent in traditional job evaluation.

Furthermore, market programs are far more understandable and acceptable to supervisors and employees than traditional job evaluation programs. In the traditional evaluation approach, for instance, no one can ever really satisfactorily explain why a salesman is in a higher grade than, say, an accountant. But if the answer is that salesmen at a given level are *paid* more than accountants at a given level, that is simply describing what exists. The company did not make these judgments; the labor market did. The market has valued work done and the experience that goes with doing the work. These are clearly more objective than subjective job evaluation decisions and therefore tend to be more acceptable to employees. Staff must make sure, however, that survey data are valid and that benchmark jobs do not reflect unusual or temporary market conditions.

GROUPING AND GRADING

The results of job evaluation under either point evaluation or factor comparison plans are total points assigned to various jobs. These, in turn, establish the relative value among all jobs. Theoretically, it is possible to give dollar values to all jobs in direct proportion to the points assigned.

This is administratively impractical, however, since it would create as many different pay grades as there were jobs in the company. Also, since even very small changes in duties would probably require adjustments in total points, pay grades would be changing constantly. The results of job evaluation can never be accurate enough to justify such fine distinctions, so for technical as well as administrative reasons jobs should be grouped into pay grades.

The establishment of pay grades is a complex process. Fundamentally, it involves grouping in such a way as to (1) place jobs of the same general value in the same grade, (2) insure that jobs of distinctly different value are in different grades, and (3) provide for a smooth progression of point groups. The pay grades established should fit realistically into the existing pay relationships within the company and should conform reasonably to pay patterns in the labor market.

This means, technically speaking, that the results of job evaluation are first inspected to locate the natural cutoff points and to be sure that groupings are reasonable and logical. The smooth progression that is the best fit statistically is then determined, and these results are again examined for logical internal relationships existing in the labor market. In other words, it is necessary to inspect both the results of job evaluation and the labor market survey before determining final cutoff points.

After this process is completed, all jobs that fall within the cutoff points are considered to have the same basic value. For instance, all jobs which total between 361 and 400 evaluation points might be placed in pay grade 6 (see Figure 10).

While administratively sound, this process raises some difficulties

It is relatively easy to defend the placing of job D (382 points) and job E (379 points) in the same pay grade. The difficulty comes in explaining why job F (362 points) is in grade 6 while job G (359 points) is only in grade 5. Such distinctions can be justified only on practical grounds—if pay grades are to be established at all, there must be some cutoff points. Borderline jobs will always exist and, as long as point groupings are based on a smooth progression, the cutoff points are at least consistent and impartial. Borderline cases should be reviewed carefully, however. Many companies place borderline jobs in the next higher ranking whenever there is reasonable doubt.

The ultimate result of job evaluation is the grouping of jobs of similar value into the same pay grade—and the creation of a logical and consistent series of pay grades from the lowest to the highest. Dollar values must then be put on the pay grades—which involves pricing the structure. Before getting to this, however, we must consider several important questions involving the use of job evaluation.

USE OF JOB EVALUATION

Job evaluation is the cornerstone of a formal wage and salary program. Without a realistic determination of relative job worth, it would be difficult, if not impossible, for management to establish a formal program. Specifically, the job evaluation process plays a key role in the following ways:

- Job evaluation is the most effective means of determining internal pay relationships.
- Evaluation can be used as an instrument for effecting the company's basic pay policies.
- Equitable base pay relationships set by job evaluation serve as a foundation for incentive or bonus plans and merit increase programs.
- Job evaluation provides a reasonable basis for personnel moves. Unless relative job levels are correct, managers will not know whether a personnel move represents a promotion, a transfer, or a demotion.
- Useful controls over wage and salary costs can be greatly aided by job evaluation.
- Job evaluation provides a realistic foundation for gearing company pay scales to wages paid by competing companies.
- Job evaluation assists managers in meeting day-to-day pay problems. This, in turn, contributes to the reduction of employee

grievances, to higher employee morale and productivity, and to decreased turnover.

– By serving as a framework for decision making and a method of control, job evaluation makes greater delegation of pay decisions possible and thus conserves the time of top management.

These are the important advantages to be gained from job evaluation. However, the establishment of a job evaluation program may mean a substantial increase in costs—including the salaries of staff personnel, the time that managers devote to the evaluation process, administrative costs, and possibly costs for outside consulting services. Top management must, of course, weigh these costs against the potential benefits.

Problems of Design

Most of the technical problems associated with designing a job evaluation plan are the concern of staff specialists and outside consultants. However, two problems have special relevance to the individual manager. These are selection of the factors to be used to measure job difficulty and assignment of point values.

As for the selection of factors, experience has shown that there are a number of requirements:

– Each factor must have some relationship to job difficulty or job value.
– In combination, the factors should correlate reasonably well with job difficulty.
– The factors selected must be both observable and measurable.
– Important elements of every job must be measured by one or more factors.
– Every factor should serve to help distinguish between jobs.
– Two factors should not measure essentially the same characteristic.

The assignment of point values within each factor is important because it establishes the relative significance of the factors used in the plan. For example, if the maximum assigned to the factor "know-how" is 200 points, and the maximum assigned to "working conditions" is 100 points, then the plan says, in effect, that know-how is twice as important as working conditions in determining job difficulty.

There is no one correct set of factors or point weightings. Many different combinations have been used successfully. Ideally, factors and weightings are geared to the level and nature of jobs covered, the type of business, and similar considerations. Therefore, it is dangerous to copy an existing plan, even one that has been successful elsewhere, unless pertinent conditions are similar.

It is apparent, even from this brief description of technical problems, that the job evaluation yardstick itself, as well as the job evaluation process, is basically subjective. Unless the difficult decisions involved are made by experienced persons, the plan can result in distorted pay relationships or can become an administrative burden without purpose.

Problems of factor selection and point weightings are becoming increasingly complex as the number and different types of jobs continue to increase. Most job evaluation plans and particularly those canned plans which have been in use for many years tend to undervalue professional positions, to overvalue the importance of supervision of assets and numbers of people, and to result in serious inequities in middle-level positions.

Problems of Measurement

There are a number of problems of measurement which may be encountered by evaluators. For instance, most jobs include heterogeneous duties which are difficult to measure. If these duties were evaluated separately, they would frequently result in different job classifications. As a general rule in such cases, evaluation is based on the principal duty performed as a regular part of the assigned job. In this way—assuming, as should be so, that the employee spends most of his time working at his highest level of skill—credit is given for the highest skill the job requires.

A similar problem, frequently encountered in smaller organizations, is the "combination job," in which two or more separate sets of duties are performed by one individual. In hourly paid jobs each set is often evaluated separately, and employees are paid at different rates according to the number of hours spent at the different types of work. For most salaried jobs, however, this is not practical; jobs are classified and evaluated on the basis of the higher-level or more difficult set of duties.

Another problem in job evaluation is whether jobs should be measured on the basis of minimum, average, or maximum requirements. Generally, evaluation is based on minimum job requirements because of the great difficulty of determining either average or maximum requirements. As long as all jobs are measured consistently in this manner, the final results of evaluation will not be influenced.

Still another problem of measurement involves jobs that cannot really be judged by the rules. Frequently, for instance, secretarial positions are classified strictly on the basis of the boss's stature, regardless of the work performed. As a result, a secretary to a vice president may be classified as an executive secretary even though she never takes shorthand and really is assigned only lower-level clerical work. Many technical jobs are also classified in a manner inconsistent with the job evaluation program. This is because the duties of technical personnel are not rigidly defined. Such employees may be moved from one assignment to another on the basis of their background, experience, and skills and the work which is available.

Finally, there are a number of special evaluation problems which a company may face. In rapidly growing organizational units, for instance, it may not be possible to specify exact job duties, and the work assigned may depend on the types of people who can be recruited. In addition, changes in organization or technological methods may cause mass upgradings or downgradings. In these circumstances, what may be good evaluation techniques may be very bad business practice. Finally, in trainee positions a straightforward evaluation of job duties would result in unrealistic classifications, since the work assigned is intended largely to prepare the trainee for future responsibilities.

Accuracy of Results

Unfortunately, there is no objective method of assessing just how precise job evaluation is in determining relative job worth. It is not possible to *measure* the accuracy of job evaluation; it is possible only to *judge* accuracy. There are a number of practical tests that the manager can apply in judging the accuracy of his job evaluation program:

- Does the program result in more logical pay relationships than those which might exist without it?
- Does evaluation facilitate the solution of daily problems?
- Are the results acceptable to employees?
- Does job evaluation contribute to that rather indefinable quality of good human relations?
- Does evaluation help to answer or to avoid employee grievances concerning pay classifications?
- Do the results of evaluation agree reasonably with established paths of job progression?

- Do the results correspond realistically to existing market pay relationships?
- Does the evaluation program tie in with the company's operating needs?
- Do the results justify the additional costs?
- Does evaluation provide top management with a technique which helps to put company policies into effect? At the same time, does it provide reasonable control of company wage costs?

The final test of accuracy is management experience. Does job evaluation guide managers in making reasonable judgments with respect to relative job worth? Observation of many programs and their results, particularly in the past few years, leads to the conclusion that with a sound evaluation plan two reasonable men, both of whom know the job being measured, will not disagree on more than one of ten factor judgments. This means that there will probably not be differences of more than one pay level in more than one job in 30. In any judgmental exercise, this represents a high degree of accuracy.

Improving Results

The usefulness and accuracy of the job evaluation program depend on how well the program is conceived, how well it is geared to the individual company's situation, and how well the evaluations are carried out. This last consideration is, of course, a question of how well managers use the evaluation tools which have been provided. Various techniques can be used to increase the accuracy and usefulness of evaluation results.

For example, the very order in which jobs are compared can affect the quality of evaluation. The first jobs evaluated should be those with which the manager is generally familiar and in which the duties are fairly standard. The results of these evaluations can then be used as an additional yardstick for slotting other jobs. Also, since it is usually easier and more accurate to compare jobs whose duties are related, the evaluator may find it helpful to select families of jobs—for instance, all bookkeeping and accounting positions.

Another way in which evaluators can improve their effectiveness is by screening their judgments for personal biases or prejudices. For example, managers frequently form preconceived notions about where a job should fit and then proceed to justify them. This is a little like cheating at solitaire, and those who are guilty of this error might ask themselves what plan was used to arrive at the preconceived notions.

Care must also be taken to evaluate the job rather than the individual on the job. Finally, it is important to avoid the "halo effect"—that is, the tendency to be influenced in one's overall ranking of a job by the ranking assigned to the job's dominant factor.

Each of these techniques helps the evaluator to increase the effectiveness of his evaluations. However, all are dependent on his know-how and his conscientiousness. Perfunctory evaluations do not yield satisfactory results; evaluators must have the time to do the job and must be required to do it well. Most important, no evaluation system can be effective unless it is used. Every manager must use the plan, and management must require that it be followed throughout the organization. If someone has a better system, let him propose it; then his may become the system used by everyone.

MANAGER'S ROLE IN THE EVALUATION PROCESS

All managers participate in the job evaluation process. Just how they participate, and to what extent, will depend on circumstances. Most companies have assigned the responsibility for evaluation decisions to staff specialists. There are several reasons for this: specialization generally means greater efficiency; staff specialists tend to be more objective; greater consistency is obtained when a limited number of persons interpret and apply the job evaluation plan in different departments; and staff specialists are held strictly accountable for results.

It is interesting to note, however, that a few companies have recently had good results from reversing the traditional line-staff roles in job evaluation. Under such an approach, line supervisors have the responsibility for making evaluation decisions, and staff specialists have the right to review and appeal. The basic advantage of this approach is that it utilizes the line manager's knowledge—the knowledge about the job—which is critical to successful job evaluation. In addition, it involves the manager in meaningful participation in a responsibility that is essentially a part of his job. A framework system and controls can be developed to prevent the judgments of some managers from getting far out of line from those of other managers and thus causing inequities within the organization.

Even when staff specialists evaluate jobs, line managers still have the basic responsibility for reviewing both the job analysis and the results of job evaluation. This review carries with it the authority to approve or appeal. Managers also have the obligation of keeping the program up to date. It is vital that they report changes in organization, job assignments, and methods of work to insure that classifications are kept current.

In carrying out the program, managers should not try to circumvent the system in order to obtain what may seem like operating advantages. For instance, the manager who presses for identical classifications for a large number of jobs may think that this will ease the problem of assigning employees to jobs and avoid employee complaints. Actually, he is creating inequities in pay relationships which will probably lead to more serious problems than those he was trying to solve. Another tempting, but highly dangerous, practice is to deal with basic personnel problems by artificially upgrading employees. The manager who yields to employees' pleas or to the pressure of circumstances and who attempts to solve difficult personnel problems in this manner is only creating inequities which will result in greater problems in the future.

Individual managers have a fundamental responsibility for explaining job evaluation to employees. It is neither possible nor desirable to make job evaluation experts out of employees; but the manager should see that they understand such basic aspects of job evaluation as these:

- The reasons why the company established a job evaluation program.
- The way job evaluation works.
- The fact that the program is concerned with measuring the job, not the person on the job.
- The fact that job evaluation seeks only to establish relative job worth.
- The fact that the job evaluation plan is applied consistently to all jobs.
- The factors which are used to determine relative job worth and how and why they were selected.

Staff personnel can help to explain job evaluation by preparing booklets or by holding meetings with employees. It is the supervisor, however, who is the closest to his employees, and he should know best what they do not understand about the plan. Furthermore, he can take advantage of his discussions with employees on specific pay questions or grievances to re-explain and resell the program.

5

PRICING JOB VALUE

THE PURPOSE OF JOB EVALUATION is to establish the relative difficulty of jobs within the company in terms of points or rankings and in terms of pay levels. The next step is to translate these data into a pay structure. This involves first pricing the pay grades and then setting up pay ranges for each grade.

STEPS IN JOB PRICING

The process of pricing the pay structure is summarized in Figure 10. Translating points into job grades has already been described and is summarized in columns A–C. The remaining columns illustrate the method used to assign salary dollars to each of these pay grades.

Once jobs have been grouped into pay grades, it is possible to price them all by surveying pay levels for comparable jobs in other companies. Not every position can be surveyed, of course, since many of the jobs in a company are unique. When jobs have been grouped, however, only a limited number need to be priced in each group. The pay structure can then be established on the mathematical principle that things which are equal to the same things are equal to each other.

Figure 10. **Illustration of steps in pricing the pay structure.**

STEP 1: COLUMN A *Evaluation Results* Express pay relationships only in terms of total point values for each job evaluated.	STEP 2: COLUMN B *Group Jobs* Choose logical cutoff points; group jobs with about the same number of point values. Determine cutoff points by number of grades needed, job groupings, and market pay relationships.	STEP 3: COLUMN C *Grade Jobs* Establish pay grade by "best fit" point groupings. Develop smooth progression (40 points per pay grade) for consistent and impartial treatment.
Job A 427 points Job B 427 points Job C 418 points	418–427 points	Grade 7: 401 or more points
Job D 382 points Job E 379 points Job F 362 points	362–382 points	Grade 6: 361–400 points
Job G 359 points Job H 340 points Job I 338 points	338–359 points	Grade 5: 321–360 points
Job J 299 points Job K 297 points Job L 295 points Job M 291 points Job N 291 points Job O 283 points	283–299 points	Grade 4: 281–320 points
Job P 250 points	250 points	Grade 3: 241–280 points
Job Q 223 points	223 points	Grade 2: 201–240 points
Job R 190 points Job S 188 points Job T 170 points	170–190 points	Grade 1: Under 200 points

In Figure 10, seven of the jobs in column D are assumed to be comparable to jobs in other companies which will be surveyed. Since jobs D, E, and F have been grouped into grade 6, all will receive the same pay. This figure will be set when job E is priced.

From the survey of other companies, base salaries for each pay grade are established. In Figure 10 the actual salaries (column E)

	STEP 4: COLUMN D	STEP 5: COLUMN E	STEP 6: COLUMN F
	Conduct Survey	*Establish Base Salary*	*Establish Pay Ranges*
	Select "key" jobs. Survey comparable companies to determine average weekly salary paid.	Determine best fit from wage survey consistent with basic company wage policy.	Provide for individual compensation on the basis of merit or length of service (15 percent spread; 6 percent between grades).
A	$198	$196	$160–$229
E	$175	$177	$146–$208
H	$166	$162	$133–$188
K	$155	$154	$127–$179
M	$143	$146	$121–$171
P	$140	$133	$112–$156
Q	–	$121	$102–$142
S	$105	$110	$92–$127

represent the "best fit" from the survey results. These salaries reflect a company policy of establishing base pay levels equal to the average paid by the companies surveyed. The result is a smooth percentage progression in base salary between grades.

The next step in job pricing is to establish pay ranges around the base salaries. In Figure 10 the base salaries were used as the midpoint for the ranges. Once salary ranges have been set, individual compensation based on performance and other considerations can be determined. Ranges also give the company needed flexibility in hiring new employees, in administering salaries to deal with special situations in labor markets, and in handling other administrative problems.

PRICING THE STRUCTURE: THE SURVEY

In determining dollar values for the pay structure, management must consider such factors as financial characteristics of the business, growth objectives, profitability, and the nature of the firm's operations. Primary consideration, however, must be given to levels of pay in competitive firms—not only to establish equitable salary levels but also to make sure that pay levels are sufficient to attract and retain qualified people. The primary method of determining competitive levels of pay is the market survey.

Market survey reports are available from a number of sources, including management organizations, government agencies (particularly the Bureau of Labor Statistics), various types of employer associations, and some consulting firms. Such information may be used for pricing a company's pay structure and is by far the quickest and least costly method of surveying.

When more specific or detailed information on pay levels is required, a company may have to conduct a survey on its own or, if possible, in conjunction with a group of companies. Four steps are essential in undertaking a direct survey: determining the companies to be surveyed, selecting the jobs for comparison, deciding what supplemental data should be obtained, and conducting the survey in a technically sound fashion.

Which companies are chosen for comparison can be a critical factor, for if a firm lacks significance in terms of the purpose of the survey, the results will be meaningless. Actually, in a large number of labor markets almost any hypothesis can be proven by carefully selecting the companies to be surveyed. For valid results, a firm should be chosen on the basis of questions such as these:

- Does the company really compete for available talent? Have any of the firm's employees left to go to companies on the list or to similar companies—or vice versa?
- Are the company's operations comparable to those in the survey list?

- Are there enough jobs in common to make the survey reasonable?
- Is the company a product competitor or is it reasonably comparable in terms of economic and operating characteristics?
- Is the company large enough to provide a sufficient number of comparisons to make the survey meaningful?
- Does the company have a reasonably sound wage and salary program?
- Can the company be counted on to supply accurate and reliable data?

Under the best of conditions, selecting companies for a survey is not an easy task. No two companies are alike—even two companies of equivalent size in the same type of business. Furthermore, it is difficult to categorize any company by the type of business it conducts both because of the diversity of operations in any enterprise and because of the increasing number of multiple-business companies.

To complicate matters, most businesses operate not in one labor market but in a number of different markets. One medium-size company with three locations found that it was actually competing significantly in seventeen different labor markets. Even within a single employee group, labor markets can be highly diversified. For example, among management personnel the market for manufacturing managers may be very different from the market for financial managers. Another difficulty in selecting companies for a survey concerns staff versus operational positions. In staff jobs there is a very high transference among industries. In fact, professional and staff personnel identify more with their field of work than with current employers.

After suitable companies have been chosen, the surveying firm must select jobs for comparison. The usual technique is to pick out "key" jobs within the company and to get rates for comparable jobs in each of the companies being studied. Key jobs in this case means jobs which represent a good cross section of the company's pay structure; generally, at least one job from each pay grade should be included. It is also helpful if the key jobs constitute a sampling of the various operating units and functional units of the company. Finally, the jobs selected should be representative of those found in the companies to be surveyed.

The value of the survey data depends to a considerable extent on how carefully key jobs are selected and how well they match jobs in the cooperating companies. In order to make sure that jobs are truly comparable, the firm should have an analyst write out survey job descriptions and discuss the key jobs with the companies surveyed.

After the survey data have been collected, the analyst must tabulate and then summarize the results. When the data are to be presented to management, the analyst usually prepares a summary which points up major findings and conclusions.

A typical format for such a summary is shown in Figure 11, which compares the data collected with the recommended company pay structure. Charts like this provide management with a clear idea of how its pay compares with competitive rates in the firms surveyed. Such data can, of course, be quite misleading unless management has some understanding of the method of collection and the statistical composition of the material. The information in Figure 11 does not, for instance, give the total market area picture; it represents only the rates paid by those companies surveyed. This may be a small propor-

Figure 11. **Data from area salary survey compared with recommended company pay structure.**

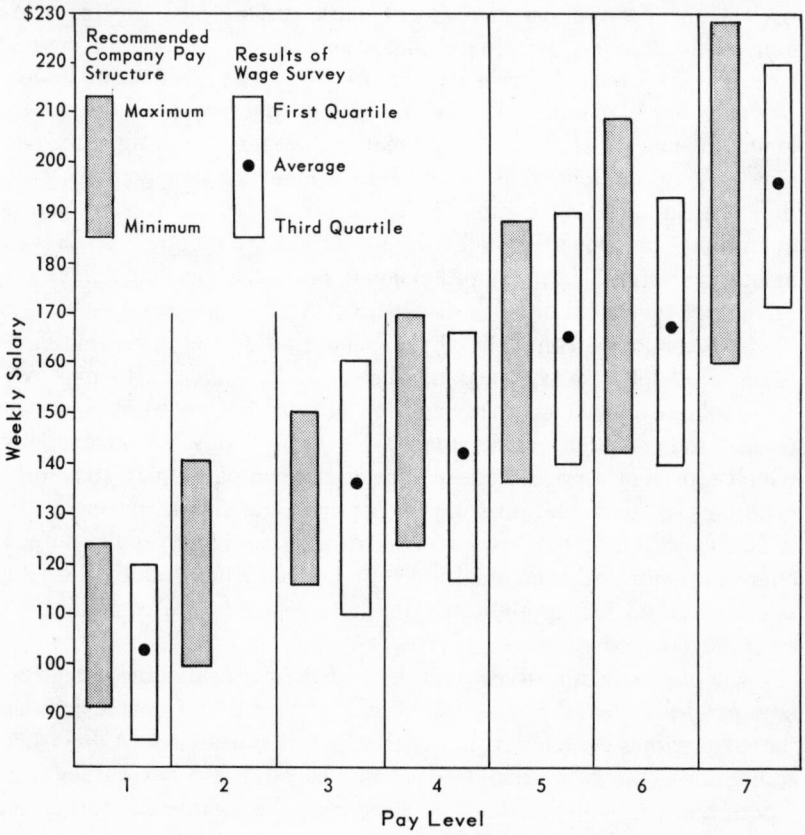

tion of the total in large market areas. Furthermore, only the quartile range is shown, not the total dispersion of rates. Conceivably, these quartile figures could represent 50 percent of the jobs but only 10 percent of the dispersion of rates paid by the companies surveyed. Finally, the data give no indication of how many rates were reported, whether there was good coverage in each pay grade, whether all companies surveyed gave information relating to each grade, or whether a few large companies dominated any of the data presented. Such statistical imperfections suggest that survey results should be regarded as only a broad indication of the labor market situation.

Studies show that when pay surveys are properly conducted, they are accurate within 5 percent for operations positions and 10 percent for top-level positions. The typical dispersion from highest pay to lowest pay (even excluding the top and bottom 10 percent) is over 50 percent for clerical positions and as much as 200 percent for management positions. Thus even the best surveys are not scientifically accurate, and management has considerable latitude in setting a "competitive pay structure."

PRICING THE STRUCTURE: OTHER CONSIDERATIONS

While the survey is an important factor in translating job evaluation points into a pay structure, the company must consider other basic factors, such as the competitiveness of the labor market, the availability of labor (especially in critical-skill occupations), and the rate at which employees are being recruited. Ordinarily, a company that is faced with rapid build-up and large recruitment requirements tends to set its pay structure somewhat higher than it might otherwise.

Information with respect to pay of employment candidates can be a low-cost supplemental input to survey data. Such information represents only a special part of the overall market, but it does provide a measure of the "in-market." Carefully evaluated against relative qualifications of candidates, it can be valuable; employment information presents "replacement cost" data, just as survey information presents competitive pay data.

The level of the company pay structure may also be influenced by the quality of the workers that management hopes to attract. For example, a company may set base pay high in order to obtain the most capable people. The success of such a practice depends, of course, on the company's ability and willingness (1) to outbid other employers for higher-caliber employees, (2) to screen and select more capable individuals, and (3) to utilize them. On the other hand, a company may deliberately enter the labor market with wages which are geared only to the average, on the assumption that average proficiency will serve the company's needs. Management may even intentionally pay wages which are somewhat below average because it believes that it can still attract the number of workers that it needs, or because of the economics and competitiveness of its own business as compared with others in the labor market.

Generally, companies attempt to keep their structures competitive with those of other firms in the product market. Here again, however, a company does have some choice, because high wages do not necessarily mean high wage costs. The importance of product-competitor factors depends mainly on the competitive nature of the business, but it should also be influenced by such considerations as the following: productivity levels, ratio of wage costs to total costs, present level of profits, business forecasts, ability to pass on higher wage costs to customers through price increases, and product differentiation. Most important of all is the fact that the level of wage costs is more a function of number of employees than pay levels.

There are other operations-oriented considerations which may be relevant under certain conditions. A company may, for instance, use pay administration to encourage employees to move into certain types of work or areas of the business. Such a strategy aims at allocating business resources. Or a company may adopt a strategy of protecting key human talent by deliberately paying above-average salaries to employees with critical skills or with hard-to-replace experience.

Finally, changes in pay over a period of time must be taken into account in pricing the pay structure. Clearly, a company's decision to increase its pay at a faster or slower rate than other firms will affect its future efforts in recruiting and its competitive position. A company must also consider pay changes because employees are sensitive to them. General pay increases have gained considerable publicity, particularly in recent years. When employees read or hear about increases which are more generous than those granted by their own company, morale suffers, and the turnover rate may increase as well.

Employees are extremely conscious of changes in the cost of living. They recognize that unless their salary increases at least as fast as the cost of living, their standard of living will decline. In a dynamic economy such as ours, people expect a continued improvement in their standard of living. They therefore tend to look to the company for pay increases which at least keep pace with, and hopefully outpace, increases in living costs.

It should be apparent even from this brief summary that a company cannot depend solely on the results of a labor market survey to carry out its pay policy. All the considerations mentioned above are important in company pay decisions and should be given some weight when the pay structure is established or changed.

CHARACTERISTICS OF TRADITIONAL PAY STRUCTURES

Table 4 shows a typical company pay structure covering all positions in the firm. The table illustrates not only the technical features of the structure but also how pay levels for different groups of employees overlap. Since managers must use such a structure to make pay decisions, it is essential that they acquire some knowledge of its basic characteristics.

Several technical features deserve attention. The minimum salary level in each pay grade should roughly reflect the pay needed to hire most candidates with minimum qualifications in that grade. The progression from the minimum of one grade to the minimum of the next higher grade will vary depending on the jobs, the nature of the labor markets, the job evaluation system used, methods of pricing the job, the diversity of jobs, and company compensation strategy. The usual variations in progression from one pay grade to the next higher pay grade are from 6 to 10 percent for operations jobs, from 7 to 12 percent for middle-level positions, and from 10 to 15 percent for professional and management positions. Of equal importance, particularly to operating managers, is the fact that this progression should follow some logical pattern—for example, the same percentage spread between all grades. Otherwise, it will be impossible for managers to explain or justify pay ranges.

The within-grade spread will vary depending on two factors: the company's method of compensating individual performance on the job and the opportunity an employee has to determine work effectiveness. When the company follows a merit pay policy, the range tends to be greater for higher-level jobs. The logic here is that higher-level employees have a greater opportunity than operations employees to exercise initiative, utilize efficient work habits, and develop other qualities which increase personal productivity; in addition, higher-

Table 4. **Typical salary structure.**

	Salary Range ($000)			*Percentage Spread*	
Pay Grade	*Minimum*	*Midpoint*	*Maximum*	*Between*	*Within*
31	77.0	100.0	123.0	10	60
30	70.0	91.0	112.0	10	60
29	64.0	83.0	102.0	10	60
28	58.0	75.0	92.0	10	60
27	53.0	68.0	83.0	10	55
26	49.0	62.0	75.0	10	55
25	44.0	56.0	68.0	10	55
24	40.0	51.0	62.0	10	55
23	36.0	46.0	56.0	10	55
22	33.5	42.0	50.5	10	50
21	30.0	38.0	46.0	10	50
20	28.0	35.0	42.0	10	50
19	25.5	32.0	38.5	10	50
18	23.0	29.0	35.0	10	50
17	21.0	26.0	31.0	10	45
16	19.0	24.0	29.0	10	45
15	18.0	22.0	26.0	10	45
14	16.5	20.0	23.5	10	45
13	14.5	18.0	21.5	10	45
12	13.8	16.5	19.2	10	40
11	12.5	15.0	17.5	10	40
10	11.3	13.5	15.7	10	40
9	10.0	12.0	14.0	10	40
8	9.3	11.0	12.7	10	35
7	8.5	10.0	11.5	10	35
6	7.7	9.0	10.3	10	35
5	6.8	8.0	9.2	10	35
4	6.5	7.5	8.5	10	30
3	6.1	7.0	7.9	10	30
2	5.6	6.5	7.4	10	30
1	5.2	6.0	6.8	10	30

level employees have less opportunity for promotion than operations employees. As a result, the within-grade spread generally varies from 0 to 30 percent for operations jobs, from 25 to 40 percent for middle-level positions, and from 30 to 100 percent for management positions. This means that there is an overlap of three to four pay grades in most situations; that is, the maximum of a pay grade will be within the range of a grade which is three or four levels higher.

The maximums of pay ranges are particularly difficult to establish; they are even more difficult to defend. There is some theoretical maximum for every job, and regardless of how well a person performs he will reach a point at which further improvement either is limited by the nature of the duties assigned or adds nothing to the operation. This reasoning is sound, except perhaps for higher-level management positions. The questions are always: At what point should pay maximums be established? How should they be administered? What does the manager do when an employee reaches the top of his range?

There is no scientific means of determining where maximums should be placed. As indicated earlier, pay ranges should reflect to some extent the individual's potential contribution on the job. The company can also be guided by the maximums reported by other companies in the area. Regardless of what maximums are set, however, some employees will eventually reach the top of their range. For a person with potential for greater responsibility, the ideal solution is promotion. Because higher positions are not always available, a manager should start exploring the possibilities for promotion before such an employee reaches the maximum of his range. In this respect the manager must take a broad view and be willing to part with a capable person who deserves promotion.

Actually, promotional opportunities are almost always available for high-talent employees in any company, even when business is declining. Few companies have such an overabundance of able workers that the manager cannot, with some planning, take advantage of their talents. Promotions need not be to new jobs; they may take the form of additional responsibilities in the same job—responsibilities which justify a higher-level pay classification.

There remains, however, the problem of the employee who has reached the maximum of his range and who is not really capable of assuming greater responsibilities. If the structure has been properly set, such an employee is already receiving top pay for top performance. He can still look forward to sharing in general increases granted by the company and to benefiting from adjustments in the pay structure. He can also expect the advantages which generally come with years of company service: longer vacations, higher pensions, and greater job security.

There are other characteristics of pay structures which are of general interest to managers. For example, pay relationships between jobs in the company structure are set by techniques of job evaluation and job grading and logically do not change over a period of time. On the other hand, labor market pay relationships are influenced by supply and demand, industry composition in the market, collective bargaining agreements, and other factors. Furthermore, pay relationships in a market area will change—and sometimes dramatically. Finally, multilocation companies with a single evaluation plan must realize that pay relationships between jobs may vary from one market area to another.

Such characteristics suggest a need for flexibility in administering pay structures. Management must keep in close touch with employment and turnover activity, as well as survey data, to make sure that administratively determined pay relationships conform to actual relationships in relevant labor markets. When exceptions exist, they should be made. Any plan that earmarks more than 2 percent of the jobs as exceptions is probably in trouble, but a plan that has no exceptions is probably in trouble also. The essential point is that managers should deal with exceptions by exempting them from the system, rather than by adjusting the system.

Explaining Pay Structure to Employees

The process of setting up and pricing the pay structure is so technical that it does not lend itself readily to simple explanation. However, it is generally only necessary to get across a few basic ideas to employees:

- Pay grades are established to reward employees for different levels of skill, responsibility, and knowledge.
- The structure is uniform in its nature and administration.
- The structure is competitive. Usually phrases like "as much or more than," "equal to," and "the going rate" are sufficiently detailed, provided they are accurate.
- A range of pay, from minimum to maximum, is established to reward employees for experience and performance.

If the company's policy is to pay average rates with respect to the labor market, it would not necessarily be correct to tell employees that the pay for a given job is equal to rates paid by any company in the area for that job. Pay relationships vary somewhat within each company, and the fact that a company pays the average rate means that some companies are paying less and some are paying more. No company pays more than every other company for every job, and employees tend to quote the higher-pay situation outside their company. Therefore, answers to specific pay questions must be answered in general terms.

Employee information on pay levels tends to be less precise than company information; and, as already noted, despite improvements in survey methods, company information is far from scientifically accurate. Facts cited by individual employees are usually based on newspaper reports, conversations with friends, a specific job offer, or similar circumstances. Frequently, two companies have quite dissimilar jobs, and comparative information is plainly inaccurate. Therefore, the supervisor is well advised to discuss serious questions of area pay with staff specialists to make sure that the basis for their answers is sound.

6

INDIVIDUAL PAY ACTIONS

JOB PRICING IS IMPERSONAL and considers the level of work which is performed. In individual pay administration, on the other hand, management must decide whether all individuals in jobs of the same level should be paid the same and, if not, just how different levels of pay should be determined. Differences in individuals' total compensation may be due to differences in salary within ranges or to bonus payments.* Bonus payments will be considered in a later chapter. This chapter deals only with variations in individual base pay or salary.

GENERAL ADJUSTMENTS

There are pay actions under which all employees receive essentially the same pay increases. These general adjustments may be the same dollar amount or the same percentage increase. They may be granted to all employees in the company or to all employees in a given department, location, or group. General adjustments include changes in the pay structure, which affect every employee's potential for

* Premium payments such as overtime and shift differentials also affect current pay.

future increases, and general increases, which provide every employee with the same dollar or percentage increase.

Adjustments in the Pay Structure

Pay structures must be adjusted from time to time in order to keep the pay program up to date. If adjustments are not made, the structure will no longer be competitive. In recent years pay structure adjustments have been upward, providing increased pay opportunities to employees. This pattern can be expected to continue in the foreseeable future.

Various economic factors are generally considered when pay structures are revised. The most important single factor is changes in pay rates in competitive labor markets. In effect, the company sets its pay structure in some position relative to the labor market to maintain a competitive posture; as labor market rates change, the structure must also change if it is to remain competitive. Another factor that must be considered is changes in the cost of living. As a practical matter, changes in the cost of living correlate closely with changes in levels of pay in the labor market.

Finally, a number of administrative or business considerations must be taken into account in adjusting the pay structure. These include the financial capacity of the company and changes in its compensation strategy. Also, from time to time technical adjustments in the structure must be made. The pay of some groups of employees may move upward either faster or slower than other groups, and this must be corrected by changes in the structure.

It must be noted, of course, that these considerations result only in changes in the pay structure; they do not necessarily mean changes in an individual's pay. Some companies do adjust the pay of employees in relation to changes in the structure. Even if a company does not do this, the range for every job increases and therefore the potential for future increases is enhanced whenever the pay structure is adjusted upward.

General Increases

General increases refer to pay adjustments granted to all employees or to a group of employees. As indicated earlier, they may be granted to employees when the pay structure is adjusted upward. They may also be granted when single rates are in effect or when a company has a very informal and unstructured pay administration system.

General increases go to everyone—for the purpose of maintaining or improving the level of real earnings.

Usually, the justification for general increases is that there are economic factors which apply to every employee regardless of his length of service or performance. To the degree that this is true, there is indeed equity in giving everyone the same increase. Unless this is done, some employees will receive less pay for the same work. For the company, these across-the-board increases represent true expense spending, as do increases in taxes or in the cost of utilities, materials, and so on. When general increases are granted, the company is paying more for essentially the same levels of performance.

Sometimes general increases are tied to the cost of living. This can be done, however, only when there is some measure of changes in an employee's living costs. The only available measure of cost-of-living changes is the Bureau of Labor Statistics' consumer price index, which reports changes in the price of items in the "market basket" of a typical factory worker with a family of four. Thus cost-of-living adjustments can logically be applied only to factory workers or to employees at equivalent income levels.

Generally, unless pay increases at least match increases in the cost of living, the real earnings of employees decline. This amounts to pay decreases for employees. As a practical matter, employees aspire not only to have their standard of living maintained but to have their real earnings power increase. To employees, therefore, cost-of-living increases represent necessary income adjustments.

Effect on Merit Program

When general increases are tied in with a merit increase program, it is extremely important for managers to recognize that some part of an employee's increase really represents a general increase. Nothing makes an employee more cynical than to see a factory worker, for example, receive a 6 percent general increase and then to get an increase of his own, supposedly for merit, which also amounts to 6 percent. To avoid this, some companies have separated merit increases and general increases. Others, which have integrated the two, have found it wise to explain to employees frankly that part of the increase is really a general increase or cost-of-living increase. Employees who continue to perform adequately in their jobs tend to get the general increase automatically. Any additional increase represents an improvement in pay and can be explained on the basis of improved performance or other considerations.

INCREASES WITHIN RANGE

There are four basic approaches to determining individual pay movement within a salary or wage grade: the single-rate approach, the informal approach, the automatic approach, and the merit approach. Frequently, elements of one are found in the others.

Single Rates

It is a mistake to think that pay differences based on merit are necessary or desirable within every job classification. Such differences are appropriate only when employee performance can vary significantly on the job. For instance, under a day-work system where the learning time on the job is relatively short, single rates are frequently paid to all employees on jobs of similar difficulty, because everyone is required to work at about the same pace in order to attain standards. In many simple office jobs, also, performance is relatively constant because the routines are so specified or schedules are so set that there is little opportunity for individual effort to affect output materially.

Step rates are often used in conjunction with a single-rate system. For instance, an employee may be given a starting rate while he is learning the job. His pay then progresses by steps to the standard rate as his performance increases to job standard. Typically, the learning period is relatively short—certainly a year or less.

There has been widespread use of single rates in factory positions. This is because factory jobs have relatively short learning periods and fairly well-prescribed standards in terms of quantity and quality of performance. To vary pay under these circumstances would be to pay a premium for no purpose or to penalize without basis. Employees tend to view such variations as favoritism. To the employee, the standard of equity is "equal pay for equal work."

Increasingly companies are applying this logic to operations jobs in offices, since many operations positions have the same characteristics as factory jobs: there is a relatively short learning time, and standards of performance are fairly well prescribed. Here again, there is a compelling logic to adjust to a single-rate structure.

The Automatic Approach

Under the automatic approach to pay increases, both the amount of the increase and the period of review are usually predetermined, so that the line supervisor has no discretion in the matter. In jobs where employees need only to gain experience or familiarity with the routines in order to attain standard performance, the automatic approach has proved useful and practical. It is used under essentially the same conditions as the single-rate system, except that longer learning periods exist. For such an approach to be effective, there must be well-defined standards for work performance, and progress toward standards must be fairly uniform for all workers. The automatic approach is also likely to be used when a union is not willing to allow management to retain the sole right to advance employees in pay or when management does not do a good job of observing and appraising the performance of employees.

The major drawback to the automatic approach is that it removes individual performance or merit from compensation decisions. This means that the only incentive an employee has is to stay with the company long enough to reach a satisfactory level of pay and, of course, to work at job standard. Obviously, when this system of pay increases is applied to jobs in which employee output can vary, it can have serious consequences.

Another problem with the automatic policy is that it is an extremely inflexible approach to wage and salary administration. Once it is adopted, it may be difficult to change even if the economic circumstances affecting company operations change materially. In fact, in some companies or in some sections of companies, the automatic approach is in effect by reason of practice and precedent rather than policy. This happens where supervisors have, with great uniformity, granted employees a fixed amount or percentage increase at regular intervals.

The Informal Approach

Under the informal approach to pay administration, supervisors make individual pay decisions without formal guides or controls. To be effective, an informal system requires that the supervisor know the employee well and be in a position to observe him regularly. It also requires a small operation, so that decisions can be consistent or at least compatible between groups. Finally, the informal system requires that managers have basic facts available as to rate of pay, prior increases, and so on. It is usually helpful for a manager to maintain at least a tickler file to make sure that there is some regularity in the frequency of review.

Except under these conditions, it is doubtful whether managers have sufficient skill, experience, and judgment to make good pay decisions without guides and controls. Under the pressure of daily operations, most managers cannot devote sufficient time and effort to obtaining and analyzing all the information needed to make intelligent pay decisions.

There are several drawbacks to an informal system—which is really little system at all. For one thing, each manager may have somewhat different standards. Such differences lead to inequities and to confusion on the part of employees regarding what is expected of them. In addition, lack of companywide standards may result in pay decisions that are influenced by personal favoritism. Finally, because there are no standards or guides for increases, it is difficult to explain pay raises to employees. For these reasons, the informal approach usually has a low level of acceptance among employees.

Simply requiring the approval of higher-level management on pay decisions does not necessarily overcome these problems. Managers tend to rationalize their pay recommendations in whatever terms are necessary to gain approval. Furthermore, unless higher-level managers are informed about the day-to-day performance of employees, approval reviews will not necessarily bring about more equitable or logical pay decisions.

The Merit Pay Approach

If differences in individual performance and output are important to a company, then some basis for compensating employees for these differences should be established. Otherwise, grievances, unrest, and even turnover among the company's best employees may result. A merit system is a management practice designed to gear differences in pay to differences in work accomplishment.

Merit pay systems assume that performance can be observed with reasonable accuracy even when it cannot be objectively measured. Thus the first step in a merit pay program is supervisory evaluation of employee performance. This evaluation process is essentially the same as that used in employee appraisal, which is also concerned with judging performance. It is what is done with the evaluation which often distinguishes the two processes. Merit rating is traditionally used to determine pay increases, while appraisal, particularly in recent years, is usually reserved for training and development. The following section focuses on administering merit pay increases; methods of performance appraisal are treated in the next chapter.

MERIT INCREASE PROGRAMS

One of the unfortunate problems of a merit pay program is one of semantics. More often than not, merit pay increases really mean increases granted within a range. Such increases include adjustments reflecting economic considerations (for example, cost-of-living changes) and in some cases adjustments reflecting improved performance.

Administration of a merit pay program involves three considerations: how often pay should be reviewed, who should get increases when the review is conducted, and what size increase should be granted. In addition, there are considerations of budgets and other guidelines to assist managers in making merit pay decisions.

Frequency of Merit Review

Frequency of consideration for merit increases depends on two factors: the level of an employee's job and the length of time the employee has been on the job. Job level is a factor because it takes longer to observe improvements in performance in higher-level jobs than in lower-level jobs. Employees in higher pay grades, therefore, should be reviewed less frequently than those in lower pay grades. Time on the job is a factor because performance progress generally follows a learning curve. An employee tends to learn rapidly during his first months on the job; the rate of improvement then slows down markedly, and after a while performance does not increase at all. Thus employees should receive more frequent reviews when they are new on a job, and the interval should become less frequent with time.* The merit review schedule shown in Table 5 illustrates how these principles may be translated into concrete guides.

Number Receiving Increases

Not all employees improve their performance in a given period. Just how many do improve depends a great deal on the rate of growth of the organization and the capacity and motivation of employees. It is rare, however, that more than 50 percent of a company's employees will improve their performance substantially enough in a year to

* One of the many problems of merit pay plans is that factors such as job level and time on the job are relevant to the performance part of a merit pay increase but not to the economic part of the increase. For administrative reasons, therefore, some review should still be made at fixed intervals—usually once each year.

Table 5. **Number of months between consideration for merit increases.**

	Length of Time at Current Job			
Pay Grade	*Less Than 1 Year*	*1–3 Years*	*3–10 Years*	*Over 10 Years*
1–8	3	6	12	12
9–16	6	12	12	18
17–30	12	12	18	24
Over 30	12	18	24	24

warrant a strictly performance-related increase. In many organizations this figure may be as low as 10 percent. As noted, however, merit increases really include amounts for economic adjustments as well as improved performance. Therefore, under merit rating programs typically 80 or 90 percent of the employees receive upward pay adjustments.

Of the remaining 10 or 20 percent who do not get an increase, the majority are employees whose pay is above the maximum of their range. Others may not get increases because they are going to retire during the course of the year, because their health is bad, or because their performance has been below standard.

Amount of Merit Increases

Generally speaking, it is not considered wise to grant an increase of much less than 5 percent to operations employees,* 7 percent to middle-level employees, and 10 percent to management and professional employees. It is doubtful that a supervisor can judge merit and other factors so accurately as to justify increases smaller than these amounts. Even the methods of determining economic changes in the marketplace are not so refined as to justify increases of much less than 5 percent. Moreover, to employees, such increases after taxes may represent only nominal amounts which do not motivate them to improve performance and which may actually have a negative effect on their attitudes.

Supervisors should bear in mind that pay progress is a function of both the amount and the frequency of pay increases. Thus if a

* Smaller amounts may properly be granted to employees under a cost-of-living escalation practice or contract.

significant merit increase cannot be justified for an employee, it is probably wiser to delay the period of increase than to give the employee frequent small increases. Some companies have devised imaginative methods for dealing with the problem of minimum merit increases. One such method, which has several employee relations advantages, is the lump-sum merit increase. Under this plan, an employee is granted—in advance—the whole annual amount of the merit increase. Thus an employee who is earning $12,000 per year and is eligible for a 4 percent increase would receive a $480 payment on the first of the year and then continue to receive $1,000 per month in salary for the balance of the year. On the first of the following year his monthly pay would go to $1,040. At this time he might receive another lump-sum merit increase.

The maximum limitations on merit increases are more difficult to determine. Theoretically, there should be no limit to an individual's salary progress except the limit of his own performance improvement. As a practical matter, however, merit pay increases in excess of 20 percent should be carefully reviewed from the point of view of budget, motivation, and effect on attitudes of other employees. Again, in such situations a supervisor should bear in mind the timing of raises. If an employee's performance progress is so exceptional that an unusually large merit increase is warranted, it might be wiser to grant more moderate increases more frequently. Moreover, under this approach the increases would more closely match the actual progress of the individual.

The company's pay structure, and any changes in that structure, also impose ground rules affecting the amount of merit increases. Any merit increase which is less than the percentage adjustment in the pay structure since the employee's last increase represents a decline in pay. Another consideration in determining the amount of increase

Table 6. **Years to go from minimum of pay range to maximum, assuming 3 percent annual upward adjustment in pay structure.**

Percentage Spread Within Range	*Average Annual Percentage Merit Increase*				
	4	*6*	*8*	*10*	*12*
20	17	6	4	3	2
30	23	8	5	4	3
40	37	13	8	6	4

is the time that it would take an employee to reach the top of his range at a given rate of pay progress. Table 6 shows how long it would take an employee at the minimum of his range to reach the maximum of his range under different pay-range spreads and rates of increase.

Merit Increase Budgets and Guides

Many companies provide business units and individual supervisors with various aids for making merit increase decisions. Two of the most frequently used are budgets, which establish the total amount of merit increases that may be spent, and merit increase guides, which indicate appropriate amounts of increases under varying circumstances.

Allocated budgets are the simplest guide in the merit rating program. In a department, for instance, whose payroll is $14,000 per month, the manager may be granted a total budget of $1,120 (8 percent) for merit increases. There is nothing, of course, which says how the supervisor may spend this money. He could grant 8 percent increases to all employees or he could grant large increases to some employees and nothing to the rest. The merit budget approach, therefore, sets a limit on the total amount that can be spent and grants maximum latitude to the supervisor in spending it. Frequently, the budget also is intended to set a minimum: the supervisor is expected to grant the budgeted amount in increases.

Another and far more refined aid to pay increase decisions is the merit increase guide, illustrated in Table 7. In this case various suggested percentage increases are established on the basis of employees' performance and the position of the current pay within the pay range. The logic of using these criteria is that employees at a given level of performance should receive pay at approximately the same position in the range; if an employee is performing at about the same level as other employees who are receiving much higher pay, he should receive higher percentage increases so that he moves more quickly to his appropriate level within range.

It should be noted that there is an implicit budget in the merit increase guide. If, for instance, all the employees in a given department were in the 50 percent, or midpoint, band position,* then the merit increase guide in Table 7 would call for a merit budget increase of 8 percent of that department's payroll.

* Band position is a way of expressing progression through a range and is here calculated as: (Actual salary − minimum salary) ÷ (maximum salary − minimum salary).

Table 7. **Merit increase guide: suggested percentage increases based on performance and position of pay within range.**

	Position Within Range					
Performance Level	*Below Minimum*	*First Quartile*	*Second Quartile*	*Third Quartile*	*Fourth Quartile*	*Above Maximum*
Outstanding: fully qualified by knowledge and experience; meets all performance standards of position	16	14	12	10	8	6
Intermediate	14	12	10	8	6	4*
Average: performs generally good work; meets or comes close to most performance standards	12	10	8	6	4*	0
Intermediate	10	8	6	4*	0	0
Acceptable: new to position or requires more knowledge and experience; a performer at minimum levels	8	6	4*	0	0	0
Intermediate	6	4*	0	0	0	0

* It is preferable to give 4 percent increases as 6 percent increases at eighteen-month intervals.

PERFORMANCE PAY INCREASE PROGRAMS

In the past few years a number of leadership companies have evolved a "performance pay increase system" to replace the traditional merit increase system, which was originally developed to reward employees with higher pay for better performance. However, because merit increases typically represent partly a reward for better performance and partly an adjustment for all employees because of economic changes, much of the hoped-for incentive value of the program has not been realized. At best, most employees are confused as to how much their merit increases are really for better performance—whether these are "merit" increases or "merited" increases.

In some cases, too, there has been more than confusion. Employees have been told, in effect, that they are getting a merit increase as a reward for improvement. At the same time, they see other employees getting general increases which are as great as or greater than their so-called merit increases. This creates a credibility gap, and frequently such merit increases become disincentives.

To meet this situation, many companies are attempting to strengthen merit increase programs. Some are communicating to employees exactly what part of the merit increase represents an economic adjustment and what part reflects improved performance. Others are attempting to guide and control the system so that most employees will receive that part of the increase which is designed to adjust for economic changes, and then a limited number of employees receive significantly larger amounts, with the difference truly representing reward for improved performance.

Other companies have abandoned the merit increase program in favor of a "performance increase" approach. In its simplest form, a performance increase program represents a combination of general increases plus merit increases, with the merit increases solely representing a recognition of improved performance.

Under the performance increase plan, economic factors are considered from time to time—usually once each year—and the pay structure is adjusted accordingly. Up to this point, of course, the procedure is exactly the same as under a merit increase program.

In the performance increase system, however, all employees get approximately the same pay increase at this time—usually an across-the-board amount which approximates the percentage by which the structure was adjusted upward. Also, under such programs there is room for exceptions. These may be for the same reasons that employees do not get increases under a merit program: declined performance, poor health, or impending retirement. Under economic increase programs, however, withholding of an economic increase must usually be justified in writing.

The annual review for economic adjustments considers adjustments for special reasons. These may involve review of questionable classifications or problems of internal relationships; special reviews for a group, department, or profession because of labor market experience; or reviews for any other personal or administrative reason.

These increases truly represent increased expenses. They are higher pay for the same levels of work. They are just another major item among many others which, in an inflationary economy, represent the continuing increase in the cost of doing business.

In addition to economic increases, supervisors may recommend individuals for performance increases. Generally, the amounts recommended must be significant—typically at least 6 percent in addition to the economic increase.

Performance increases must be justified in writing. Thus the process for reviewing recommendations for performance increases is the crucial part of a performance increase system. Obviously, if increases are based on the writing skill of the reviewer rather than on real performance improvement, the whole system can become a very expensive charade. To avoid this danger, many companies require certain procedures in addition to written justification. These include:

- Field interviews conducted by personnel staff
- Development of performance criteria
- Personal presentation to high-level management of all performance increase recommendations
- Earmarking of employees who receive performance reviews for promotion

Typically, there are no limits on the number of performance increases which may be granted. Few organizations are so endowed with talent or so productive that they can't use all the increased performance they can get. Nor are any budgetary or financial controls imposed. Rather, control is exercised through the review of recommendations, which must clearly demonstrate that an employee's performance has improved.

Unlike economic increases, performance increases do not represent expense spending. They are, in fact, a form of investment spending, for while the company is paying out more money it is getting higher levels of performance in return. In this sense net wage costs have not increased at all and may actually decrease.

The performance increase approach represents a very dramatic change in wage and salary practices, equivalent perhaps to the shift some 30 years ago from automatic and informal pay increases to merit increases. The approach recognizes the need for economic and administrative increases—and treats them as a necessary business cost in an inflationary economy. Management actions to offset such increases include price changes, increased emphasis on labor productivity, and changes in the business.

The emphasis is now on performance increase, which usually focuses on increased productivity on a given job or greater value from incremental addition of duties. This focus requires improved definition, observation, and measurement of performance. It inevitably leads to emphasis on improving performance.

Some companies feel that the shift to a performance increase approach is a cosmetic change. They argue, as noted earlier, that the same results can be obtained by modifying the merit increase approach and separating performance increases from economic increases. But if this is really done, the firm has, in fact, shifted to a performance approach. In many firms, the merit approach has been stretched, modified, and adjusted as much as it can be. What is needed is a new model—and that is the performance increase approach.

OTHER INDIVIDUAL PAY ACTIONS

There are, under both the merit and performance increase approaches, certain other pay actions which must be considered. These include hiring rates of pay, pay changes for various job moves, reevaluation and inequity adjustments, and pay actions under special situations.

Hiring Rates of Pay

It is generally sound practice to hire a new employee at or near the minimum of the pay range which has been established for his job, assuming the pay structure fits realistically into the labor market. In theory, applicants with minimum qualifications should be hired at the bottom of the pay range, and hiring rates should increase with experience.

If inexperienced employees are hired much above the lower third of the pay range, they will have little opportunity to obtain increases as they learn the company's operations and improve their performance. Furthermore, such a practice may create inequities: employees who seem better qualified during the recruitment process may not turn out to be truly superior to those already on the payroll.

Unfavorable employment experience of this type may lead a supervisor to think that the company's pay structure is inadequate. Employment experience is, in fact, one of the most practical tests of the adequacy of a pay structure. However, it is important to recognize that success in employment depends on a number of factors, including:

Adequacy of the pay structure
Correctness of pay classifications
Range of hiring rates established within pay levels
Labor availability
Employment requirements
Recruiting requirements

Screening techniques
Number of employees being recruited
Time permitted for hiring

All these factors are crucial to the employment process. For example, unnecessarily high employment requirements are frequently an obstacle to effective recruiting. Or the recruiting techniques themselves may be the problem; in the labor shortages of recent years imaginative and aggressive recruiting methods are frequently not only appropriate but justifiable from the cost point of view. As a rule of thumb, $1 per year more in starting pay is the equivalent of $5 in extra recruiting costs.

There are two special situations which frequently cause difficulty with respect to determining appropriate hiring rates. The first situation involves jobs whose duties are somewhat indefinite, so that the appropriate classification is also uncertain. This problem is sometimes caused by uncertainties in operations—for example, the uncertain impact of a new product or the effect of computer technology. Frequently, however, the question to ask is this: If the supervisor cannot determine what work must be assigned to a new employee, how can he be sure that he needs the new employee?

The second difficult hiring situation involves jobs with rapidly emerging responsibilities. For example, a supervisor may be hired to run a department which, within months, will increase from 30 to 300 employees. Usually, the correct course in this situation is not to classify the job according to current circumstances but to set the hiring rate in relation to future responsibilities. This should only be done, however, when resources are committed to the change. Companies should realize that it frequently takes a better man, with a higher rate of pay, to build an organization than to run an organization.

Promotional Increases

Promotion can be defined as a move from a job in one pay grade to a job in a higher pay grade. It follows that an employee should receive a pay increase when he is promoted; otherwise, he would be doing more without receiving more.

Sometimes a promotional increase is deferred until the employee has proved himself in the new job. Such a practice is inequitable in the sense that it does not apply to an employee who is recruited for the job from the outside. Furthermore, it is illogical in the sense that the company has better opportunities for screening men inside than it does men outside. Finally, deferment of the increase reflects a doubt as to the ability of the individual to perform the new job and may actually undermine the employee's self-confidence.

In determining how much of a promotional increase should be granted, the supervisor must consider a number of factors: the magnitude of the promotion, the employee's position within range in the new job, and the pay progress the employee might reasonably have achieved through merit increases if he had not been promoted.

The ground rules one company has established for promotional increases include the following.

1. Generally speaking, pay progress of a promoted employee should be greater than it would have been without the promotion.
2. The salary of a promoted employee should be raised to at least the minimum of the pay level of his new position.
3. The promotional increase should in no case be less than 5 percent.
4. When a promotion of more than one pay grade is involved, the minimum promotional increase should be 3 percent per pay grade.
5. Promotional increases should never exceed 20 percent. In the event that a greater increase is required to satisfy one of the other ground rules, the matter should be referred to the personnel policy committee and data should be supplied *with respect to compensation and selection.*

Frequently, promotions do not involve a move to a distinctly different job with a higher pay grade. Rather, they reflect emerging job duties or a series of additional assignments over a period of time. None of these new duties may in itself warrant a change in pay classification, but their cumulative effect may in time justify a reevaluation and redescription of the employee's position. If the position does fall into a higher pay grade and the employee is effectively performing his new duties, he should be eligible for a promotional increase. Such an increase need not be precisely labeled as promotional, however.

Frequently, such promotions are handled in the normal salary-planning process, recognizing that the higher pay level warrants a larger increase but not identifying which part of the increase is merit and which part is promotion. This practice is typical for all groups of employees under a performance increase plan and for professional employees under any system.

Upgrading

Upgrading occurs when a given position is reevaluated and assigned a higher pay level. A job may be upgraded when the scope of its duties and responsibilities has increased, even if no additional responsibilities have been assigned. Or upgrading may just reflect new or changed thinking on the part of the evaluators.

Some companies handle upgrading exactly like promotion, reasoning that upgrading does indeed reflect increased levels of responsibility regardless of the causes. Other companies establish the higher pay classification but permit no pay action at the time of the upgrading. This course is logical, for instance, when the scope of duties in the future might equally well decline as increase. It also avoids the possibility that reevaluation is imprudent and will later be regretted. Companies which follow this approach do, of course, consider the higher pay grade in determining future merit or performance increases, so that upgrading enhances income opportunities in the long run.

Downgrading

Downgrading occurs when a job is reevaluated and placed in a lower pay level. Only rarely does a company reduce the employee's rate of pay in such a situation, however, since the changed classification in no way reflects his performance. Almost invariably company practice is to establish the new pay classification, so that the employee's income opportunities in the future are diminished. Downgrading involves problems of manpower planning and placement, because if the employee was performing properly at the higher-rated job, he is now being underused.

Demotions

Demotion, the opposite of promotion, is a move from a job in one pay grade to a job in a lower grade. A demotion may occur because the employee's job has been eliminated or substantially changed and there are no jobs available at his current pay level. Or it may occur because an employee has failed to perform properly.

Demotion involves broad personnel questions as well as compensation questions. Employees whose job levels have been reduced without prejudice should logically be "selected" for demotion. Demotion, like downgrading, also involves manpower planning and placement questions. Company pay practices vary greatly with respect to employees who are demoted without prejudice. Some companies continue their former rate of pay, but this may create inequities if a demoted employee receives more money than others who are performing as well, or even better, in the lower-level job. Other companies follow the practice of reducing the employee's pay so that it is in the same relative position in the lower pay grade as it was in the former pay grade.

When an employee is demoted because of unsatisfactory performance, a different situation exists. Normally, disciplinary demotions call for cutting the employee's pay so that it fits the classification of the new position. This may be done by reducing pay in a single action or, if undue hardship would result, by withholding pay increases over a period of time. In disciplinary cases many companies follow the practice of discharging the employee rather than demoting him, on the grounds that in the long run discharge is in his best interest as well as the company's.

Reevaluation and Inequity Increases

Reevaluation increases refer to special adjustments in the pay of recently hired or promoted employees in recognition of demonstrated abilities and aptitude beyond those assessed when the employees were placed in their jobs. Such increases have the virtue of correcting past mistakes. Their existence, however, may encourage ultraconservatism in hiring rates or even loose employment screening procedures.

Inequity increases generally refer to those that cannot be classified elsewhere. When used, the term tends to reflect the fact that practical considerations such as market competition and internal pay relationships are being considered in setting the employee's pay. The same objective can be achieved without such a label, however, if the pay increase program is broad enough to allow supervisors to review all pertinent factors in reaching pay decisions.

Special Situations

Red-circle situations. A red-circle situation occurs when an employee is paid more than the maximum of the pay range in which his position is classified. There is seldom any question of reducing pay in red-circle situations; rather, the problem is whether to withhold further increases.

Good business practice dictates that in such cases the employee's pay should be "frozen"; that is, he should not be eligible for increases until the structure has been adjusted upward to the point that his pay is within range. This is desirable for three reasons. First, unless pay-range maximums are enforced, they are meaningless. Second, in a red-circle situation the employee is being paid more than an outstanding rate for his performance. This is already an inequity, since he receives more money than others within range who are doing outstanding work. Third, unless the company has unlimited resources, any additional amount granted to red-circle employees must be made at the expense of other employees.

Sometimes supervisors are too apologetic toward employees who are ineligible for merit increases because they receive red-circle rates or are at the top of their range. The fact is that if the company's pay structure is properly set, these employees are receiving outstanding pay. One large firm in the glass industry takes a positive approach to such situations. Employees who are at the maximum of their range are identified on the company bulletin board as people who have demonstrated superior performance and have been rewarded with outstanding pay.

Some companies allow modest and infrequent increases in red-circle situations, so that the structure catches up gradually with the incumbent's pay. Special types of controls are necessary when such a practice is followed.

Gold-circle situations. A gold-circle situation occurs when an employee's pay exceeds the maximum of his evaluated pay level but red-circle ground rules do not apply. Basically, there are two possible gold-circle situations. First, the incumbent may be in a training position, performing work that does not reflect his capabilities or the level of duties he is qualified for. Second, the incumbent may deserve a promotion to a significantly higher level but for the time being no opening is available. In both cases, the usual practice is to exempt the employee from the pay structure until such time as he can take his proper place in it.

Green-circle situations. A green-circle situation occurs when an employee's pay is below the minimum of his job classification. In theory, all employees should be raised to the minimum of their range as a matter of equity. However, when a company is faced with a large number of green-circle cases, either because of a job reevaluation project or some major organizational change, there are practical drawbacks to raising everyone immediately to the minimum. For one thing, significant costs may be involved. For another, inequities may be created between the newly raised employees and those who were already at the minimum of the range. Furthermore, there is always the danger that either a position has been overclassified or the employee in it is underqualified. For these reasons, careful review and phasing-in periods are frequently appropriate.

Silver-circle situations. Some companies grant long-service employees pay increases even when such increases are not justified on the basis of performance. These situations are sometimes labeled silver-circle increases. Some companies, however, put these increases in the same category as the 25-year service pin. When such increases are clearly only for long service, are identified as such, and are separately budgeted, they can be of some value. It goes without saying that they should not be granted at the expense of other employees who deserve pay increases for improved performance.

7

APPRAISING PERFORMANCE

THE MAJORITY OF EMPLOYEES in the American labor force have their pay administered under the merit pay system, the performance increase system, or a variation thereof. These systems involve some review and appraisal of how well employees perform their job duties. Thus, while the process of appraising performance is a separate and important employee relations function, it also has an important bearing on administering individual pay.

There are a number of methods by which companies appraise performance for compensation and other purposes. Many firms use traditional merit rating techniques. Increasingly, however, companies are relying on either performance appraisal systems or some program of management by objectives. Finally, there is an emerging trend in some companies to use performance rating systems as only one of many inputs to pay increase decisions. This chapter examines each of these techniques for appraising performance, along with its implications for merit increase or performance increase programs.

MERIT RATING TECHNIQUES

Under almost all traditional merit rating systems, there is some formal process by which employee performance is measured. A variety of specific techniques have been developed, all of which have two things in common. First, they represent some method for appraising performance. Second, their primary objective is to serve as a guide to analyzing performance for the purpose of making pay decisions.

Thus the essential difference between merit rating techniques and performance review techniques lies in how they are used. Merit rating techniques are generally designed to determine and/or justify a pay increase. Performance review techniques are generally designed for much broader purposes, for example, as an input to training and organizational development or as a method of translating enterprise goals into individual performance standards. In these circumstances, better pay decisions are a byproduct of performance review. Obviously, the relationship between the pay decision and the performance review is vague and indefinite.

Because of the narrow purpose for which they are designed, most merit rating techniques also have three limitations. First, they can at best only guide managers' thinking about employees' performance, potential, or personal qualities (which is not their main objective). Second, they represent only an inventory of information relevant to a given pay situation. They do not tell the supervisor how large a merit increase should be granted; nor do they explain why these conditions of performance exist or how performance might be improved. Finally, they offer no scientific or objective means of evaluating performance and thus cannot be used as a substitute for managers' judgment. The right technique for a given company is that which best guides the judgment of its managers.

The principal techniques used for merit rating programs are performance factor rating, graphic rating scales, checklists, grouping and ranking, job appraisal, and the critical-incident method. A basic understanding of all these techniques is important to the manager who administers salary programs. Each technique can be helpful to the supervisor in performing his duties, even if it is not a formal part of the company salary administration program.

Performance Factor Rating

The most widely used merit rating technique is performance factor rating, illustrated in Figure 12. Under this system, a number of factors or criteria of job performance are identified and usually described. Examples of such factors are quantity of work, quality of work, attitude, effort, and cooperativeness. The supervisor rates the employee's degree of excellence with respect to each factor. The exact

Figure 12. **Performance rating form.**

	Level of Performance				
Rating Factor	Unsatisfactory	Below Average	Average	Above Average	Outstanding
Quantity of work					
Quality of work					
Attitude					
Effort					
Cooperativeness					
Overall rating					

rating system used is left to the supervisor's discretion; generally, however, ratings are done by comparing relative performance of employees.

One of the major problems with performance rating is the difficulty of identifying factors which truly measure performance. As a practical matter, few factors correlate directly with job performance. There is, for instance, no necessary correlation between the attitude of the person and the kind of job that he does. Even factors such as quantity of work pose problems. In many jobs the quantity of work need not be judged—it can be measured by objective count of units produced or other quantitative techniques. In other jobs what is done is as important or more important than how much is done. For instance, an employee may perform a high quantity of work which is of little value to the organization. Under a performance rating system his output might deserve a very high rating, but in terms of useful work to the company it should receive a low rating.

Another problem with performance rating, as with many other rating techniques, is that it allows the supervisor considerable latitude. Even when supervisors conscientiously try to apply such programs, each will have somewhat different standards as to what constitutes unsatisfactory, average, or outstanding performance. Moreover, there is opportunity for a supervisor to "rig" the results—to fill out the rating form to justify the pay decision he has already made. If company policy requires that these ratings be discussed with employees, the completed rating sheet may cause confusion, embarrassment, and difficulties with subordinates.

Graphic Rating Scales

Another widely used type of merit rating inventory is the graphic rating scale, illustrated in Figure 13. Under this system, which is quite similar to point evaluation, the supervisor rates employee performance in terms of prescribed factors or traits. Each degree of each trait is defined and the manager selects that degree which best describes the employee's performance. Usually degrees and factors have point weightings so that an overall rating can be obtained arithmetically.

The problems associated with graphic rating scales are similar to those encountered in point evaluation plans and factor comparison systems. The traits that identify job performance, and the various degrees of those traits, are extremely difficult to define and measure. Moreover, factors of performance have different significance in different jobs. For example, persuasive ability is often the most important single trait for a salesman, but it typically has little importance for a research scientist. Finally, merit rating frequently includes an evaluation of personal qualities as well as specific measures of job performance. These traits, such as initiative, dependability, and ability to work well with others, are particularly elusive and difficult to define.

After the factors have been selected, the next task is to define them and establish degrees within traits. This process raises all the problems already noted in connection with job evaluation factors and degrees. If anything, it is even more difficult to define human traits than to define job characteristics.

Checklists

The checklist is a merit rating inventory that is especially helpful to supervisors when used in connection with performance factor rating or graphic rating scales. In the checklist technique, a number of statements are prepared, each relating to employee performance. The supervisor then checks those statements that best describe the work of the employee.

Part of a checklist, designed to be used in conjunction with the graphic rating scale, is shown in Figure 14. Note that the checklist examines employee performance in far greater detail than the rating scale can. A checklist attempts to pinpoint ways in which the employee is doing well or failing to measure up to performance standards. It also indicates the important points that a supervisor should consider in judging performance in relation to a given factor.

Figure 13. **Graphic rating scale.**

Employee's Name: _____ *Employee's Classification:* _____ *Department:* _____

TRAIT	A	B	C	D
Quality of Work: Consider quality of work produced by employee regardless of quantity.	Often makes mistakes. Work usually unsatisfactory. 1	Part of time maintains passable quality level. 3	Usually does a good job. Makes few errors. 5	Consistently does an excellent job. Few errors. 7
Quantity of Work: Consider the quantity of work produced by the employee regardless of the quality.	Takes a long time to accomplish little. Output low. 1	Produces reasonably satisfactory volume of work. May need pushing. 3	Produces the required amount of work. Needs no prodding. 5	High production. Exceeds quotas regularly. Completes job quickly. 7
Cooperativeness: Consider the extent to which the employee cooperates with fellow employees and his supervisor.	Does not get along with others. Indifferent. Causes friction and trouble. 1	Fair teamworker. At times inclined to hang back. 2	Gets along satisfactorily with associates. Meets others halfway. 3	Goes out of his way to cooperate with others. 4
Dependability: Consider how reliable the employee is and the extent to which you can trust him to carry out your orders conscientiously.	Requires frequent checking or follow-up. Cannot be relied upon without close supervision. 1	Reliable in the performance of most duties. Needs follow-up where assignments are not routine. 2	Carries out instructions adequately. Generally reliable and needs only occasional follow-up. 3	Carries out instructions conscientiously and promptly with excellent results. No need for follow-up. 4
Initiative: Consider the extent to which the employee uses initiative in the performance of his duties and works without constant supervision.	Routine worker. Needs constant supervision—waits to be told. 1	Sometimes at a loss in other than routine situations. Frequent checkup required. 2	Resourceful. Needs little supervision. 3	Performs excellent job with very little supervision. Seeks additional tasks when has time. 4
Knowledge of Work: Consider the employee's knowledge in his particular field; his mastery of all phases of job.	Does not know enough about most phases of his job. 1	More knowledge of some phases of the job would be desirable. 2	Has satisfactory knowledge of practically all phases of his work. 3	Has excellent mastery of all phases of his work. 4

Figure 14. **Checklist of job performance, office positions.**

TRAIT	ASSESSMENT		
	YES	NO	COMMENT
Quality of Work:			
1. Have there been specific instances when employee made important mistakes?	___	___	_____
2. Are mistakes frequently made because of carelessness?	___	___	_____
3. Are mistakes made because of inexperience or lack of knowledge of the job?	___	___	_____
4. Does employee learn from mistakes rather than making the same mistakes frequently?	___	___	_____
5. Is employee's attitude good when mistakes are called to his attention?	___	___	_____
6. Are mistakes made regularly or just at irregular intervals?	___	___	_____
Quantity of Work:			
1. Is quantity of work as high as should be expected?	___	___	_____
2. Does quantity of work vary from time to time?	___	___	_____
3. Does employee do some jobs significantly faster than others?	___	___	_____
4. Could the employee increase his speed significantly?	___	___	_____
5. Does employee look for quicker ways of doing things?	___	___	_____
6. If quantity of work could be increased, could this be done by—			
a. More effort	___	___	_____
b. Wasting less time	___	___	_____
c. More experience and know-how	___	___	_____
d. Closer supervision	___	___	_____
e. Other (specify)	___	___	_____

Grouping and Ranking

Another way in which the manager can evaluate performance is by grouping or ranking the employees in his unit. The easiest grouping technique is slotting employees into broad categories: excellent, good, average, and so forth. Ranking is simply a matter of identifying the best performers in the group and then evaluating the remaining members in relation to them. Though grouping and ranking is a relatively crude rating technique, if used thoughtfully it can be of help to supervisors in relating pay to performance.

Direct Appraisal

Some companies have adopted a system of direct appraisal to evaluate how well employees perform their work. The appraisal rating form consists of a list of assigned duties taken from the employee's job description. Opposite each duty is a space for the manager to assess, first, how important that duty is in the overall job and, second, how well the employee is performing it. This method goes to the heart of performance evaluation, particularly for pay purposes, by directly assessing how the employee is performing the job.

There are two major drawbacks to direct appraisal. First, it is very costly, since a separate appraisal form must, in effect, be prepared for each job. Second, the results are imprecise as far as justifying pay increases is concerned, since there is little way to relate ratings between jobs when no point weightings are assigned. That is, it is difficult to determine, in any arithmetic manner, relationships between merit rating conclusions and pay decisions.

Critical-Incident Method

While this method does not lend itself directly to merit rating, it can be of assistance to supervisors in the merit rating process. A supervisor can, for instance, maintain a separate folder or data sheet for each employee in which he records incidents that illustrate either unusual accomplishment or particular job failures. Similarly, the supervisor can take notes on incidents which illustrate particular characteristics of the employee's work. Such written case histories can be valuable to the supervisor in preparing merit rating inventories and in discussing ratings with employees.

INCREASING THE EFFECTIVENESS OF RATINGS

It is obvious that even the most excellently conceived and designed merit rating system will not automatically yield valid ratings. The skill with which the techniques are used is as important as the soundness of the method itself. To the staff specialist, this means that technically appropriate systems must be provided to the line supervisor. To the line supervisor, it means that the success of the program depends to a considerable extent on his skill and effectiveness in rating.

The quality of the manager's ratings will naturally depend on the amount of time and thought he invests in the process. His willingness to take pains, in turn, will depend on what is required of him and whether he believes that merit rating genuinely helps him as a manager. If he finds that it improves both the performance of his employees and the quality of his personnel actions, he will be strongly motivated to develop skill in rating.

There are several ways by which supervisors can improve the quality of their merit ratings. One is through careful and accurate observation of the employee's performance. Just as the reliability of job evaluation depends on conscientious job analysis, so the value of personnel evaluation depends on careful observation of work performed. Obviously, ratings based on casual and infrequent observation can be misleading and unfair.

Another way in which managers can improve their ratings is by tabulating the results into summary profiles. Such a procedure can help them to spot errors or inconsistencies in rating and can facilitate comparisons among employees. Still another helpful procedure is simply to rate each employee more than once. The supervisor can rate all his employees, put the ratings aside, and rate all of them again after two or three weeks, without referring to the previous results. He may even use an alternative method for the second rating.

Finally, supervisors can improve their merit ratings by consulting with other managers—for instance, by cross-checking their ideas and experiences. Discussions with competent staff personnel may also prove helpful. The specialist who has had the opportunity to sit in on rating sessions with many supervisors will have a broader knowledge of merit rating than the line manager, who does this work only periodically. In addition, staff specialists can help supervisors bring more impartiality into the merit rating session. They can clarify points in the rating process, provide information on the objectives, purposes, or details of merit rating, and make constructive suggestions on a variety of problems.

In all this, of course, the manager must have a thorough understanding of the rating process. He should know something about merit rating in general, as well as how the system works in his company, what objectives the company has set, what personnel actions are based on ratings, and how the system may affect daily operations.

Above all, managers must guard against the tendency to project themselves or their views into the rating process. Specifically, a manager should try to avoid rating employees on the basis of some preconceived idea; subconsciously comparing subordinates with himself; allowing judgments to be influenced by prejudices; and permitting one or two incidents to influence the rating of a whole year's performance. He should also guard against judging potential when he is being asked to judge current performance; relying completely on the face that an employee shows him; or rating a man unfairly because he is stronger in some characteristics than the manager.

Problems of Merit Rating

Despite the basic soundness of the merit rating approach and the time and effort that have gone into developing it, merit rating has not always achieved the objectives which have been established for it. Many managers and employees have come to oppose merit rating, and in some organizations true merit rating either has undergone significant modification or has been completely abandoned. The failure of merit rating programs can be attributed to several factors:

- The measurement of observed performance is not considered accurate enough to serve as a basis for making pay decisions.
- The merit rating program has been poorly designed or is technically unsound.
- The program has not been administered properly.
- Merit rating has become a form of gamesmanship between line and staff.
- Merit rating objectives have been in conflict with basic objectives of the company, of employees, or of individual managers.

Accuracy. It is probably fair to say that really conclusive studies on the accuracy of merit rating have never been conducted. This is because of the virtual impossibility of setting standards for measuring accuracy. There is little doubt, however, that even the most formalized merit rating program is a highly subjective process. Human judgments based on only a partial knowledge of the qualities judged and measured against an imperfect yardstick are bound to yield results which are far from perfect.

The fact that merit rating results are not completely objective or scientifically accurate does not, however, mean that they are not useful. They must be judged on the basis of their relative effectiveness over other techniques and on their potential to improve managers' pay decisions. Judgments about performance and translations of those judgments into personnel actions are an inherent part of the management process. The question of accuracy is really: How accurate is judgment?

The real test of merit rating is whether the process results in *improvement* in judgments.

Technical soundness. The technical problems concerning merit rating have been examined at great length by personnel specialists. Probably the greatest of these problems is overemphasis on technique. Some staff specialists, faced with problems in merit rating, direct their energies to those aspects of the plan which they understand best—the technical features—and lose sight of its broader aspects.

To be successful, a merit rating plan must meet several technical requirements. First, it must be a reflection of, or a natural extension of, normal management practice. Second, it must be appropriate—not the cleverest or most excellent plan but one which is suited to circumstances. Third, it must be usable—and this means that it must be understandable, believable, and realistic in terms of time demands. Finally, the merit program must be sound in terms of form, structure, and methodology.

Poor administration. Too often, managers sustain a high degree of enthusiasm during the design and installation of a merit rating program and then assume that the job is done and the problem is solved. In fact, design and installation represent the beginning, not the end. It typically takes three years of implementation before a merit program becomes an integral part of management practice in an enterprise.

Gamesmanship in merit rating. Some merit rating plans have failed simply because they have become a game rather than a management process. The game has taken many forms, but basically it involves having the supervisor rate a subordinate's performance and then having staff or high-level management use the rating to disapprove a recommended increase or to dictate what increase may be given. The teams are sometimes staff versus line, sometimes one level of line versus a higher level of line. Almost always, the players concentrate on winning the game at the expense of solving pay problems. Not only are such games silly and expensive, but they undermine the supervisor's integrity and ability to perform his job.

Conflicts of objectives. Underlying many of the problems of merit rating are basic conflicts of objectives. One of these is the fact that merit rating is not regarded as equally advantageous by all employees or all managers.

Rewarding higher performance with higher pay is important and beneficial to the company, which gains through lower unit costs. It is also important to those employees whose performance is better than average and to those managers who use the system to promote more efficient operations. However, gearing pay to performance is contrary to the self-interests of others. For instance, employees who perform below average will object to merit rating because they may receive less pay than they would otherwise. Supervisors may oppose the process because they lack the time or skill necessary to carry out the program, because they are uncomfortable with appraisal, or because they prefer a more personalized approach.

Another basic conflict involves the degree of authority granted to managers in merit rating. Some researchers argue that managers are "playing God" when they rate employees, particularly when ratings are based on personal characteristics. Such a criticism, however, overlooks the fact that business must always be authoritarian to some extent and that managers must in one way or another evaluate the performance of subordinates and take appropriate action. Merit rating is merely one technique which attempts to refine this process and make it more objective.

On the other hand, many managers argue that merit rating restricts their absolute authority. Supervisors who so contend are correct. Merit rating is a company system intended to both guide and control managers. While the emphasis should always be on guiding them, the element of control is also essential. Top management cannot delegate such an important function without providing standards to guide lower-level management.

Another conflict involves the perfunctory manner in which merit rating is sometimes applied. In some companies forms are completed, filed, and forgotten. The process becomes mere routine and serves no purpose for the employee, the company, or the supervisor. Other companies seem to pay great attention to the merit rating program on paper but disregard it in practice by granting automatic raises and allowing all employees to reach the top of their range within a fairly standard period of time. Under such conditions, merit rating becomes a matter of empty form.

The most important conflict of objectives in merit programs is one of basic purposes. Even when pay reviews are properly tied to merit rating techniques, the process can become mechanical because managers tend to decide first what pay increases they want to give and then figure out what type of merit rating they must submit in order to justify the increase. While it is easy to criticize line managers who engage in such practices, it must also be recognized that this sometimes happens because the basic objectives of merit rating are in direct conflict with those of pay review, making it impossible to tie wages solely to merit rating. As will be discussed later, performance is but one important element to be weighed in making pay decisions. Furthermore, review of performance can serve much broader objectives than simply guiding pay decisions. This fundamental conflict of purpose between merit rating and personnel actions is at the heart of many of the problems of merit rating.

PERFORMANCE APPRAISAL

As noted earlier, performance appraisal and merit rating are similar in that they are aimed at measuring job performance. The primary difference between the two processes lies in their objectives. Merit rating is specifically designed to guide managers' thinking about pay decisions. The primary objective of performance appraisal is to improve the effectiveness of people at work. The knowledge gained in the process can be helpful in making pay decisions, but it is strictly a byproduct of the appraisal system.

Objectives of Performance Appraisal

Performance appraisal is, therefore, essentially a personnel development technique. In addition, it can serve to achieve any or all of the following objectives: improved employee performance, determination of training needs, manpower inventory, manpower control, improved personnel decisions, and organizational development.

Improved employee performance. Probably the most important single purpose of performance appraisal is to improve the performance of individual employees. To achieve this objective, the appraisal process must include (1) analysis of employee performance, (2) development of specific plans for improved performance, (3) implementation of the plans, and (4) year-end review—which starts the process over again.

Determination of training needs. Well-executed performance appraisals can play a major role in determining group training needs. The supervisor's written analyses of the strengths and weaknesses of individual employees can assist staff personnel in establishing general objectives for group training programs and in tailoring these programs to the needs of specific employees.

Manpower inventory. The performance appraisal process also provides useful input to the preparation of inventories of manpower skills. Written records of supervisory appraisal can be valuable as future references, either when the employee is promoted or when a new man takes over the operation of the department. From a broader point of view, the manpower inventory can be of material assistance in management planning. By matching the skills and abilities of employees against planned business strategies, management is in a better position to provide for orderly growth or change.

Manpower control. Effective manpower control above operations positions is a major problem in many large enterprises. The knowledge gained from job analysis and performance appraisal can assist management in determining the proper number of persons required to conduct the business and achieve the goals of the enterprise.

Improved personnel actions. Performance review can aid managers in making more realistic and equitable personnel decisions. These include the identification of employees for promotion purposes and the reassignment of employees within the operating unit to utilize their skills better. The information gained from performance appraisals can also serve as a basis for disciplinary action or, when ability and performance are part of the employment security policy, as a guide to managers in scheduling layoffs. Finally, the results of performance appraisal are a key input to individual pay actions.

Organizational development. Training and development of people, manpower management, effective personnel actions—which are the primary objectives of performance appraisal already identified—are part of the managerial activities which are collectively a part of organizational development. OD, in the minds of top personnel executives, means those activities designed to improve the effectiveness of people at work (which is what personnel management, as contrasted to personnel administration, has always meant). Performance appraisal is, in this context, a key analytical tool in organizational development.

PERFORMANCE APPRAISAL TECHNIQUES

Performance appraisal is more a process than a technique. The critical element is not the specific technique which is used but the degree of thought that goes into the process. Some experts maintain that the best appraisal form is a blank piece of paper. Such a view is perhaps more idealistic than practical, but it does point out the fact that the objective of appraisal is to elicit *thinking* about an employee's performance—with the specific purpose of planning developmental activities which will improve that performance. Because of this, there are just about as many effective appraisal programs, techniques, and procedures as there are companies which use them; each is properly a unique management process. These techniques may be grouped into three general approaches to appraisal: supervisory appraisal systems, management review systems, and goal-setting programs. Any company program might well include elements of all three of these approaches.

Supervisory Appraisal Systems

Supervisory appraisal systems are those that start with some formal analysis of a subordinate's performance by the immediate supervisor. In addition, the process logically and properly includes:

- Observation of employee performance.
- Completion of appraisal form.
- Comparison of work actually done with job duties assigned.
- Identification of a few (usually two or three) of the employee's strongest skills and planning of developmental activities to exploit these strengths.
- Identification of two or three areas in which the employee needs the greatest improvement and planning of developmental activities to strengthen these weaknesses.
- Counseling of employees on their strengths and weaknesses.
- Planning and implementation of specific training or developmental activities for the employee.
- Use of information from appraisal to reassign duties in order to increase the effectiveness of the work unit.

The supervisory appraisal process is enhanced whenever performance standards—criteria of what is expected—can be identified. Ideally, performance standards are objective, but in most positions only a few quantitative standards can be established. Determination of performance standards enables managers to review performance of job duties against some objective criteria. This, in turn, gives managers a more concrete basis for identifying areas in which the individual employee needs to improve his performance.

Supervisory appraisal is, of course, not aimed at just identifying the strengths and weaknesses of employees or the ways in which they fail to achieve or exceed performance standards. The ultimate objective is to use this information to identify developmental activities which will improve the operations of the work unit. The development of standards of performance assures that the appraisal process is truly geared to the operational needs of the enterprise and creates a more logical order of priorities as to where improvements can most effectively be made.

The specific techniques available, as well as the appraisal systems and the problems associated with supervisory appraisal, are properly part of a study on training and development rather than salary administration. As a tool of compensation administration, however, appraisal can be quite helpful and usually serves as a substitute for traditional merit rating techniques. Appraisal is valuable not so much because it provides a specific guide for pay actions but because it enhances the knowledge of the supervisor about the job performance of employees. This knowledge is the cornerstone for making equitable pay increase decisions. But those who look to the appraisal process as a mechanical system for identifying or justifying pay increases would be disappointed. Supervisory appraisal does not result in specific or tangible conclusions with respect to pay actions because it is designed as a developmental tool rather than as a compensation mechanism.

The performance review helps not only the employee who is appraised but also the manager who does the appraising. The process of studying job duties, setting work standards, and observing employee performance is bound to increase the supervisor's knowledge of his operations and his understanding of the problems involved. The observation of performance will help him to see what obstacles prevent his employees from doing their best work. Similarly, it may reveal ways in which the manager himself can become a more effective supervisor.

Management Review Systems

Management review systems involve direct top management review of the appraisal process. In addition, while the immediate supervisor is still the key player, these systems call for inputs from all managers who view the work of the employee and for more direct participation by staff.

Management review systems start with field interviews by trained personnel staff. First the immediate supervisor is interviewed and taken through the appraisal process, in a manner customized to that supervisor's operations and circumstances. Other managers who view the work of the individual are also interviewed (though not, of course, as intensively).

In all this, the personnel staff interviewer is a reporter; his job is to pose the right questions and record information in a systematic and consistent manner. The final product is an appraisal report identifying the strengths and weaknesses of the employee and outlining an individual development program. This report is reviewed by the immediate supervisor, who then presents his appraisal in person to his supervisor.

This process is repeated upward, with each level of supervisor reviewing in detail the appraisals of second-level subordinates and making general conclusions and plans. Eventually, this became a personnel summit meeting, with key managers making employee appraisal reports to top management.

Management review systems involve high time costs. But the quality of information they provide and their effectiveness in achieving objectives are also very high. Clearly, appraisal is an integral part of the management system where this process is followed.

In management review systems pay actions are not generally discussed, since this would make the review session too long and would direct attention away from the principal objectives: appraising manpower talent and developing plans for improving employee effectiveness. Occasionally, personnel actions (including pay actions) of outstanding persons are discussed as part of individual development programs.

Goal-Setting Programs

Goal setting is a third variant of the performance appraisal process. It differs from other appraisal techniques primarily in methodology. Under goal setting, appraisal is accomplished by first establishing goals or objectives for each position. Actual job performance is reviewed at the end of the process by comparing achievements against objectives.

Goal setting also differs from other appraisal techniques in its objectives. Supervisory appraisal and management review systems are essentially organizational development methods. In contrast, goal setting is basically a technique or style of management. However, because it does examine jobs and performance against jobs, it is a form of appraisal. And because it enhances knowledge about how well people perform, it can assist supervisors in making sound pay decisions. Under goal setting, better pay decisions are a byproduct of a basic management style.

Goal setting—or, as it is sometimes called, management by objectives—begins at top company levels, where overall corporate objectives are established. These objectives are then broken down into subgoals at successively lower levels. Thus each manager and each employee participate in establishing specific goals to be achieved during the year. A simple example of a goal-setting exercise is presented in Figure 15.

Many companies have instituted goal-setting programs in the past dozen years—MBO has become a contemporary personnel fad. All these

***Figure 15.* A goal-setting exercise.**

PROJECT TARGETS FOR FISCAL YEAR 19—

Position: Plant Personnel Manager *Incumbent:* R. J. Ricky

	Target Date
1. Conduct community fringe-benefit survey; review with corporate office; submit recommendations.	February 1
2. Bring all office and exempt-position descriptions up to date.	February 1
3. Conduct survey of terminated employees per memo dated November of previous year; present results at April management meeting.	March 1
4. Investigate possibility of middle management plant incentive compensation program; report company practices and prepare written report of feasibility.	July 1
5. Reduce lead time in factory recruiting to seven working days, with no increase in cost per hire.	Fiscal year
6. Develop and recommend management skills training program for foremen.	August 1
7. Conduct management skills program.	October–November

Approved: _____

Adapted from the program of a large pharmaceuticals company.

efforts have been costly, most have done little harm, and a few have been successful—contributing in a meaningful way to improved operations and more effective management of human resources. Those which have been successful tend to have the following characteristics:

- They are top-down—goals are set first for the chief executive officer.
- Goals for individuals are geared to enterprise goals.
- Goals for individuals are derived from goals of the individual's supervisor.
- Goals are related to assigned job duties.
- Goals are always of two types:
  1. Criteria of performance for principal regular job duties.
  2. Special projects to be achieved this year.
- Only principal goals or objectives—and those identifiable before the appraisal period begins—are established.

– Goals are set down in writing and are:
  1. Partially quantifiable, partially not.
  2. Invariably brief—never more than two pages long.

The goal-setting exercise in Figure 15 is a very simplified model, presented for illustrative purposes only. The actual process starts by establishing certain criteria or standards for the performance of assigned job duties. These are essentially supervisory appraisal systems or management review systems. The process also involves the translation of enterprise objectives into individual goals.

The goal-setting process is elaborate and interrelated with the management process, not the compensation program. This is illustrated in Figure 16, which shows the goal-setting program followed by a number of leading companies. Essentially, goal setting starts at the top, and each organizational level can set its goals only after goals of the next higher level have been established. Frequently, goal setting is an integral part of the operational planning process. The inputs to goal

Figure 16. **The goal-setting process.**

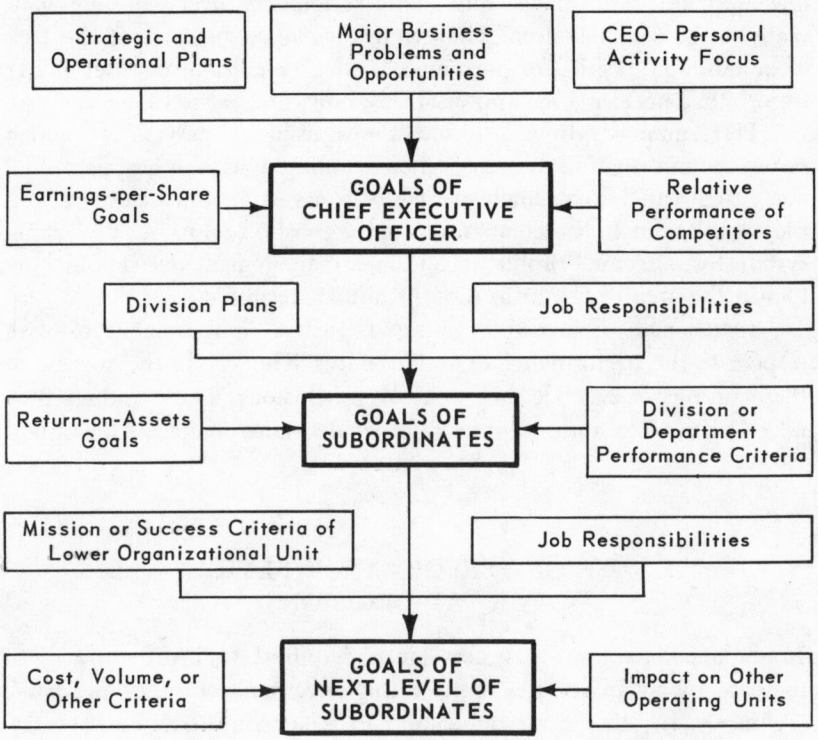

setting at each level are the goals of the immediate supervisor, financial goals of the unit, nonfinancial goals of the unit, strategic plans, and each employee's job responsibility.

Goal setting cannot be the sole basis for individual pay determination; but it can be a valuable aid, provided that realistic goals are established. The process must not focus on the demonstrable at the expense of the pertinent; it must not become either elaborate or mechanical; and there are no mathematical relationships between goal setting and salary discussion. As a tool for making pay decisions, it lacks precision. It only enhances knowledge of job performance and therefore assists the supervisor in making better individual pay decisions.

Performance Ratings

Performance ratings are a relatively new idea in personnel administration. The rating form is a simple document which calls for a rating of overall job performance. Sometimes separate ratings are made of an employee's current job duties and of his potential for future development. Performance ratings are statements of conclusions—generally without explanation. They were developed because of the lack of quantifiable results for personnel actions (including pay decisions) from either performance appraisal programs or goal-setting programs.

Performance ratings are sometimes used as part of a human resources information system. When combined with other personnel data, they can be extremely valuable in assessing the health of employee relations in the company, as a diagnostic tool or early warning system for personnel problems, and as a management decision-making tool in the area of the utilization of human resources.

In essence, performance ratings represent final conclusions with respect to the performance of subordinates. The key to the success of these ratings is a frank statement of conclusions. These ratings may never be used to audit or reverse other decisions made by the supervisor.

USE OF PERFORMANCE REVIEW FOR PAY DECISIONS

In some companies the supervisor is required to justify any merit increase by means of the merit rating inventory or other personnel technique. In other firms the same end is accomplished by a central auditing of recommended pay changes, using the completed merit inventory forms. In both cases, an attempt is made to establish a direct relationship between the recommended pay increase and the merit rating results. This objective is a logical extension of the basic goal of merit rating—tying pay within ranges to the individual employee's performance. However, such a rigid relationship assumes that (1) performance is the only factor which should be considered in determining an individual employee's pay within range; (2) evaluation by merit rating is designed only to determine merit increases; and (3) evaluation of performance is an extremely accurate process. Actual experience indicates that none of these assumptions is correct.

An Approach to Individual Pay Actions

The traditional approach to merit rating can be modified without losing the basic objective of relating individual pay within ranges to individual performance. The modified approach suggested here involves the recognition that merit rating or performance appraisal can only give insight into the excellence of performance.

Figure 17 shows the proper relationship between performance review and compensation review. Performance review is the cornerstone of management actions designed to utilize the employee resources of the company more fully. It has a number of important purposes; helping to make more realistic pay decisions is only one of them. At the same time, employee performance is only one important factor that managers must consider in making pay decisions.

These statements suggest a new emphasis in the preparation of merit rating inventories, or in otherwise evaluating individual employee performance. They also call attention to the need for a broader look at individual pay decisions. Finally, the close connection between performance review and compensation review demonstrates the desirability of physically separating the two processes. This does not, of course, mean that performance should not be considered in pay decisions. The greater knowledge that the manager obtains through appraisal should be an important factor in these decisions.

Pay Decisions in Perspective

Pay decisions must be viewed in the proper perspective as regards the overall objectives of performance review. Performance cannot be the only factor considered in making merit pay decisions for several reasons. First, if a company were to tie merit increases rigidly to per-

Figure 17. **Relationship between performance review and compensation review.**

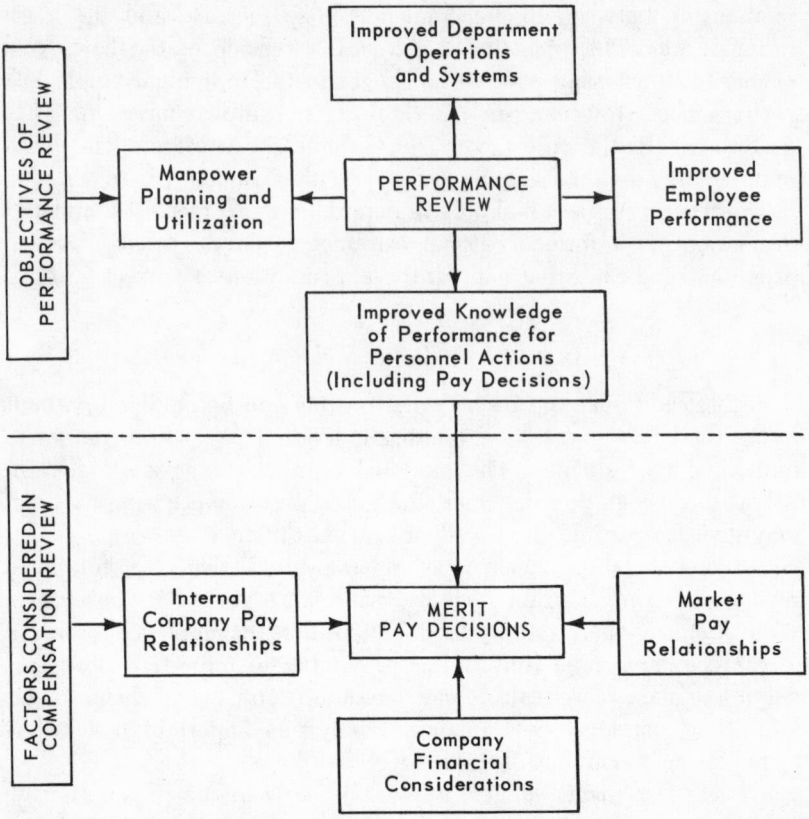

formance, it would have to increase an employee's pay every time his performance improved. In practice, however, a formal wage and salary program sets a maximum value on each job. If these maximums are enforced, the employee who has reached the top of his pay grade and who still improves his performance cannot have his pay increased. By the same token, if merit increases were tied only to performance, an employee would automatically have his pay cut when his performance declined. In most cases this is not considered practical, unless performance declines to the point where some disciplinary action is necessary.

Second, while merit rating techniques can bring reasonable results, it is a mistake to consider them so accurate that each additional improvement in job performance is worth an equal increment in pay.

Third, it is sometimes necessary to grant an employee an increase because of pay inequities even though such an increase is not justified on the grounds of improved performance. Finally, because of short-term financial considerations, the company may not be able to grant an increase at a particular time.

To sum up, managers must consider many factors in deciding so-called merit increases. These include:

- The employee performance review
- Company pay relationships, which include:
  1. The individual employee's pay history
  2. The employee's present position within his pay range
  3. The experience the employee has had in his present position
  4. The period of time since the employee's last increase
  5. The amount of the previous increase
  6. The pay relationships within the supervisor's department
  7. The levels of pay received by employees doing similar work in other departments
- Labor market considerations, which include:
  1. Pay experience with newly hired employees
  2. The pay received by employees doing similar work in other companies in the labor market
- Operating considerations, which include:
  1. The importance of the work being done
  2. The financial budget which the company has assigned for merit rating purposes

All these factors strongly influence individual pay decisions. They are frequently in conflict in the sense that if each were considered separately different decisions might result. When such conflicts arise, the supervisor must make some compromise, since none of the factors can be neglected for long.

It is important to note that the individual supervisor cannot independently judge the importance of every factor relating to individual pay decisions. Some factors, such as employee performance, must be assessed primarily by the immediate supervisor. But other factors, such as company pay relationships and market area comparisons of employee earnings, can be evaluated only by trained staff personnel. Still other factors, such as the merit rating budget, are the responsibility of top management.

8

PLANNING, CONTROL, AND ADMINISTRATION

THERE ARE A VARIETY of other general aspects of pay administration which are important to the success of the program. These include company practices with respect to salary planning, control and administration, and outside forces—such as labor unions, the federal government, and society—which have a direct and important effect on pay administration.

SALARY PLANNING

The complexity of the factors involved in individual pay decisions suggests the need for some organized approach to salary planning. The difficult job is to identify the pertinent factors, give them due consideration, and arrive at proper pay decisions. Many companies have introduced formal planning activities to assist in this process. Even when there is no formal system, many managers have devised their own planning methods to help meet their basic pay responsibilities.

Need for Planning

Systematic salary planning is essential if managers are to relate pay to performance in a realistic and equitable manner for all employees. There is also a great need for salary planning because of the amount of money involved. Pay progressions between grades are generally no higher than 10 percent. However, within-grade progressions generally range from 30 to 60 percent. Thus three to six times as much money is involved in within-grade planning as in the determination of proper pay classifications.

Another reason for salary planning is the number of people who are involved in making individual pay decisions. Generally, even in a decentralized organization, only a limited number of people are responsible for final decisions relating to pay classifications, and they need only consider the analysis of job duties and the job evaluation yardstick. Determination of pay increases within range, however, involves decisions by many supervisors, who operate under different circumstances and who have diverse backgrounds and perspectives. These managers must consider not only the performance of duties but also market pay relationships, the financial budget provided for them, the pay history of each employee, and other factors.

Techniques of Planning

The salary planning process should include the following elements: (1) providing sufficient background information to the manager so that he has a factual base for considering increases; (2) preplanning by the supervisor of both the amount and the time of increases for all employees within his unit for a full year's period; (3) counseling by staff specialists to assist the manager in interpreting the complex data involved in pay decisions and to insure that company policies and practices have been observed.

The type of information required for effective salary planning depends, of course, on the types of jobs which are being considered. Basically, it includes detailed data on the pay history of employees, facts relating to internal pay relationships, and at least benchmark information on pay relationships with competing companies. Summary pay data can be recorded on a salary-planning worksheet, such as that in Figure 18, and supplemental information on pay histories and competition data can be prepared separately for more detailed examination.

Note that the salary-planning worksheet in Figure 18 contains columns for a "performance rating" as well as for an "X" rating. The supervisor checks the "X" column if he has considered factors other than employee performance in recommending pay increases. The performance rating is really an overall conclusion as to how well the employee performs on the job. And in this case the conclusion is not necessarily related to any method of control.

Figure 18. **Salary-planning worksheet.**

Department: Data Processing *Supervisor:* I. Johnson *Budget:* $6,600

POSITION	NAME	CURRENT SALARY	PAY GRADE	PERCENTAGE BAND POSITION	TOTAL PERCENTAGE INCREASE FROM 1/1/70	LAST INCREASE AMOUNT	LAST INCREASE PERCENTAGE	LAST INCREASE DATE	X	PERFORMANCE RATING	PLANNED INCREASE AMOUNT	PLANNED INCREASE PERCENTAGE	PLANNED INCREASE DATE
Manager, systems	P. Thompson	$15,670	IX	45	24	$1,160	8	3/15/72		18	$1,100	7	3/15/73
Manager, operations	L. Jones	14,930	VIII	57	32	1,600	12	7/1/72		24	1,500	10	7/1/73
Programmer	J. Smith	12,360	VI	55	18	810	7	2/1/72		15	740	6	2/1/73
Programmer	T. Gray	10,250	VI	11	–	–	–	–	x	20	1,540	15	9/1/73
Computer operator	S. Lee	10,660	IV	67	15	510	5	2/1/72		10	0	0	–
Computer operator	C. Thomas	9,800	IV	45	23	550	6	5/15/72		17	690	7	5/15/73
Computer operator	M. Cook	8,670	IV	17	–	–	–	–		20	870	10	2/1/73

Total Preplanning: $6,440 Average Preplanning: $920 Total Increase: 7.8%

Total After: _____ Average After: _____ Variance: _____

The experience of a number of companies indicates that preplanning of salary increases has a number of distinct advantages:

1. Preplanning brings consistency and objectivity to the supervisor's determination of pay increases.

2. Preplanning is the only efficient way of considering all relevant information. Otherwise, the supervisor would have to organize and review all the data on an employee each time a pay raise came up for review, going through the same process and much the same information many times during the year.

3. Preplanning is the only realistic manner of estimating merit budgets, since it enables management to predict the impact of merit increases on operating costs.

4. Preplanning assures equal treatment for all employees regardless of what time of the year their pay reviews are due. Unless this is done, some employees may suffer because of operating circumstances or other conditions which influence management's willingness to grant increases at a particular time.

5. Preplanning of merit increases by all supervisors within a company or operating unit insures that employees as a group are being treated in a consistent manner compared with other groups.

6. Careful preplanning can make possible a true delegation of pay decisions to the lowest levels of supervision and can facilitate approval procedures.

Preplanning is effective because the basic personal qualities that determine performance—intelligence, self-motivation, energy, attitude, and so on—generally do not change dramatically in a year's time. However, these factors may change if the employee's work environment changes. For this reason, salary planning should never become a rigid and inflexible instrument for pay decisions. If an employee does perform more efficiently than was anticipated, management can and should consider giving him a higher performance increase when his review date occurs.

The worksheet in Figure 18 relates only to salary planning. Some companies, however, use this system to provide for organized, one-time planning of other important personnel actions. These include bonus awards and individual pay actions with respect to promotion, transfer, recognition, termination, or reorganization of duties.

SALARY CONTROLS

The idea of salary controls is sometimes not well received by managers, who feel that it restricts their latitude in making pay decisions. Nevertheless, controls of some sort are necessary if the company is to make sure that (1) top management is informed as to how well the salary program is being implemented, (2) managers in different sections of the company are administering the program with reasonable consistency, and (3) company policies and practices are being observed.

Budgetary Controls

Experience indicates that one of the essential elements of successful salary administration is an effective budgetary system. Budgets serve primarily as control devices. As noted earlier, however, they are also necessary for effective delegation of salary actions to the first level of supervision. Finally, budgets serve as useful guides for individual managers. A budget tells the manager how much he should spend to make sure that the employees in his unit are being treated fairly in relation to employees in other sections of the company or in other companies in the labor market.

There are two types of budgets—payroll and merit. Payroll budgets involve total dollars of payroll allocated to various operating units. These gross figures are affected by pay increases of all types and, more important, by the number of persons in each unit at the beginning and end of each measurement period. Such budgets are valuable in financial forecasting, cash management, and other accounting controls. They do not serve any useful purpose in controlling individual pay decisions or the equitable distribution of pay increase dollars.

A merit budget, on the other hand, specifies the amount allocated for performance increases to each division, department, section, and unit of the company. It tells supervisors how much they may spend and also how much they should spend in total for performance increases for those on the payroll.

One method of preparing merit increase budgets is the control curve, illustrated in Figure 19. To determine a control curve, only three points need be established. These points are labeled X, Y, and Z in Figure 19. Point X is fixed in the sense that if maximums of pay ranges are to be enforced, the merit increase budget should be zero when the average band position is 100 percent. Point Y is also fixed and represents the average band position for the entire business unit.

Determination of point Z—the average percentage pay increase contemplated for all employees—is more difficult and requires some analysis and decisions on the part of management. This percentage should equal the average merit increase which management feels ap-

Figure 19. **Merit budget control curves.**

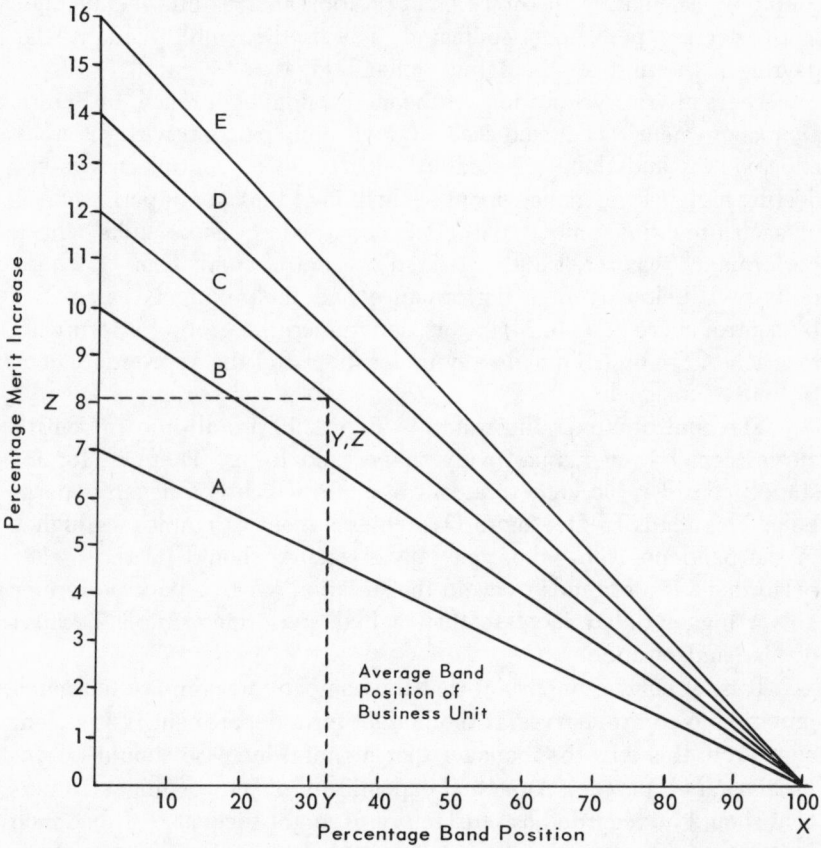

propriate for the year. It should be selected on the basis of such factors as the following:

- Competitiveness of company pay levels in the labor markets
- Information on other merit increase budgets and amounts granted by competitors in the labor market
- Financial ability to pay
- Cost-of-living trend since the last adjustment of the salary structure
- Company compensation policies
- Increases in productivity in the work group

Once point Z is established, a control curve, C, can be drawn by connecting point X with the intersection of points Y and Z. Management can use this curve to determine the appropriate budget for every unit simply by calculating the unit's band position and reading the average merit increase percentage indicated. This is then multiplied by the payroll of the unit for the actual dollar budget.

There are many variations of the merit budget approach. In Figure 19, management recognized that different units perform with different effectiveness and therefore established a series of control curves—reflecting higher-level management evaluation of the overall performance of each operating unit, department, and section. Those units whose performance was rated high operated on control curve E or D. Those units with below-average performance had their budgets calculated by control curve A or B. Managers determined the group performance for each of the units immediately under them and the appropriate control curve for each.

The control curves illustrated in Figure 19 are all linear. Control curves can, however, take many shapes and forms. There is, for instance, considerable logic to a control curve which is a negative parabola. This tends to give more favored treatment to employees higher in the band position—who, generally speaking, should be the higher performers. It also tends to avoid the situation where a poor performer gets a bigger dollar increase than a high performer simply because of his band position.

It is, of course, important that the company not impute too much precision to control curves. If the budget for a department is 8 percent of payroll, this tells the manager that his total increase should be *approximately* 8 percent. An actual expenditure of plus or minus 10 percent should be regarded as satisfactory. It might seem at first that such latitude would encourage managers to spend more than amounts budgeted. In practice, however, many supervisors spend less than their budgets.

For individual managers, control curves are only a first step in determining individual increases. Supervisors can determine the band position for each employee and see what percentage increase is indicated for that individual. They should then consider performance and other relevant factors in arriving at pay decisions.

Statistical Controls

Properly presented, statistical reports can serve not only as a control device but as an appraisal device for top management. Statistical controls are most effective when they are combined with budgetary controls. Budgetary control devices guide before the fact; statistical devices report after the fact.

One type of statistical control is the salary-planning sheet, described earlier in the chapter. Another basic type of control is a report comparing amounts expended for merit and other increases for each unit with amounts budgeted. Other useful control devices include reports on the number of positions which have been reevaluated and the results of reevaluation; data on the dispersion of job classifications by organizational unit and analysis of significant trends in dispersion patterns; information on money expended by units for increases other than merit increases; and reports on grievances with respect to pay classifications or pay changes.

If properly geared to the business, these reports can tell management a great deal about how well salary administration programs are operating. They can also give valuable insight into the effectiveness of supervision.

Personnel Audit

The development of personnel audit techniques has led to more organized and rigorous review of compensation practices and other personnel activities. The concept of the personnel audit is relatively new and in its early stages. Essentially, personnel audits aim at assessing the use of human resources, just as financial audits gauge the use of physical assets.

Personnel audits are not, of course, legally required; they are designed to serve management purposes. These include, among other objectives, checking personnel programs to insure that they are effective, consistent with company goals, and properly administered; identifying opportunities for improving employee productivity; and developing concrete ideas to exploit such opportunities—ideas that should in themselves pay for the cost of the audit.

Unlike their counterparts in the accounting area, personnel audits are neither comprehensive nor detailed. Rather, they involve identifying key areas and sensitivity points in personnel administration and reviewing these areas through statistical analyses, observation, and personal interviews. Also, unlike financial audits, personnel audits are intended primarily as a strategic tool—to improve the management of human resources. Therefore, they are only secondarily control devices.

In one company a personnel audit in the compensation area—made at the corporate level and in two operating divisions, the central research lab, and the purchasing department of another operating unit—included the following procedures: analysis of dispersion of jobs by pay level, review of performance patterns, interviews of a sample of supervisors, and comparisons of benchmark positions against market data. In addition, career pay progress of fast-track employees was examined, personnel staff activities were analyzed, and management incentive awards were reviewed. This audit resulted not only in an assessment of the pay program but in a number of immediate actions which improved the program.

Control by Approval

Approval requirements, the most traditional method of management control, provide management with the opportunity to review each pay action. They also have some control value in keeping higher-level management informed about people.

Approval requirements alone, however, have proved inadequate as control devices. Unless a higher-level manager knows the facts surrounding each individual pay change, it is difficult for him to approve, disapprove, or modify that change. Only immediate supervisors, who have information about such crucial questions as employee performance, the possibility of quitting, relationships within a group, and the potential of individual employees, are in a position to make pay decisions. Thus, in the reviewing process, the higher-level supervisor should concentrate on making sure that all relevant factors have been considered and that the immediate supervisor has done a thoughtful job in reaching decisions. It is also helpful for the reviewing supervisor to discuss pay changes with the personnel representative before submitting them for higher-level management approval. In this way he can be sure that the immediate supervisor has complied with policies and ground rules and that the action is consistent with company practices.

Frequently, approval requirements have become obstacle courses. Just how many approvals should be obtained depends on company organization and the type of pay program in effect. It is hard to believe, however, that there is any real need for—or any genuine value in—obtaining approvals from more than the immediate supervisor, one personnel representative, and the next two higher levels of line management.

Figure 20 illustrates one company's policy on review of pay recommendations. As shown in the figure, the immediate supervisor is accountable for thinking through each pay situation and making

Figure 20. **One company's policy on review of pay recommendations.**

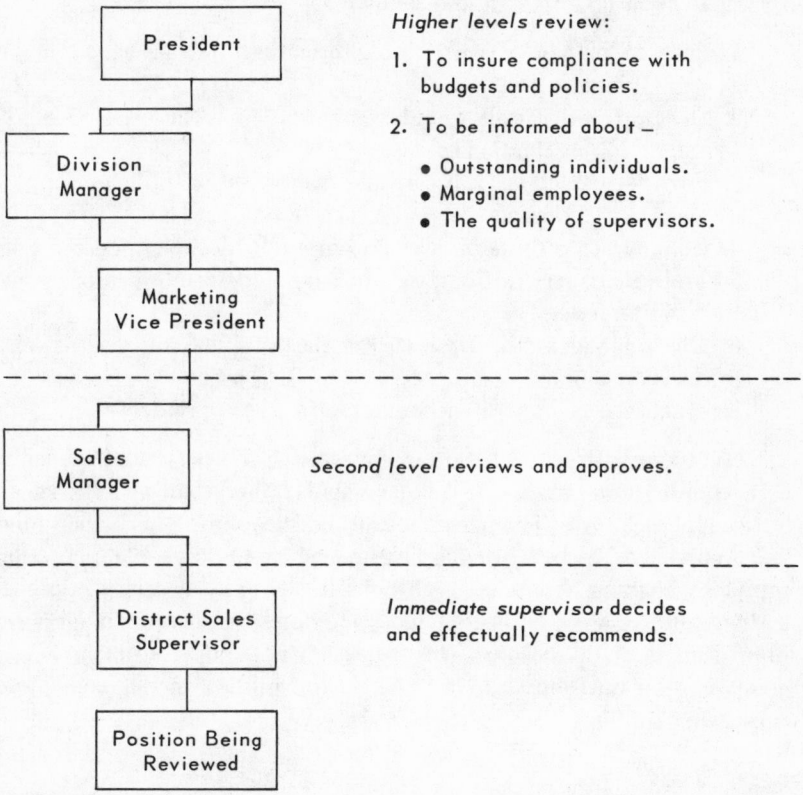

recommendations in line with established policies and guidelines. Pay recommendations for individuals are approved at the very next level. Higher levels of management review the results in various departments to assure compliance with company policies, to obtain information on individual employees, and to assess the performance of immediate supervisors.

Control by Influence

One effective, though indirect, method of control may be described as control by influence. This approach involves taking constructive steps to train managers to make sound pay decisions in the first place, rather than following a punitive approach of correcting mistakes after they are made. Such a policy considers individual review, not as a means of reversing the supervisor's decisions, but as an opportunity to help the supervisor make better decisions. Constructive actions that a company can take include the following:

1. Provide managers with the information they need to make equitable pay decisions.
2. Develop and install sound compensation techniques (for example, job evaluation).
3. Provide managers with sensible compensation policies supplemented by constructive and logical ground rules.
4. Communicate these policies and ground rules to supervisors.
5. Train managers in the basic thinking and techniques of sound salary practices.
6. Give managers the time to do a careful job of making pay decisions.
7. Make managers truly accountable for their pay decisions.

Another constructive action involves using the personnel specialist as a counselor or advisor to management rather than strictly as an instrument of control. The personnel specialist can bring his background and knowledge to bear on helping managers to solve compensation problems, making concrete suggestions in the area of salary administration and related subjects, and generally assisting managers in improving their operations. This approach not only results in better compensation decisions but contributes to building management and preserving staff.

OUTSIDE CONTROLS

All companies are to some extent influenced in their programs and decisions by outside forces or controls. For example, whenever employees are represented by a union, the collective bargaining agreement must be considered in designing the pay program. Similarly, government regulations and, in recent years, community and social pressures have an important bearing on pay decisions.

Collective Bargaining Agreements

The National Labor Relations Act requires employers to bargain in good faith with certified union representatives on all matters relating to "wages and conditions of work." These matters include not only pay rates of employees but also techniques, practices, and procedures which affect employee earnings. Thus, among organized employees, the collective bargaining agreement represents a policy guide for supervisors. Management can be certain that its actions will be closely audited by union stewards.

Labor leaders generally have not favored the techniques associated with a formal wage and salary program. They have usually opposed job evaluation and have almost invariably objected to merit rating programs which gear earnings to management judgments of work performance.

The major objection raised by union leaders is that the techniques of wage and salary administration are a substitute for collective bargaining. They recognize, for instance, that if job evaluation guides the thinking of managers and union leaders, the determination of individual pay relationships is largely removed from collective bargaining. In addition, labor leaders sometimes see a formal plan as primarily a management guide rather than a system to benefit employees. They are reluctant to accept unilateral management judgments—particularly if these judgments are based on a system which, in their opinion, does not necessarily result in more logical pay actions than those which could be obtained through collective bargaining. Finally, union leaders have criticized some pay techniques on the grounds that they are too complicated for workers to understand. Some have even voiced the fear that the more intricate procedures are really management tricks designed to hide continuing discriminatory practices.

Companies are naturally defensive about such union attitudes, but the plain fact is that there is some merit in all these criticisms. However, it is not necessarily the techniques which are at fault but rather the ways in which they have been used. Management's insistence on the importance of techniques is not necessarily a matter of deception, though some deception is no doubt part of the gamesmanship of collective bargaining. In many salary programs the problem is simply improper application or overuse of techniques. In fact, many of the criticisms raised by unions are also concerns frequently voiced by managers about their own pay programs.

In companies that have established mature collective bargaining relationships with unions, labor representatives have participated with management in the development and administration of pay programs. In some cases unions have come to regard the techniques not only as a valuable management-labor guide for reaching agreement but also as a means of explaining the results of these agreements to their members. In other cases unions have seen the various techniques as methods of getting more for workers. For instance, some have found it to their advantage to bargain for upgradings through job evaluation, rather than to bargain on the basis of overall job worth. In this way they can use each factor judgment under the evaluation plan as a means of achieving upgrading. Also, during periods of government wage controls, unions have accepted job evaluation programs as a necessary means of getting government approval for pay increases.

Supervisors must exercise the same care in interpreting and applying collective bargaining agreements as they do in carrying out company policies. Experience has shown that the following points are particularly important in the administration of a labor agreement:

1. Management must take great care in assigning employees to their proper pay classifications.
2. When an employee's job assignment changes, his position should be reevaluated promptly.
3. Managers must thoroughly understand the provisions of the collective bargaining agreement. They should know, for instance, whether a new position must be discussed with union representatives before it is established.
4. Pay progression practices in the collective bargaining contract must be strictly followed.
5. Managers at all levels should be familiar with the provisions of the grievance system, should know which pay questions are subject to grievance handling, and should understand how pay grievances are processed.
6. Managers must be alert to the possibility of "whipsawing" by unions—that is, using one request for a change in pay grade as a basis for gaining upgradings for many other positions.

Government Regulations

The various federal laws affecting wage and salary practices are another important control on pay decisions. While managers should always seek the advice of legal counsel on specific questions, there are certain basic legal requirements which should be understood by all supervisors who are involved in the administration of wage and salary programs. A single violation of the law by an uninformed supervisor can result in a substantial fine, a penalty payment, loss of government business, or court action.

Overtime payments. The Fair Labor Standards Act requires that covered employees be paid time and one-half for all work over 40 hours per week. This law, along with subsequent administrative decisions, spells out in great detail the conditions under which an employee may be exempted from overtime pay requirements. The supervisor should recognize that the company has no discretion here; he must check carefully with the personnel staff and with legal counsel with respect to the status of any questionable positions.

Minimum wages. There are also legal requirements as to the minimum wages which can be paid to employees. Compliance with federal minimum wage laws is generally a matter of companywide practice. Supervisors, however, should be cognizant of the laws and should recognize the impact of minimum wages on pay differentials within the company.

Rates of pay for government contractors. The Walsh-Healy Act requires employers who engage in certain types of government contract work to pay the "going rate" in the areas where the work is performed and to pay overtime for work in excess of eight hours a day. Failure to meet this requirement can involve the company in considerable legal difficulties.

Antidiscrimination laws. Discrimination with respect to pay because of an employee's race, color, creed, or sex has always been contrary to good business practice or social justice; it is now prohibited by law.

Pay stabilization. Government pay guidelines or controls are another legal factor to be considered in the company pay program. The controls established during World War II and the Korean War, plus the more recent phases of pay controls under the Nixon administration, suggest that some form of pay controls are a recurring, if not permanent, part of government policy.

Social Pressures

During recent years there have been increasing social pressures on companies with respect to use of human resources and specific personnel practices. These pressures have to do with equal employment opportunities for minority groups and women, safe and reasonable working conditions, and corporate responsibility toward the community and its environment.

Some of these social pressures have a direct effect on pay administration. There is, for instance, great sensitivity with respect to equal pay for equal work for minority groups and women. This is manifested in various government regulations, but the actions of employees may frequently put pressure on companies to do better than the requirements of the law. The company should be sensitive to existing social and community pressures and should take them into account in designing and administering its compensation program.

ADMINISTRATIVE AND TECHNICAL MATTERS

The various administrative and technical considerations involved in a wage and salary program are primarily the concern of top management and the personnel specialist. However, the individual supervisor should at least be cognizant of them, and a few of these matters are outlined below.

Interface Problems

The existence of different groups of employees within a company may lead to interface problems. For instance, if the merit budget, rate of pay progress, or salary structure applied to operations jobs is different from that applied to administrative positions, pay relationships between the groups may become distorted. This not only may create inequities but may impede the transfer of employees. Consequently, it is critically important that the company use a single structure for all groups of employees. Benchmark positions should be selected from each group, and pay levels should be set regardless of job evaluation results.

Pay practices generally vary from one group of employees to another. For instance, office workers tend to receive pay increases more frequently than middle-level or management personnel. On the other hand, management and middle-level employees often have more flexibility in terms of work hours and timekeeping procedures than office personnel. These differences are derived from the nature of the duties performed by each group. It is important that the supervisor be aware of such differences and the reasons for them. Otherwise, he may not be able to administer the salary program equitably or explain pay differences to employees.

Career Compensation

Some of the questions which supervisors face in wage and salary administration involve career patterns of income improvement for employees. Figure 21 shows three common patterns. Curve A illustrates the typical pattern of income improvement for a single job or a family

Figure 21. **Hypothetical career compensation curve.**

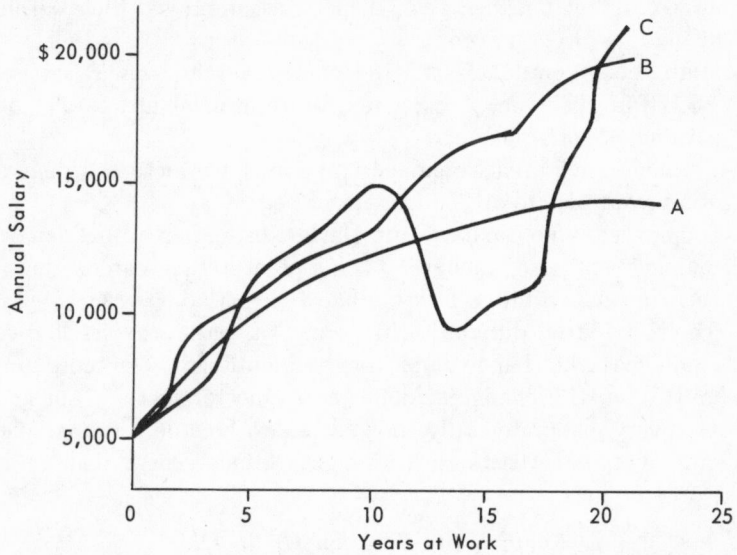

of jobs (such as mechanical engineer I, II, III, and so on). Note that income improves rapidly when the employee first comes on the job; pay progress then slows down gradually until the employee receives only modest gains.

Most employees, however, do not spend their entire career at one job or even at one level within a family of jobs. Their career curves then resemble curve B, which is essentially a series of A curves joined together. Alternatively, the income curve of an individual may be quite irregular. Frequently, for instance, it will show a distinct upward thrust between the ages of 30 and 40. Or a person's income curve may actually decline at some period. This pattern is represented in curve C.

Information not only on the shape of career curves but also on the amount of overall pay progress can be valuable to management in establishing wage and salary programs. Unfortunately, little concrete information is available in these areas. The few studies which have been made show some interesting facts:

- In a West Coast engineering laboratory 200 engineers with an average of fourteen years' experience improved their pay at a rate of 11 percent per year.
- Among 374 middle management employees who were seeking new positions and who had an average of twenty years' experience, average annual pay improved 13.5 percent.

- In one company more than 1,000 nonexempt employees who had an average of fourteen years' experience improved their earnings at the rate of 6.5 percent per year.
- High school graduates starting at an average annual salary of $3,500 in 1965 can be expected, by retirement at age 65, to be earning $25,000 per year.
- Employees who reach managerial status have increased their pay at an average rate of 17 percent per year.
- Employees who achieve top levels in either professional or management positions have at some point in their careers doubled their income within a three- to five-year period.
- There is little difference in terms of pay progress between employees who change employers frequently (three or more times) and those who change seldom (two times or less) or not at all. One very elaborate study showed this to be true for a sample of employees in several industries over a fifteen-year period.

Keeping the Program Up to Date

Supervisors sometimes feel that the problems of pay administration have been solved once a formal salary administration program is installed. Actually, of course, unless a program is kept up to date and adapted to changing circumstances, the company will very shortly have no program at all.

To keep the program up to date technically means (1) updating job information (and perhaps job descriptions) so that existing position information always accurately reflects duties assigned; (2) updating evaluation judgments so that evaluations represent management's best thinking, guided by the evaluation program and market pay data, as to the relative worth of all positions; and (3) updating the pay structure so that it is indeed reasonable and competitive.

The most difficult aspect of keeping the program up to date is adapting it to changing circumstances within the company or in various labor markets. Staff personnel are usually responsible for making recommendations, but certainly the day-to-day experience of supervisors can be a useful input. Most companies have found it necessary to make some sort of compensation program review at least once every five years to make sure that management has responded properly to changing circumstances.

Such technical adjustments in the pay program can be achieved rather simply. The most difficult problem is to keep the program up to date substantively. Essentially, this requires that supervisors *use* the system which is in effect and do so with good judgment, for the key to the success of any good technique is sound management practice.

Explaining Pay Decisions to Employees

The basic objective of pay administration cannot be accomplished unless the supervisor can explain his decisions adequately to employees. As a general rule, the supervisor should not discuss pay increases exclusively in terms of performance. Rather, he should point out that performance, while a basic consideration, is only one of many factors to be evaluated in making individual pay decisions.

Some managers rebel against the idea of having to explain a raise. Employees, however, are interested in getting not just any raise but the raise they think they are entitled to, and it is the task of the manager to explain why he decided on the particular amount he did.

Traditionally, supervisors have discussed both the employee's performance and the resulting pay increase at the same time, in a session commonly called the "postmerit-rating interview." However, if there is logic in separating performance review from compensation review, there is also logic in discussing performance and pay increases at separate times. Unless this is done, consideration of the merit pay increase is likely to dominate the interview.

Ideally, the manager discusses performance with each of his subordinates whenever appropriate circumstances warrant. These discussions should focus primarily on summarizing what has already been covered in the periodic performance review and on examining ways in which the employee's work might be further improved. If these review sessions are handled well and the supervisor has been working with the subordinate throughout the year, the groundwork for the discussion of the pay increase will already have been established. The pay increase interview can then deal primarily with why the supervisor arrived at the particular amount of increase.

Explaining the amount of a raise is not always an easy matter, particularly if the supervisor has had to judge a number of conflicting factors in arriving at his decision. Because of this, and because of the importance of the pay increase discussion, the manager should review the facts which led to the decision before meeting with the employee. He also should attempt to anticipate the employee's reactions to his explanation and prepare himself accordingly. During the session, the supervisor should make sure that the employee understands how the decision was reached and what factors (including performance) were considered. The employee should then have an opportunity to comment on the decision—free from fear of reprisal.

Just how well the employee accepts the pay decision will, of course, depend on several factors: the size of the increase, whether he is impressed by the manager's thoughtfulness and thoroughness in making the decision, and the degree to which he understands the company's merit rating program.

Cost of Wage and Salary Administration

The cost of wage and salary administration varies substantially. A true cost estimate must include some measure of the supervisor's time and the employee's time, as well as a measure of the expense of staff work and outside consulting services. The total cost depends on the level of the jobs covered and the nature of the program. The following guides might apply to a program covering supervisory, administrative, and technical personnel: (1) cost of installing the program—$100 to $150 per employee; (2) cost of administering the program—.25 to .5 percent of the payroll.

These costs will be substantially higher for programs covering management and professional employees and somewhat lower for programs covering operations employees. In any case, of course, the costs are considerable. Because of the size of the investment, the program should certainly contribute significantly to the solution of company pay problems and the achievement of company goals.

9

WAGE INCENTIVE PLANS

THE PRIMARY CHARACTERISTIC of wage incentive plans is that there is a direct and predetermined relationship between output, or performance, and total pay. These plans are used primarily for factory workers, although occasionally they are applied to clerical jobs as well.

THE WAGE INCENTIVE APPROACH

Bureau of Labor Statistics surveys have revealed that the overall percentage of factory workers who are paid under wage incentive programs is declining. About 33 percent of all factory workers earned incentive pay in the period 1951 to 1958; this figure declined to less than 30 percent by 1963 and to about 20 percent by 1970. The chief reason for this decline is mechanization—the substitution of machines for human labor. In general, operations that lend themselves best to incentive pay programs are those that are easiest to mechanize.

Logic of Incentive Plans

Wage incentive plans and merit rating plans have two major characteristics in common. In both systems, job rates are determined through job evaluation. In both systems, individual employees are paid a premium for performance above specified requirements.

The logic behind individual premium payments is that people vary in almost every possible respect: in strength, vitality, ability, and desire to produce on the job. Because of these differences, a group of employees—all qualified to do a given job—can perform at widely divergent speeds. Both merit rating and incentive plans assume that if the company gears extra pay to extra work, each employee will tend to produce to the maximum of his ability.

Incentive plans attempt to motivate employees to perform above a standard by creating a direct relationship between physical units produced and compensation. The standard specifies how many units of output are expected in return for the job rate. In theory, this calls for an equal effort from all employees. Any production above this minimum is assumed to be the result of greater effort, and the employee is given additional pay in direct proportion to the extra amount he produces. Since the incentive approach assumes that the output can be physically counted, it is applicable primarily to production jobs.

The wage incentive approach represents a unique concept of worker payment. Other systems pay the employee for the time he is on the job, and it is the task of management to utilize that time effectively. Under the incentive system, the employee's pay is geared primarily to the number of units produced, regardless of the time involved.

Whether a wage incentive plan can be successfully applied to a given operation depends on several factors:

– Pay levels and practices already in existence must be reasonable and must include hourly rates and fringe benefits which are competitive. Problems in the basic pay structure or its administration may well be magnified by the incentive program.

– The operation to be performed must be easily measurable.

– The operator must be able to have a significant effect on output. If the timing of the operation is largely controlled by the speed of a conveyor belt or machine, his extra effort will have very little effect on measured output.

– The operation time for a full cycle must be short enough that the operator's extra effort can show itself in the measured output.

– The labor relations environment must be such that the program can be introduced in a spirit of cooperation and understanding of the objectives to be attained.

– There must be a commitment by management to spend the time and money necessary to initiate and maintain the program. This usually means a larger industrial engineering staff and increased attention to the handling of grievances, at least until the program is well established.

Types of Incentive Plans

Over the years, individual companies have developed a bewildering array of incentive plans. Some of these are quite direct and simple to understand; others are extremely complex and technical. The most widely used are the piecework plan, the Taylor differential piece-rate plan, the Halsey gain-share plan, the standard hour plan, and various point incentive and group incentive systems. There are, of course, innumerable variations and combinations of these.

The piecework plan. Under the piecework plan, the employee receives a fixed price or wage for each unit he turns out. This plan was the first incentive system to be developed and is one of the most popular in industry. It has the advantage of establishing a direct relationship between what a worker produces and what he earns.

Taylor differential piece-rate plan. The differential piece-rate system, developed by Frederick W. Taylor, is similar to the piecework approach except that two rates are applied. The higher rate is paid when the worker equals or betters the standard established for his job; the lower rate is paid when output is less than standard. This arrangement provides workers with an incentive to produce at least the standard.

Halsey gain-share plan. Under the gain-share plan, a standard time is established for each task, and the employee receives a base rate of pay for production completed within the time. If he finishes the task in less than the time allotted, he receives a bonus, or percentage premium, which is generally equal to half the percentage saving in time. Bonus earnings are added to base earnings and an earned rate is calculated for the purpose of computing overtime hours.

Standard hour plan. The standard hour system is similar to the Halsey gain-share plan except that employees receive a 100 percent premium for improved output. Thus a 10 percent increase in productivity would result in a 10 percent increase in pay.

Point incentive systems. Point incentive systems set a standard time for each operation, taking into account periods for rest or relaxation. The standards are translated into point values, and incentive pay is then geared to the employee's ability to perform in less than standard time. Since all jobs are measured in points, it is possible to make simple comparisons of performance on jobs that have dissimilar work cycles.

Group incentive systems. The various techniques described above are often applied on a group basis in situations where several employees work as a team. In such cases, it is not practical to apply incentives individually; they are based on the output of the group as a whole, with each member sharing proportionately in the bonus.

Methods of Determining Work Standards

Responsibility for selecting the appropriate incentive plan for a given operation and for deciding which method to use in setting standards is usually the shared task of the industrial engineering specialist and the personnel specialist. All incentive pay programs require a predetermined standard, and their success in attaining the basic objective of gearing pay directly to production depends on the standard's accuracy.

Standards may be established in three different ways. The simplest way is to base them on past performance—to analyze production records and take some percentage of past work attainment as the standard for the future. This approach is, of course, extremely hazardous. Records reflect only what workers have done, not what they can do. Experience has shown that past performance may represent as little as 30 or 40 percent of a reasonable standard of work. This is particularly true in companies where methods have been loose, supervision has been lax, or scheduling and production planning have been faulty.

Because of the pitfalls of basing standards strictly on past performance, most plans include some form of time and motion study, carried out by a trained industrial engineer. The engineer observes the operation, records the time necessary to accomplish it, and judges the worker's efficiency in performing the task. The accuracy of time and motion studies depends on how closely the engineer observes the job and how well he estimates the worker's efficiency.

A third and still more refined method of determining work standards uses preestablished time values for every conceivable type of worker motion. These values are based on years of observation and study in many different production situations. Since worker efficiency is already built into these time values, the industrial engineer need only observe and record each motion and attach the established time value to it. The standard for that particular task is then set after making proper allowances for rest and downtime. This method not only eliminates a large area of variability due to individual judgment but also permits more careful study of the job.

ELEMENTS OF A SOUND WAGE INCENTIVE SYSTEM

Some of the prime advantages of wage incentive systems are that they have been in use for many years, they have been thoroughly developed and tested, and there are thousands of case histories from which to draw information. In addition, relatively few new techniques have been developed in recent years that introduce any degree of risk. Experience with these plans has shown that certain requirements are essential for their success:

- The program must be technically sound.
- The standards established must be guaranteed to employees.
- Reasonable incentive earnings must be maintained.
- Basic work methods must be enforced.
- A balance in total pay relationships must be preserved.
- The program, including work standards, must be kept up to date as methods, materials, and equipment change.
- The program must contribute to higher productivity and to the long-range growth and success of the company.

Technical Soundness

A successful wage incentive plan must meet several technical requirements. First, it must have some sound and reasonably objective means of setting work standards. Otherwise, it would be impossible to judge whether increased worker effort was the primary cause of increased production. Second, the incentive system must be understandable to employees. The plan should be so simple that workers, knowing the amount they produce each day or each hour, can determine for themselves what their incentive earnings should be. Third, the incentive formula should establish some direct relationship between the earnings of the employee and the quantity and quality of his output. Finally, incentive earnings should be sufficiently generous to convince workers that they are being adequately paid for their extra effort.

Guaranteed Standards

If there is one single factor that is responsible for employee and union opposition to incentive programs, it is rate cutting, which has occurred in every industry where incentive plans have been in effect. Certainly, when a worker has increased his earnings because of his own application or ingenuity on the job, he will resist any cut in the rate. Not only has rate cutting resulted in direct and obvious retaliation by employees who quit or strike; it has also led to such practices as collusion to withhold work or to peg the output on the job.

Thus any successful wage incentive program must make some provision for guaranteeing work standards. This does not mean that the standards can never be changed. It means only that management promises not to change the work standards unless there is a genuine change in methods, materials, or equipment on the job. When the job does change, a new standard should be set.

Reasonable Incentive Earnings

If standards are set so high that only a few workers can earn premium pay, then there is not much incentive in the incentive program. With reasonable effort, most workers should be able to attain some incentive earnings. In addition, the incentive plan should contain special provisions for breakdowns in equipment, problems with materials, and other delays or interruptions in work. On the other hand, work standards and controls should not be so loose that incentive earnings constitute a disproportionate share of total pay. Average premiums of 15 to 25 percent are generally considered proper. Finally, incentive earnings should not become a substitute for general increases in base pay—increases warranted by upward trends in industry wages or increases in the cost of living. The incentive system will soon run into trouble if the company expects to eliminate general pay raises for employees.

Enforcement of Work Methods

Under a sound incentive plan, the company should engineer each task to determine the best method, set standards based on that best method, and require workers to follow it. This assumes that it is management's responsibility to improve methods, equipment, and material, while it is the worker's responsibility to apply himself reasonably to the job, following the methods that have been established. Unless this procedure is adopted, employees may improve the methods so much that they either earn an unreasonable amount of incentive pay or attain high incentive pay with minimum effort.

Balance in Pay Relationships

The question of setting consistent standards and applying them uniformly has an important bearing on gross pay relationships in the company. If standards are not set consistently on all jobs, some workers may be able to attain higher incentive earnings without any additional effort. By the same token, some employees may work harder to improve methods than others. In either case, gross earnings on different jobs will vary widely, and workers on jobs with relatively low base rates may be able to earn considerably more than highly skilled workers.

Contribution to Successful Operations

A final requirement of a sound wage incentive plan is that it contribute to the long-range success and growth of the business. Otherwise, the investment necessary to establish and administer the plan cannot be justified. This requirement has many ramifications.

For example, personnel policies must take into account the worker's skill, versatility, length of service, and any other attributes which may be important to the company in the long run. In addition, the company must adopt procedures and controls to insure that greater output is not obtained at the expense of poorer quality. Again, the entire wage incentive program must be acceptable to union representatives; otherwise, the company may become embroiled in repeated negotiations over standards, work methods, and incentive earnings. Finally, the incentive plan should not seriously impede the flexibility that the company needs in assigning work and in transferring employees; nor should establishment of the plan lead to the deterioration of management practices.

INSTALLING THE PLAN

The first and foremost consideration in adopting a wage incentive plan is communication. Fear of the unknown and resistance to change are two great hurdles that must be overcome before a new plan or a change in an existing plan can be adopted. In companies where employees are organized, the union must be informed of the new plan in the early stages. Eventually, certain parts of the plan may become negotiable items to be clarified and inserted in the contract.

Equally important are communications with supervisors and workers in the shop areas. The plan must be formally presented to these groups, and the presentation should include some history of past experiences to show how the need for change arose. The system should be discussed in detail, and the advantages and disadvantages both to the company and to employees should be thoroughly disclosed. To the extent possible, workers and supervisors should be involved in the planning process—their practical knowledge can be of help in avoiding many pitfalls.

In addition, general guidelines for administering the plan should be thoroughly discussed with all concerned. Some workers, for instance, will undoubtedly try to "beat the system." The safeguards against such a practice and the policies for handling infractions should be openly discussed. Everyone should be made aware of the changes that the plan will create in worker-supervisor relationships—for example, pressure by workers to get rates increased, new worker grievances, and new problems associated with materials handling, machine downtime, and other procedures.

Above all, the discussions should attempt to dispel the long-standing fears of employees that incentive plans will lead to sweatshop conditions, rate cutting, or other practices. It is important that employees be informed of management's real goals and of their part in helping the company to attain them.

Paperwork systems must be developed to provide for the accurate reporting of all events of interest in the system and for the eventual control reports that come back to supervisors. It will be necessary to tie the system into inventory control, quality control, waste or scrap control, and, most important, payroll and cost accounting.

Concurrent with the development of paperwork systems, plans must be devised for improving manufacturing methods. Before incentive pay standards can be set, it is necessary to be certain that the most efficient method of manufacture is being used. This involves establishing the proper sequence of operations, setting up the tooling for each task, and making detailed time and motion studies to determine the best possible combination of worker movements and machine speeds and feeds.

The selection of which items to develop standards for can best be accomplished by the "usage value" approach. The unit cost of a part or assembly times its annual usage determines its annual usage value. Generally, parts with the highest annual usage value are those that are made of expensive raw materials, that are produced in great quantities, or that require a lot of manufacturing time. In a typical plant inventory about 15 percent of such items will account for more than 80 percent of the annual usage value. It is this small group of items which should be analyzed first. If this is done, the system can be made operational long before the industrial engineers finish their work. Other items can be analyzed as it becomes necessary to manufacture them.

It is important that all the analyses used to create a wage rate be carefully documented. In many cases—particularly with respect to materials handling methods—it is useful to include pictures of the work station as part of the documentation. Inevitably, changes occur in any job—through improved operator methods, new types of materials handling equipment, design changes, and so on. These changes may affect manufacturing time and the operator's earnings. Under such conditions, it may be necessary to revise the wage rate, and documentation will be invaluable in proving that the change was not due to increased operator effort.

Once work methods have been established, it is necessary to train operators in those methods. Most companies train workers on the job for relatively simple tasks. For longer sequences of operation, complex assemblies, or difficult movements, many companies have established separate training facilities, in which operators learn through visual aids and are given the opportunity to practice certain tasks before being placed on the production line.

ADMINISTERING THE PLAN

Just how well managers meet their responsibilities under the wage incentive program is every bit as important to its success as the technical aspects of the plan. Managers, particularly first-line supervisors, have responsibilities in the areas of establishing and enforcing work methods; establishing and reviewing work standards; training employees to follow correct methods; supervising work flow, materials, equipment, and the administrative aspects of incentive plans; and handling communications regarding incentives, including questions and complaints.

Proper work methods are a basic determinant of shop efficiency, and establishing them is a fundamental management responsibility. It involves the choice of the proper equipment, layout, process, and materials, as well as stipulation of the motions which workers should make. Theoretically, there is a best method for each job, and it is this method which management should seek to discover.

This responsibility should not be delegated to workers. Employees may, largely through trial and error, devise more efficient motions and techniques, but they are hardly in a position to determine equipment, flow, materials, and so forth. In fact, their innovations may have adverse effects on equipment life, work flow, product quality, or safety practices. (This is not to say that workers cannot *participate* in developing efficient methods, either formally through a suggestions system or informally through working with industrial engineers.)

The Manager's Role

Just as the manager must play an active role in determining proper work methods, so he must have some control over the standards which are set on these methods. Although it is the task of industrial engineers to establish standards, the manager concerned must at least review them, since he is held accountable for costs and employee relations. If standards are too loose, costs will be out of line; if they are too tight, trouble with employees or unions will result.

After both methods and standards are set, it is the duty of the manager to make sure that employees observe them. This involves training workers on the job, particularly if they are expected to follow company-determined standards. Job training frequently requires more than merely telling the employee what to do; the supervisor may have to show him how to do it, observe him doing it, and tell him when he is doing it improperly. The quality of job training influences not only how much workers produce but also how quickly they learn the job.

Enforcement of standards and methods also requires effective daily supervision, which includes assignment of duties, discipline, and rewards. People vary in their aptitude for different types of work—an employee who makes 30 percent more in incentive pay on one job may have difficulty attaining standard pay on another. Assignment of workers to the jobs for which they are best suited can contribute substantially to worker achievement.

In addition to proper training and daily supervision, managers must motivate workers on the job. Such motivation is an indefinable activity. Certainly it involves follow-up by the supervisor, so that workers not only know what is expected of them but are sure that the supervisor knows what they accomplish. The manager who is successful in motivating employees is one who is sensitive to work problems and to the worker as an individual, who is able to identify problems which interfere with employee efficiency, and who has a certain social grace which defies description because it is so highly individualized.

Both reward and discipline play a part in assuring proper attainment of work standards. Incentive plans are designed to give material rewards automatically. In addition, greater recognition, more rapid promotion, preferential treatment in job assignments, and other personnel devices may be utilized to reward the particularly effective worker and provide extra incentive pay for him.

For those who do not attain reasonable standards of production, some form of disciplinary action is necessary. The supervisor would be unfair to those employees who do perform effectively, as well as to the company and himself, if he did not take such action. Ideally, discipline is proportioned to the offense, geared to correction and prevention of abuses rather than to punishment, and applied only after careful investigation of facts and circumstances.

Finally, the manager of each operating department plays a key role in explaining the incentive program to employees. Unless workers believe the plan to be fair and believe that extra effort on their part will bring about commensurate increases in earnings, it is unlikely that they will be motivated to substantially increase their production. In addition, it is the job of the supervisor to handle employee questions and complaints. Many grievances concern the fairness of the standard. It is usually not enough for the supervisor to call on the industrial engineer to recheck the standard for accuracy. The manager must review it himself and make sure of its accuracy; he should not simply act as the spokesman for someone else's judgment.

Even this brief summary of the manager's responsibilities under wage incentive programs indicates that these plans require a great deal of supervision. The manager's responsibilities under incentive pay and day-work pay plans may differ somewhat in areas of emphasis, but they are equally great for both programs.

ECONOMICS OF WAGE INCENTIVE SYSTEMS

The economics of wage incentive plans, illustrated in Figure 22, have a basic impact on earnings and costs. Under most plans, employees are guaranteed a fixed hourly rate up to the point of standard production. This is an average of $4 per hour in Figure 22. After the standard is exceeded, average hourly earnings increase in direct proportion to increased output. In the figure, the increase is from $4 to a maximum of $5. At the same time, unit costs, which are a combination of direct costs of labor and materials and fixed overhead costs, drop rapidly as employees work toward standard production, and they continue to decrease as employees pass standard. This is because the increase in direct costs caused by increasing hourly rates is more than offset by the drop in fixed overhead costs. As a result, by motivating employees to produce more on the job, managers can accomplish the double objective of increasing employee earnings and reducing unit costs.

***Figure* 22. Economics of wage incentive plans.**

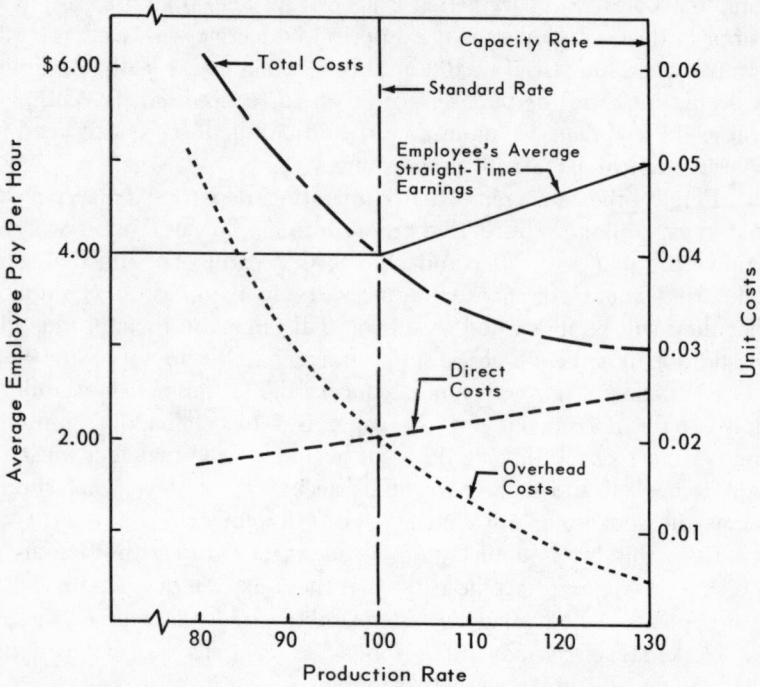

It is a serious oversimplification, however, to assume that the mere establishment of an incentive plan can motivate workers to achieve these ends.

10

SALESMEN'S COMPENSATION

IN ALL BUSINESSES distribution is a key part of company operations, and the effectiveness of distribution usually depends in large measure on the field sales force. A major portion of sales expense is personnel. Thus, from the viewpoint of both effectiveness and cost, salesmen's compensation is of vital concern to management.

THE SALES JOB

Because of the diversity of operations in most enterprises today, the nature of the sales job is difficult to identify and define. Typically, sales personnel perform at least some nonsales work, and many nonsales personnel are in some way related to the selling activity.

In a broader sense, everyone who affects the quality of the product, the service rendered, the image of the company, or relationships with customers is a salesman. Many employees devote their time to performing professional, technical, or administrative work in support of the sales effort. Some actually have direct selling responsibility even though their primary job is professional or managerial. For instance, lawyers are expected not only to perform legal work for clients but to be alert to opportunities for additional legal assignments.

Such employees, however, would not be defined as salesmen for the purpose of personnel administration or compensation. Strictly speaking, a salesman is someone who works with buyers to procure orders. The bulk of his time is devoted to this task, and it constitutes the main activity for which he is paid. Most sales positions involve a variety of duties, including any or all of the following.

Soliciting orders. Certainly every sales job entails the actual solicitation of orders. To understand the job, however, the salesman must also know the specific product line for which he is responsible; the number of customers and who they are; the total sales volume and the volume by line; the number of units, sales transactions, and buying decisions; the number of times that each customer will probably be visited; and what he expects to take place during the visit.

Servicing orders. Many sales jobs have important servicing responsibilities. In fact, it is sometimes difficult to distinguish between a solicitation call and a servicing call.

Prospecting. Part of the sales job involves prospecting—ferreting out new potential users of the company's goods or services.

"Missionary" work. The salesman may be expected to undertake direct promotion or merchandising, train customer personnel in use of products or services, or give technical advice and administrative assistance.

Accumulating information. Inherent in every sales job is some requirement for the accumulation of information—for example, information about the customer, people within the customer's organization, and potential customers in the district. The salesman may also send information to headquarters about markets, customers' requirements, forecasts, competitors' products, and new sales possibilities.

Management decisions. Many salesmen who spend the majority of their time in direct selling also have management responsibilities—for other salesmen, for office personnel, or for storage facilities. In addition, salesmen sometimes make management decisions involving credit, pricing, and product adaptation or modification.

Nonsales work. All salesmen have some administrative responsibility, which includes making reports and keeping records.

Market knowledge. Sales jobs also require an understanding of the marketing operations of the company—including the markets themselves, the competition, alternative or substitute products, distributive systems, the nature of demand for the product, the degree of product differentiation, and the sophistication of buyers. Finally, it is important to know whether the salesman handles the sales transaction independently or works as part of a selling team.

ELEMENTS OF SALES COMPENSATION

Since the basic objectives of compensation plans are the same for salesmen as for any other group of employees, essentially the same elements of compensation administration are applicable. First, as discussed above, it is necessary to understand the jobs involved. Second, there must be a method for determining the relative worth of jobs, with respect both to other sales jobs and to other positions within the organization. Third, the compensation of sales personnel must be related to compensation for comparable jobs outside the company. Fourth, outstanding individual achievement must be rewarded. Finally, administrative considerations and company ground rules, similar to those discussed earlier, must be taken into consideration. In salary administration for sales positions, as for other groups of jobs, the unique features of a compensation plan lie in its application and methodology, not in its basic requirements.

In the sales compensation area the primary emphasis is on providing the salesman with an incentive to work enthusiastically toward the particular sales goals of the company. These goals range from improved service to clients through optimization of profit to maximum increase in sales volume. The methods of creating the incentive also vary widely and range from straight salary, where the emphasis is on service to clients, through various combinations of salary, bonus, and commission plans, to straight commission, where the emphasis is on volume.

The personality traits that lead people into the sales field are often entrepreneurial in nature; thus salesmen are generally willing to assume a certain level of financial risk in order to reap the rewards of success. Incentive compensation, along with other psychological rewards, can be a big factor in the salesman's motivation.

Since a high percentage of salesmen's pay is often in incentive form, the compensation program must take into account such factors as market characteristics, allocation of districts, and assignment of personnel. All these variables have a significant effect on a salesman's performance level and therefore his income. In fact, to be sure that these essentially administrative matters are handled competently and equitably, most companies assign the administration of sales compensation to sales management instead of personnel management.

Still other factors that must be considered in designing the compensation program are geographic dispersion, number of salesmen in each district, and other characteristics of the sales force. For example, a salesman who works in an area where customers are widely separated and who must spend a relatively large portion of his time traveling will have a lower sales volume and higher expenses than a salesman working for an equivalent number of customers in Manhattan. Provision must be made to compensate for such differences so that the plan provides equal reward for equal accomplishment. Similarly, when the sales effort is performed by a group of people rather than by a single salesman, the compensation plan must provide for a method both to award the group and to distribute the award within the group.

The overwhelming variety in sales jobs is at the heart of the complexities of sales compensation. It results in a great number and diversity of sales compensation plans, as well as in the need to make frequent changes in any single compensation program. One study of nine leading companies in an industry, for example, revealed nine different sales compensation plans. It also showed that in a five-year period all nine companies had made significant changes in their programs.

Incentive Versus Base Pay

Generally speaking, companies favor some form of incentive compensation for salesmen. This is not only because of tradition but because of the importance of sales volume in the success of most businesses, the general dispersion of the sales force, and other elements of sales management. The key to determining appropriate incentive compensation is analysis of sales objectives and of the sales job and identification of those areas which lend themselves to an incentive approach. Incentive pay is usually most practical when the following conditions exist:

- The sales function involves individual sales rather than a joint effort.
- Sales volume per se is crucial to the success of the business.
- There is little product differentiation.
- The salesman is required to develop potential customers as well as sell them.
- Intangibles such as personal relationships and persuasiveness are crucial.
- The product is not highly technical.

– Preselling through advertising or promotions is not a significant factor in sales transactions.

Level of Total Compensation

The level of total compensation for salesmen is determined primarily by internal pay relationships, competitive market conditions, and the economics of the business. The most pertinent points of comparison inside the company are with sales management positions, administrative sales positions, and positions that have a supportive relationship to the sales activity. Another major point of comparison in the company is with positions from which salesmen might be recruited and those to which they might be promoted. Finally, of course, there is always the general goal of relative equity among all employees within an organization, regardless of practical considerations.

Many a salesman has earned more in a given year than his sales manager or even the president of the company. This is quite acceptable on an occasional basis, but when an individual salesman or a percentage of all salesmen consistently earn more than the sales manager, it is wise to investigate the method of compensation being used. The company should bear in mind, however, that the salesman who earns the most is, in most plans, the least costly in terms of sales expense per dollar sold.

As for comparative pay in the labor market as a whole, an abundance of data is provided by the American Management Associations' Executive Compensation Service, by various trade and sales organizations, and by research and consulting organizations. All these studies show, of course, that there is considerable variation in total compensation for comparable sales positions in different companies. This is the latitude within which management must make its decisions. A company may find that the level within its particular industry varies from the overall level for all salesmen. In this case management must decide where it must compete in order to attract and retain the type of talent needed to attain sales goals.

The economics of the business must also be considered in establishing salesmen's pay levels. Items such as breakeven points, profitability of different product lines, identification of future growth businesses and growth markets, and other economic factors will not only influence the nature of the incentive compensation plan but also, within the parameters set by the marketplace, affect the level of total compensation.

Actual levels of compensation for salesmen vary widely. One study reports that salesmen earn $7,000 to $95,000 per year; *The Wall Street Journal* recently published a story about an insurance salesman who earned as much as $100,000 a month. These figures are interesting but not very helpful.

Factors which determine the actual level of total compensation of sales personnel include:

1. *The industry.* Average pay levels for salesmen vary considerably from industry to industry. Table 8 shows data as of August 1973 on total compensation of top-level, nonsupervisory salesmen in 25 industries.

2. *The job.* Product mix, territorial assignment, and other job-oriented factors largely account for the wide variation of earnings among top men within each industry.

3. *Form of compensation.* Generally speaking, the higher the proportion of incentive compensation to total compensation, the higher the level of total compensation. It is difficult to make valid comparisons of similar jobs in similar industries, but it would appear that salesmen on incentive compensation earn about 20 percent more than those who are paid a straight salary for similar sales work.

4. *The man.* Nowhere is individual worth more intertwined with job worth than in sales positions. A salesman's effectiveness, his following among customers, and other personal attributes account to a considerable extent for the pay variations indicated in Table 8.

DETERMINING BASE SALARIES

Generally speaking, when a salesman receives all or a significant portion of his compensation in the form of salary, the same considerations which were outlined in the first five chapters are applicable in determining base salary. The only variations will be in format and technique to reflect the unique nature of sales positions. When a large part of the total compensation depends on incentive earnings, broader measures and more simplified techniques may be instituted. When straight commission is the payment method, the salesman's paycheck is his evaluation.

Use of Job Descriptions

Whether or not a company should use job descriptions for salesmen depends primarily on how many sales positions it has, how com-

Table 8. **Annual total compensation of top-level nonsupervisory salesmen, by industry ($000).**

Industry	*Average Total Compensation*	*Range of Total Compensation* *	
		Minimum	*Maximum*
Proprietary drugs	13	12	25
Building materials	14	11	29
Food	15	10	26
Instruments	16	12	21
Office supplies	17	12	33
Glass	17	14	26
Insurance	17	10	46
Metal products—heavy	18	12	26
Electronics	18	14	34
Paper	18	14	25
Automotive parts	18	12	32
Metal products—light	18	12	37
Chemicals	18	12	23
Light machinery	18	12	40
Containers and packaging materials	18	13	29
Consumer—durable goods	18	15	27
Ethical pharmaceuticals	19	12	30
Heavy machinery	19	12	32
Tools and hardware	20	14	27
Iron and steel	20	15	31
Printing and publishing	20	16	30
Electrical equipment	20	12	35
Computers	20	16	66
Fabrics	22	17	45
Services	24	11	50

* Eliminating the lowest-paid 10 percent and the highest-paid 10 percent.

plex they are, and how much is known about them by the people who make the pay decisions. Various studies indicate that between 50 and 75 percent of companies do use sales job descriptions. As a rule of thumb, a firm which has more than two dozen sales positions (not salesmen) will find job descriptions not only desirable but essential.

The format for sales job descriptions is frequently different from that for production or office descriptions. The information needed involves far more than what the salesman does; it also includes such facts as the number of customers, volume of sales, diversity of products sold, areas covered, and other data of the kind already outlined. However, if all the company's sales positions have the same basic responsibilities, the descriptions need only provide information which distinguishes among the various jobs.

Use of Job Evaluation

Most companies use some form of job evaluation when base salary is all or a major part of salesmen's total compensation. More often than not, the traditional job evaluation techniques are used, and the same plan which is used to measure administrative, supervisory, and middle-level management positions is used for sales positions.

When the basic responsibilities of all a company's sales positions are similar and variations occur only in the number of customers, sales volume, or other objective criteria, simplified evaluation techniques can be used to establish pay levels. Table 9 illustrates such a program for a metal-working company. This company used the traditional classification system to relate sales positions to its pay structure and to place salesmen in the various pay grades shown.

Merit Pay Administration

When only part of the salesman's compensation is in the form of base salary, it is desirable to differentiate between extra pay through merit increases and extra pay through incentive compensation. While it is difficult to generalize, merit pay administration usually considers

Table 9. **Simplified position evaluation for sales jobs.**

Job Title	*Pay Level*	*Sales Volume*	*Number of Lines*	*Persons Supervised*	
				Sales	*Other*
Salesman III	8	Under $500,000	1–3	0	0
Salesman II	10	$500,000 to $2,500,000	3–7	0–1	0
Salesman I	12	$2,500,000 to $5,000,00	All	1–2	0–1
District manager	14	Over $5,000, 000	All	3–10	1–5
Regional manager	17	Over $20,000,000	All	Over 10	Over 5

increased knowledge, extra experience and skill, long-range demonstrated potential, and general economic factors. Incentive compensation, on the other hand, focuses on specific contributions to the sales effort and to particular sales goals.

In practice, however, merit pay and incentive pay are frequently interrelated, and there is an unfortunate tendency to give small merit increases in years of high incentive earnings and vice versa. Conversely, in some plans which gear incentive pay to base salary, every increase in pay automatically results in an increase in bonus. To the extent possible, sound practice suggests a separation of merit pay increases and incentive pay.

Ground Rules and Problems

The only special ground rules required in salesmen's salary administration relate either to pay problems inherent in moving a salesman to a different geographic location or to special pay considerations because of incentive earnings. In many companies salesmen are moved quite frequently from one place to another—because of promotions, transfers, or simply reassignments due to changing market conditions. In such cases, special pay adjustments may be necessary owing to cost-of-living considerations, different pay relationships in the new district, or changes in a salesman's earnings potential.

In some situations a significant portion of a salesman's total income is derived from special types of incentive compensation. These include an automobile and automobile expenses, cash awards or other prizes from sales contests, expense allowances, membership in clubs, and tax deductions on home expenses because the salesman uses his home as an office. In such cases, special pay adjustments may be necessary if the salesman is moved from one district to another or from the field to the home office, since his earnings potential will be affected.

INCENTIVE COMPENSATION PLANS

Because sales compensation plans must be tailored to the company's products, organization, and other special circumstances, there are literally thousands of different incentive programs for salesmen. Most of these, however, fall into five basic categories: straight salary, commission, quota systems, bonus systems, and planned compensation. Combinations of these basic approaches may also be used.

Straight Salary

The payment of straight salary provides company management with the greatest degree of control over the sales force. Salesmen can be required to spend a portion of their time in developmental activities, research or prospecting as necessary. Straight salary provides a fixed total cost of sales payroll, but the unit cost varies as volume varies. It has the advantages of being easily understood by salesmen and of allowing trainees to concentrate on the learning process rather than on their earnings. A well-administered salary program can provide a good degree of incentive but cannot compare with some of the more direct methods that tie compensation to sales volume.

Commission Plans

Commission plans are those which, in one way or another, relate the salesman's pay directly to his volume of sales. In its simplest form, the salesman is paid X percent of each dollar of sales booked or sales shipped. The rate may vary from a fraction of 1 percent to as much as 25 percent. It may increase, remain constant, or decrease with increasing volume, although decreasing rates are not recommended. Frequently, the percentage varies with each product line or service.

Commission plans give the salesman the greatest incentive to sell the largest volume, and this single feature accounts for most of their advantages and disadvantages. On the one hand, commission formulas create the maximum incentive for sales, provide a fixed cost of sales, and usually provide salesmen with the maximum opportunity for income. In fact, studies indicate that commission salesmen earn about 20 percent more in gross pay than those in comparable jobs who are on straight salary. On the other hand, this very focus on sales volume makes it difficult to control product mix. Salesmen tend to push items which provide the greatest volume and ignore items which may be more profitable or which may have to be sold to balance the manufacturing process. In addition, commission salesmen tend to be more independent—more money-oriented and less company-oriented—which often results in increased turnover of sales personnel. Finally, commission salesmen are encouraged to neglect all duties except those which will result in direct and immediate sales.

Quota Systems

Quota plans are similar to commission plans except that salesmen are usually paid a salary for a minimum level of sales, or quota, and receive a percentage of sales over the quota. Thus, in return for salary, the company can require a variety of activities—such as customer relations, missionary work, and intelligence information from the field—as well as a minimum level of sales. The commission then provides incentive to exceed the quota.

The success of such plans depends on the correctness of the quotas established. Setting quotas requires a thorough knowledge of markets, a precise estimate of sales potential, and other statistical analyses. Quota plans are frequently geared to a district, and the money for extra compensation is accumulated from the sales of all salesmen in the district. The money is then either allocated on a pro rata basis among all salesmen or apportioned by some appraisal of each man's contribution to overall achievement.

Bonus Plans

Bonus plans may be geared to the sales a man makes above a given quota. Generally, however, they include such considerations as penetration of market, profit results, and expenses. Like quota funds, bonus funds are usually accumulated on a group basis and allocated according to individual contribution. Bonus plans take into account more of the variables of sales jobs and salesmen's duties than commission or quota plans. However, their methods of rewarding individual salesmen are less direct.

Planned Compensation

The planned compensation approach is based on such factors as career compensation progress and appraisal of the individual's potential and contribution. Under this system, management sets standards as to what an employee's compensation should be and then makes pay and bonus pay judgments which will result in a planned improvement of compensation. Year-to-year variations from the total compensation expected may occur, but these are quickly adjusted, either by salary actions or by changes in the basis for incentive compensation.

Combination Plans

Over half of all companies today use some combination plan for salesmen or even several different combination plans tailored to divisions or subsidiary companies. Such plans can be designed as salary plus commission, salary plus bonus over quota, salary plus commission plus bonus over quota, or almost any possible combination. There are several advantages to this approach. The company can retain a degree of control over sales activities and at the same time encourage volume sales. Salesmen have potential for high income but also have a base salary as a floor under earnings to reduce their financial worries.

The disadvantages associated with combination plans center around their complexity and flexibility. They are more difficult to understand and administer than other plans, and many companies find it necessary to alter them periodically. The flexibility of combination plans has led to the development of literally thousands of different incentive programs—almost as many as there are companies using them.

TRENDS IN INCENTIVE COMPENSATION

Studies over the past twenty years indicate that there is a trend away from commission plans to combination and straight salary plans for salesmen. This does not mean that there is less enthusiasm for incentive compensation. Rather, it reflects the fact that a growing number of sales positions do not lend themselves to incentive plans. This, in turn, reflects trends toward a more technological society and greater emphasis on group selling.

Partly because of these trends, and because of improved market research techniques and use of computers, incentive compensation plans are becoming increasingly complex. They tend to take qualitative as well as quantitative considerations into account in setting pay levels.

Finally, there has been some fundamental new thinking in the sales compensation area during the past few years. Some companies have instituted what may be labeled "incremental compensation plans," in which a top salary is paid various personnel for achieving a high sales level and a very high bonus rate is paid for exceeding that level. In some cases this bonus is paid in a form which gives salesmen certain tax advantages.

Other companies have instituted plans in which regions and districts are literally considered as separate business enterprises or distributorships. The company puts up the capital and exercises various controls, as would be expected in any franchised operation, but the people in the district operate almost as an independent marketing company. The latitude they have is accompanied by considerable responsibility and greater opportunity to share in the profits of the business, sometimes on a favorable tax basis.

DEVELOPMENT OF A SALES INCENTIVE PROGRAM

The development of a sales incentive program involves a logical sequence of steps: determining objectives, gathering pertinent data, establishing income levels, designing the plan, and testing and adjusting the program.

Determining Objectives

The first step in the development of a sales incentive plan is to decide what goals are to be accomplished by the program. There are many possible goals for a sales compensation plan, and the plan should be structured so that goals can be changed from time to time as conditions change. Possible goals or objectives include increased profit, sales volume, market share, or number of customers; increased sales of more profitable items; improved product mix; and decreased expenses. In addition, sales compensation plans may focus on higher volume to fewer accounts, development of a territory, or increased team effort and cooperation.

Gathering Pertinent Data

In order to attract and retain better salesmen, a company must offer its sales force a compensation program that is competitive in the personnel marketplace. To do this, management must gather information about the types of incentive plans that are used in competitive companies and the levels of income that they typically provide. Special note should be taken of what is being done in the most successful companies and the least successful companies to learn the do's and don't's of compensation in the industry.

In addition, data must be gathered on the company itself: its organization, management style, sales compensation history, and plans and forecasts of sales for the future. Product lines must be explored for both sales volume and profitability or gross margin. Historical costs of sales must be examined in depth. Management must become familiar with the sales department organization, the various methods of selling, the degree of marketing support provided, and situations in which groups of salesmen rather than individuals are actually making the sale.

Finally, existing sales administration policies should be investigated with respect to windfalls, split commissions, promotions and transfers, retirements, leaves of absence and deaths, terminations and resignations, eligibility, new products, new markets, house accounts, special accounts, and ceilings on earnings. All this information will serve to guide the plan designer in carrying out the remaining steps.

Establishing Income Levels

Information is usually available from various surveys regarding what salesmen are paid in the local area, in the industry, and in the nation as a whole. Management must first decide how it wishes to compete for sales talent and then establish income levels sufficient to attract and retain the salesmen it wants. In addition, equity of income within the organization must be considered to avoid morale problems.

Designing the Plan

There are several considerations that must be made in designing a plan that will suit the needs of the company. They are:

Objectives to be accomplished
Complexity of the plan
Past practices in the company
Practices in competitive companies
Types of sales activity

The objectives to be accomplished play a very important part in the design of the plan. As noted earlier, commission plans create the greatest incentive for sales volume. Salary plans tend to be used when service to the customer is an important goal. Combination plans attempt to serve both masters and vary widely in their emphasis.

The complexity of the incentive formula is another major factor. Generally, the more complex combination plans create just the right amount of incentive for each of the company's sales goals. But such plans run the risk of not being understood, or at least of being difficult to explain, and may lose the very incentive value that they are trying to create. A compromise must often be made between placing sufficient emphasis on company objectives and designing a plan simple enough for the salesman to understand.

Past practices in the company or industry can also affect the design of the compensation plan. It may well be that past practices have established a tradition that must be followed in order for the company to remain competitive. Management should certainly investigate this possibility to make sure that the plan will be acceptable. This is not to say, however, that past practices are necessarily correct or that innovative changes should not be made. The best approach in a given situation is a matter of judgment, and there are no pat answers.

Finally, the type of sales activity is very important to the design of the plan. For example, the salesman who sells appliances from door to door has quite different needs from the man who sells high-technology or high-priced equipment to industrial consumers. The appliance salesman spends a very short time with each customer, whereas the engineering salesman may spend many months developing his relationship with a potential customer. In the former case compensation methods tend to be toward the commission end of the spectrum; in the latter case the emphasis is on the salary end.

Testing and Adjusting the Program

It is very important to test the plan before it is implemented. It should be checked against actual sales figures for the last few years to determine what each man would have earned under the system. The extremes of high and low income generated by the formula should then be analyzed to see if they are justified and appropriate. These figures should be reviewed with sales managers. The same type of analysis should be made using sales forecasts for the next year or two in order to anticipate problems with changing product mix in the future. Adjustments should then be made in the formula either to avoid individual extremes or to alter the overall costs of anticipated sales so that they will be within budgeted or forecasted levels.

ADMINISTRATION OF SALES COMPENSATION PLANS

Special administrative requirements of the sales compensation plan include communication of the plan to the field sales force, detailed and sometimes extremely complicated recordkeeping and other administrative chores, and an almost built-in requirement for continuous audit and change.

If the sales compensation plan is really to relate salesmen's pay to achievement, to motivate salesmen to extend their best efforts, and to focus their attention on the achievement of company goals, its structure will necessarily be complex. Such a program obviously requires considerable explanation, and this task is made more formidable by the typical geographic dispersion of salesmen. As a result, most companies rely on either written communication or communication through many channels to explain the program to the sales force.

The complexity of the compensation system can also make record-keeping and other administrative chores extremely burdensome, particularly if payments are related to individual orders and individual accomplishments. Sales compensation plans generally require a separate bookkeeping system. From the standpoint of the total company operation, however, this problem amounts to little more than an inconvenience and a minor expense.

The built-in requirement for auditing the compensation program and adapting it to changing conditions can be far more costly. One well-known company recently announced that 80 percent of its sales volume in the previous year was derived from products which had been unknown to the firm five years earlier. This extreme case illustrates only one of the many factors which necessitate continual auditing. Basic statistics on earnings, sales by lines, and other indexes of sales activity and effectiveness must be kept up to date. In almost every company changes in these statistics will require adjustment of quotas, commission bases, or other elements of the plan—for new products, for changes in customer requirements or locations, for advertising or merchandising methods utilized, and for innumerable other circumstances.

In many companies the principal auditor of the sales compensation plan is the sales supervisor. Frequently, one of his major responsibilities is to make sure that the plan is properly motivating the sales force and that salesmen who are making the biggest contribution are being rewarded with the most compensation. The supervisor also has the responsibility for communicating details of the program and for making sure that his salesmen understand and accept it. Finally, he must be particularly alert to competitive changes in the labor market and changes in conditions which affect the sales job.

11

COMPENSATION OF PROFESSIONAL PERSONNEL

PERSONNEL POLICIES and practices—including those concerning compensation administration—are quite different for professionals than for other groups of employees. This is not because people doing professional work are different but rather because their jobs are different. Compensation administration must be geared to the unique characteristics of the professional job.

PROFESSIONAL JOBS

In its broadest sense, professional work involves the application of learned knowledge to the solution of enterprise problems and the achievement of enterprise goals. An individual professional might engage in a variety of tasks, but the essence of his work is the application of learned knowledge. The knowledge of the professional may be in areas of the recognized disciplines (law, economics, medicine, or one of the physical sciences) or it may be based on or derived from those disciplines. Finally, the profession may be in the recognized business disciplines, such as accounting. In any case, the knowledge applied is that acquired through prolonged periods of formal study.

Thus one group of professional jobs requires knowledge of an advanced type in a recognized field of academic study. Nonsupervisory engineers and research scientists are certainly in this group. Attorneys, economists, physicians, psychologists, and sociologists also fit the definition. Another group of professional jobs requires original and creative work, which entails innovation, talent, a high level of intellectual activity, and knowledge based on one of the traditional academic disciplines. Included in this group are editors, copywriters, artists, and industrial engineers. A final group of professional jobs requires knowledge in the basic business disciplines. Many staff positions in areas such as business planning, finance, and personnel fit this description.

The professional makes analytical judgments or decisions based upon advanced knowledge acquired through prolonged periods of formal study. With experience, the professional applies this knowledge more effectively. In essence, his job is to achieve enterprise results through the application of advanced knowledge. He manages knowledge instead of assets or people.

The key to successful personnel practices for professionals involves an understanding of the unique characteristics of professional work. These are some of the distinguishing characteristics of professional work: *

– Essentially, the enterprise is buying the knowledge of the professional—not his time or any measure of his output. This implies that what is paid for is the level and the relevance of the knowledge. It is the job of management to use this knowledge effectively.

– The knowledge of professionals—what they know—represents the assets of the group.

– The professional job involves choice—of what to do as well as how to proceed.

– To a large extent, the user—be it the company or an outside customer—is buying confidence. The layman cannot really judge the appropriateness of professional work, at least from the technical point of view.

– The professional has multiple goals. One is inevitably financial—survival if not profit. But there is also at least a secondary goal inherent in all professional work.

* For a more complete description, see Robert Sibson, *Managing Professional Services Enterprises* (New York: Pitman, 1971; distributed by R. B. Keck, Princeton, N.J.).

Figure 23. **Pay progress of professionals.**

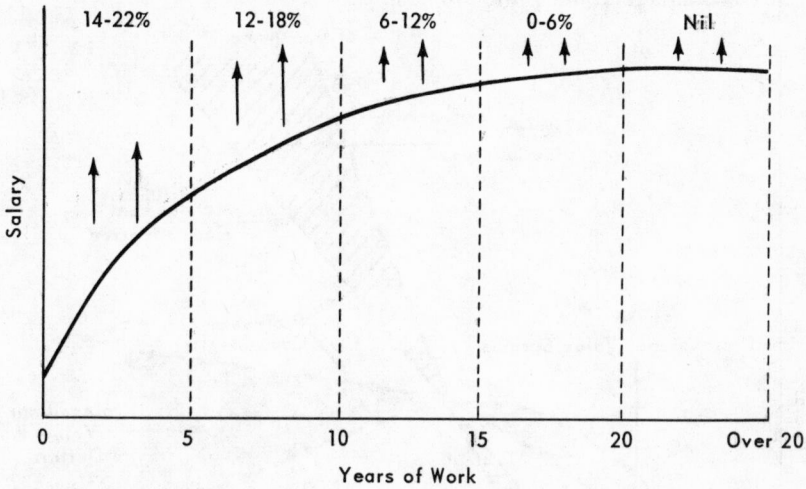

It is the application of these general definitions and characteristics of professional work which identifies professional jobs. When such jobs represent the essence of an organization's work (even though professionals are numerically a minority, as in hospitals), then that enterprise is a professional organization.

Understanding the professional job is far more than an intellectual exercise. For the practical businessman, it is the key to effective management of such work. For the staff specialist, it is the key to developing policies and practices which assist management in attracting, retaining, and effectively motivating professional employees.

PAY PROGRESS OF PROFESSIONALS

The pay increase pattern of professionals is distinctly different from that of other groups of employees. As shown in Figure 23, pay progress for professional employees is quite rapid in the first five years of work, typically 14 to 22 percent per year. In the fifth through the tenth years pay progress is still rapid but slows down to 10 to 18 percent. After the fifteenth year, the pay progress of the professional is negligible or moderate—generally 0 to 6 percent. As indicated by the arrows in Figure 23, this progress may be supplemented by inflationary forces.

Figure 24. **Comparison of career compensation and organizational value of managers and professionals.**

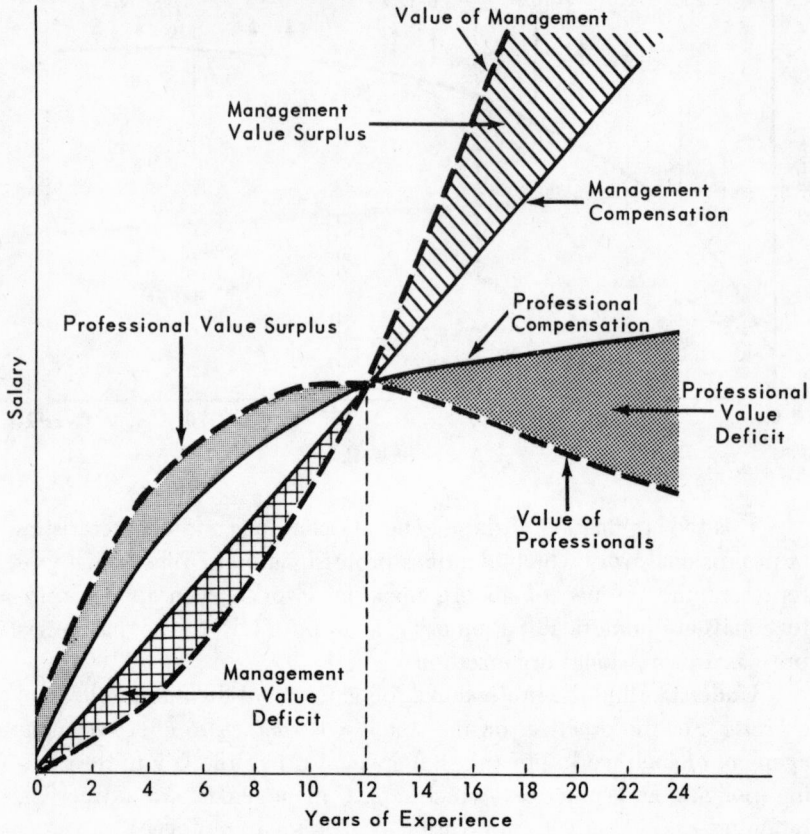

Figure 24 compares the pay progress of nonsupervisory professionals * with that of their counterparts in operational work. The figure is, of course, merely illustrative and the curves are exaggerated to point up differences. During the early years the professional, because of his faster progress, is distinctly better paid, and by the end of five years he is paid 15 to 20 percent more than his counterpart in operational work. By the end of ten years the difference is typically 20 to 25 percent. After that, however, the pay progress of the professional slows down dramatically and the pay progress of his counterpart in

* Nonsupervisory professionals are those whose primary duties involve the application of professional knowledge. Such employees may, however, have a few associates or technical assistants to assist them in their work or to relieve them of administrative chores.

product or service units continues in a rather linear fashion. As a result, the pay levels of the two are equivalent somewhere between the fifteenth and twentieth years. After that time the pay level of management personnel is much higher than that of nonsupervisory professionals.

Obviously, the curves in Figure 24 represent only average differences in pay progress. Actual career earnings for individuals in both professional and operational work seldom follow such a smooth progression. Rather, there are periods of moderate increases and periods of very rapid income growth. For the professional, rapid income progression tends to occur after three to seven years of experience. For the operations person there may be several periods of rapid growth. The first tends to occur after seven to fourteen years of experience.

The pattern of pay progress for professionals reflects the fact that they bring to the job knowledge which is immediately applicable. With relatively few years of experience, they very quickly reach a period of maximum value to the firm. This is best illustrated by career patterns in scientific research jobs, which have received the greatest attention and study. Most R&D laboratories have found that the period of maximum innovation and invention occurs among those who are out of school for about five years. After ten years or so the usefulness of the scientist as an individual contributor declines rapidly, primarily because of technological obsolescence. Most data concern experience with physical scientists, but recent studies indicate that the same pattern is true for professionals in investment work, medical research, economics, and some other fields.

Many who have worked closely with professional people feel that, if anything, they are grossly underpaid in the first years of employment in spite of their rapid income progress. In contrast, managers are overpaid in the early years in spite of more modest pay progress. This is because so many managers begin in trainee positions and need to be moved to different jobs to gain the diversity of experience required for higher-level management responsibilities.

This discussion should not suggest that professional workers inevitably reach maximum earnings after ten to fifteen years of work. Some achieve what amounts to a second or third career. Typically, the second career occurs when they are put into a position where their knowledge and experience are leveraged—that is, when they are applying their background and experience through younger professionals whose actual specialized knowledge may be greater than their own. A third career occurs for those few who achieve general management status. At this point, of course, the career pay pattern of the

Figure 25. **Career income potential in professional work.**

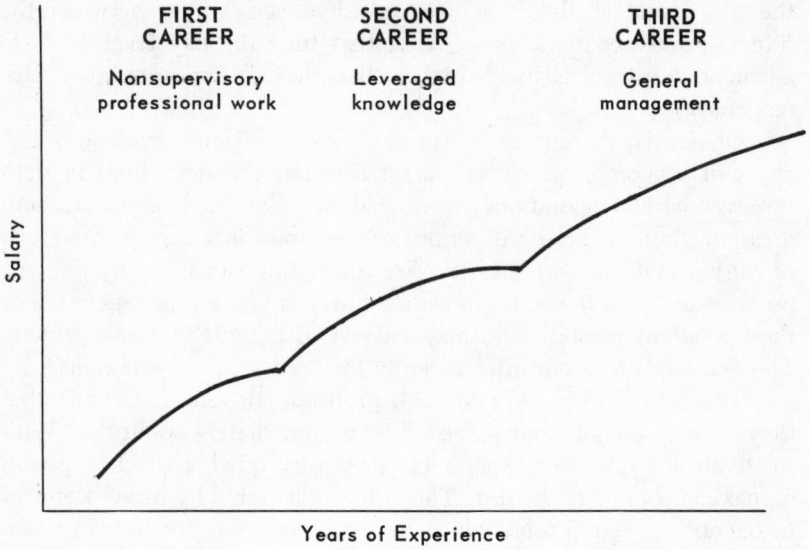

professional follows that of any manager. Pay progress for the relatively few professionals who achieve second or third careers is illustrated in Figure 25.

The professional progresses in his career as well as in his pay by performing higher levels of work—that is, by taking on assignments which are technically more difficult or assignments which require systems analysis. This progression does not represent a series of promotions in the traditional sense; rather, it is a gradual movement to more complex assignments. Generally, the levels of increasing difficulty of professional work can only be described generically. In most professional jobs there are at least three such generic levels and no more than five discernible levels.

Again, beyond this there are only two types of promotions: leverage of knowledge and achievement of managerial status. In professional work, however, there are far fewer such promotional opportunities than there are in operational work—in fact, about one-fourth as many.

In summary, the pay for professional work (like that of salesmen, who are also frequently more immediately useful to the firm) progresses rapidly at first but reaches a plateau at a relatively early stage in their careers. This income pattern, which is discernibly different from that of operational workers, is a key to effective compensation administration for professionals and has important implications for salary administration practices.

SALARY ADMINISTRATION FOR PROFESSIONALS

Use of Job Descriptions

Traditional job descriptions are not widely used for professional jobs because it is very difficult to describe professional duties within a traditional format. But if sound pay decisions are to be made, good job information must be worked up.

Generally speaking, three forms of position descriptions are used for professional jobs: modifed functional descriptions, generic descriptions, and work sample descriptions. Each has been successful in certain situations. Which of these forms should be used depends on the degree of professionalism in the work; the number and diversity of professional positions within the firm; the size, organization, and orientation of the company; and whether the descriptions are to be used solely for pay administration or for other purposes as well, such as communication of responsibilities and organizational development.

Modified functional descriptions. A functional position description identifies the various tasks performed by the employee. There are two problems with using such an approach in professional jobs. The first is that descriptions of jobs within a given discipline read about the same. For example, in the field of electronics design the only difference between the beginner and the advanced engineer is in the complexity of the components designed. As a result, descriptions of different levels of work may simply involve strings of increasingly superlative adjectives.

The second problem with the functional position description is that the assignments given to professional employees usually depend on such factors as personal ability, experience, career development, and department scheduling. Also, the level of assignments often varies greatly over a rather short period. For instance, an engineer may be asked to do extremely complex designing work one day and basic drafting chores the next.

For these reasons, functional position descriptions for professionals are most effective when they are applied to jobs that have a steady flow of work and when they deal mainly with differences between disciplines rather than those within a discipline. Even in such cases, companies have found it necessary to modify functional descriptions in three ways: (1) to confine the description of work to the most complex and most professionally advanced duties that are involved, (2) to prepare a glossary of terms which gives body and substance to the superlative adjectives, and (3) to provide examples of the types of work usually assigned.

Generic descriptions. Generic descriptions of professionals do not attempt to describe job assignments but rather seek to define in very broad terms the level of professional work involved. As shown in Figure 26, generic descriptions are relatively simple and brief. The writer, however, must have knowledge of the field and must understand what constitutes various levels of professional competence.

The generic approach has several advantages. First, it is very flexible in that it can be applied to jobs in a variety of functional fields. Second, it eliminates the great cost and sometimes great frustration of writing and rewriting functional descriptions. Finally, it recognizes that the value of professional employees must be determined basically through an analysis of individual capabilities and work performed.

The very flexibility of the generic approach, however, causes considerable difficulties in administration. Generic descriptions are so

***Figure 26.* Generic descriptions for professional personnel.**

SENIOR ENGINEER	PORTFOLIO MANAGER	ACCOUNT CONSULTANT
Responsible for design of components for radar system. Must design to customer specifications when precedents are not clearly defined. Receives only general professional guidance from scientists. Accountable for quality, accuracy, and planning of own work and for work of detail designing of engineers assigned.	Responsible for management of securities portfolio in excess of $10 million. Makes buy or sell decisions guided only by general statement of fund objectives; not required to buy or sell from list of approved securities. Performance measured against other portfolios and *Standard & Poor's* index.	Responsible for client assignments in the area of business analysis and planning—typically for firms over $200 million sales. Has business development responsibility to $250,000 per year; direct billing (at $600 per day) of $100,000 and manages billings of $250,000. Complete responsibility for analyzing and developing recommendations and for submitting them to client.

broad in scope and general in content that they do not always serve as meaningful guides in decision making. Moreover, because such descriptions classify professional employees on the basis of what they can do rather than what they actually do, the company may end up paying for services not performed.

Work sample descriptions. Probably the most useful format for describing professional work is the work sample description. There are a great variety of work sample descriptions for professional people. Many involve a listing of assignments completed by an individual. Others emphasize the highest level of professional work which the individual has demonstrated that he is capable of performing. They describe, in effect, the value of the work that can be done. Thus a work sample description for a lawyer might indicate clients served and samples of the most advanced legal work that the employee might be called upon to perform.

Use of Job Evaluation

Even though it is difficult to separate individual worth from job worth in professional positions, some basis for assigning relative values to professional jobs has use in pay administration. Several of the most widely used methods of job evaluation for professional positions are described below.

Traditional evaluation methods. Some companies still rely on one of the traditional approaches to job evaluation, described in Chapter 4, to establish pay grades for professional positions. If job evaluation is to be applied successfully to professionals, however, two basic requirements must be met. The first is total job knowledge. This knowledge may reside in the mind of the evaluator or it may be set down in job descriptions and other records of the company. The second requirement is that the job evaluation plan be appropriate. Evaluation plans that are designed primarily for production and administrative positions place heavy emphasis on such considerations as dollars of assets, volumes of sales, budgets, and numbers of people supervised. Such plans simply cannot give appropriate weighting, in terms of either value to the business or value in the marketplace, to positions whose key factors are knowledge and talent. The evaluation plan must measure these important aspects of professional work.

When these requirements are met, job evaluation can be a useful guide in pay decisions for professional employees. "Usefulness" is, however, a relative term. Because of the greater complexity and individualized nature of professional work assignments, evaluation results are undoubtedly less precise when applied to professional positions than to other types of jobs.

Generic classifications. Companies which use generic descriptions or work sample descriptions for professional positions frequently divide these jobs into four or six generic levels and then classify them into the company pay structure. Usually, the slotting is done so that the maximum of one level overlaps the minimum of the next higher level. In this way the professional moves smoothly, first within a pay level, and then from one pay level to the next as he progresses in his field.

This approach is similar to traditional job classification, in the sense that a position, however described, is classified into an existing pay level. However, it has two important differences from the classification system. First, since there are no definitions of pay levels, generic classification provides no real management guide to pay decisions except dollar values assigned. This can invite salary accommodation rather than salary administration. Second, companies which use the approach tend to classify individuals rather than positions.

Career curve approach. The career curve approach is a method specifically developed for professional jobs, particularly in engineering. In essence, it assumes that after completing their education, professional employees will progress within their disciplines at some standard rate as a result of their experience in the field. This assumed progress is usually described as a curve, in which average earnings are plotted against the number of years since an employee received his degree.

Under the career curve approach, position descriptions—if they are used at all—are not basic to the salary administration process. Rather, determination of salaries becomes a matter of looking up the number of years since an employee received his degree and then reading off the salary indicated by the curve. Generally, however, it is recognized that professionals with the same years of experience will vary in their ability. As a result, a number of curves are usually drawn representing different levels or ratings of employee proficiency. This is illustrated in the upper graph of Figure 27. In this case, the supervisor must first judge the proficiency of the employee before determining his salary level.

The validity of such an approach depends both on the supervisor's ability to place each individual in the correct curve and on the correctness of the curves themselves. The first requirement is, of course, a matter of judging performance—that is, it is another form of performance appraisal. Unless appraisal is done well, the process can become a mere rationalization of predetermined increases. As far as the second

Figure 27. **Professional career curves.**

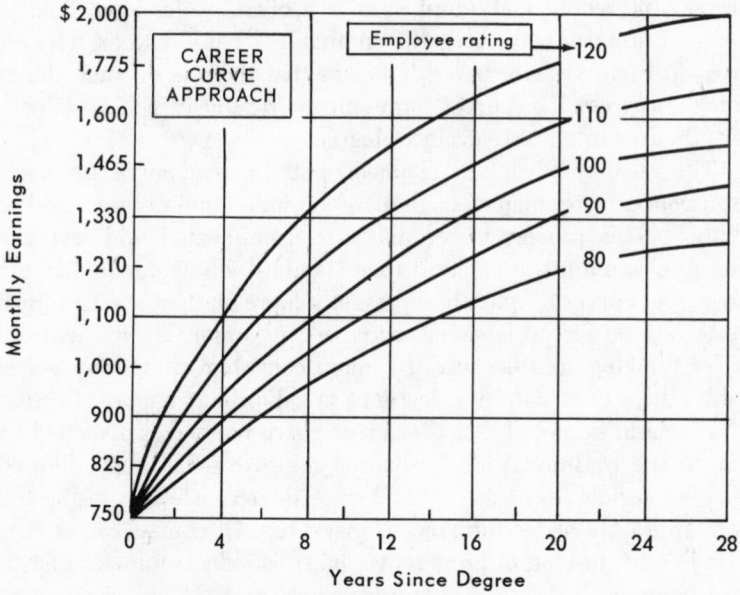

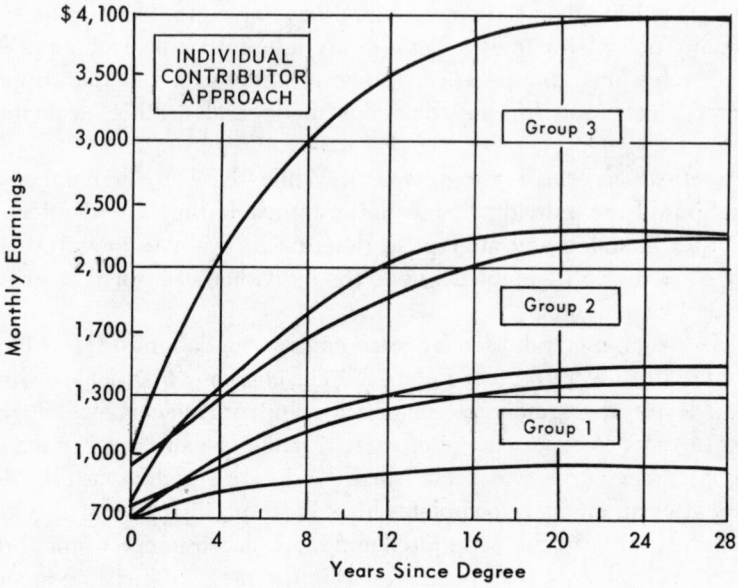

requirement—the correctness of the curves—is concerned, it is certainly questionable whether all employees in a given professional field progress in a uniform way. Actually, an analysis of the data on which the curves in Figure 27 are based indicates that there is no such thing as average progress. The curves represent the best fit of widely dispersed salary figures in each year since degree.

The greatest advantage claimed for the career curve approach is that it concentrates managers' thinking on individual progress and contribution. This process is certainly less complicated and less costly in terms of administrative effort than standard job evaluation. In addition, career curves frequently represent a more mathematic administrative technique for professional managers; it is more in line with their way of thinking, and because it is more consistent than other ways, it enables them to explain pay decisions to subordinates more effectively.

It should be noted that the career curve method is essentially the same as the traditional job evaluation approach. The only difference is that career curves measure years since degree, whereas in the traditional approach job performance is measured. Of course, career curves are regressive instead of progressive, but this reflects the fact that they are usually applied only to nonsupervisory professional positions.

In summary, the career curve approach, with a number of embellishments, has proved to be a practical, though far from perfect, method of salary administration in large engineering organizations that are engaged in advanced research and development. The approach is probably not adequate as a basic salary administration technique for other professional groups. It can, however, serve as a valuable supplementary technique for pay decisions made under other evaluation methods.

Individual contributor approach. While there are a number of variations of the individual contributor approach, they are identical in that they abandon any attempt to describe or evaluate jobs. Instead, they place the entire emphasis upon the individual's personal contribution and his potential.

One such method, used by some engineering laboratories, is illustrated in the lower graph of Figure 27. The company first defined three broad levels of engineering competency and proficiency, without regard to years of experience. For each, a range of values rather than a simple career curve was established. Under this system, within five years after an engineer completes his education, his performance and capabilities are carefully appraised and he is placed in one of the three groups. His salary is then planned within the range of curves assigned to the group. In this way attention is concentrated on the salary progress of each engineer. In addition, managers making salary decisions can consider all important factors by using the salary-planning practices already described.

Another variation of the individual contributor approach is really a resurgence of individual bargaining. Some scientists, commercial artists, lawyers, economists, and other professionals are so well known and so highly respected, or can make such a tremendous personal contribution, that their value defies any method of salary classification. They are indeed worth what it takes to get them. Some companies have developed systematic methods for analyzing such individual situations. Generally, these methods have been designed, not to establish guidelines for pay decisions, but rather to develop yardsticks for individual bargaining.

Market position classification. With the increasing availability of market data, more and more companies are using the market position system to classify professional jobs. This approach represents a reversal of the traditional job evaluation process. Under traditional job classification, a whole series of administrative exercises are performed before jobs are priced, and the pay levels assigned are based on a very limited amount of data. Under the market position approach, a representative number of jobs are priced at the outset, using extensive market survey data to determine pay levels. These then become the benchmark jobs and are at least in part the basis upon which other positions are classified.

Other positions which cannot be priced directly in the marketplace are then slotted into pay grades in comparison with the benchmark jobs. This slotting can be done by ranking or by some other evaluation technique. The market position approach is effective for professional jobs only when at least 20 percent of the jobs can be priced directly in the marketplace.

Market position classification has many advantages. First, pay relationships are established by conditions in the marketplace rather than by administrative judgments, thus assuring that the company has postured itself appropriately from the point of view of competitive pay. This is especially important when the firm competes for professional talent in a number of different labor markets. Second, market position classification involves low administrative costs. This is particularly true if positions can be priced by generic levels rather than on a job-by-job basis. Third, the market approach has a high degree of acceptability among employees. It is difficult to explain results arrived at through any job evaluation system, and if anything the problem is complicated with professional jobs. There is a higher likelihood that employees will accept the results of job evaluation when it can be reasonably demonstrated that a job has been assigned a given pay level because that is what the average pay for similar work is in other companies.

Finally, the market approach can be applied to all middle-level salary positions, regardless of the disparity in the nature of work performed or the different labor markets in which employees compete. This simplifies compensation administration and provides a more sound basis for pay for middle-level employees. Most important, it provides an acceptable solution to the age-old problem of determining the relative value of positions in different functional fields.

Professional Salary Structures

Professional salary structures may take the traditional form, with pay minimums and maximums, or they may be based on career curves. In either case, there are two steps involved: pricing the levels appropriately and developing the structure itself. If a separate structure is developed for professionals, there is the additional task of integrating this structure with those in effect for other groups of employees.

Setting salary levels for any group of employees involves consideration of company economic and operating factors, company employment experience, and data gained from market surveys. In pricing professional positions, management must rely heavily on both survey data and employment experience.

Selecting the right companies and the right jobs to survey is far more difficult for professional positions than for other types of jobs. This is because the professional tends to identify more closely with his field of work than with any individual employer or industry. As a result, many kinds of companies in many geographic areas are really competitors for professional talent, and there is a bewildering array of labor markets and competitive conditions for different professional positions. Frequently, potential competitors for professional talent are quite diverse. Many are unsophisticated in salary administration and are unable to supply valid data. Frequently, too, competitors will not cooperate in exchanging data. Thus the effort and cost involved in assuring competitiveness of salary levels for professional jobs are considerably more than in most other types of positions.

Because of the special difficulties of surveying professional positions, it is frequently necessary to use modified methods of determining competitive pay. This may involve a number of innovative or hybrid survey techniques. For example:

- Establishing college hiring rates and lowest-level management pay levels and determining intermediate levels through salary progress data.
- More intensive use of employment experience.
- Establishing link-ratio information with positions priced in available surveys.
- Conducting intensive surveys of a few key professional positions or benchmarks.

These techniques provide managers with sufficient information to make sound business judgments, with a reasonable time-cost input. The resulting data, however, are sometimes inadequate to prove or justify decisions to a critical or doubting audience.

There was a trend a number of years ago to establish separate pay structures for professional jobs and for operations jobs. Multiple structures have proven burdensome, however, particularly as the number of groups or units requiring separate structures has increased. Increasingly, therefore, most companies have found it practical to develop one structure for all groups of employees. Such a structure serves the important purpose of providing a uniform human resources accounting mechanism. Different groups or units within the firm apply this structure differently to meet their particular needs.

Table 10 illustrates how one company adapted its pay structure to professional employees. Four professional levels were established for engineering and three levels for staff positions. The senior engineer level includes company pay grades 19 through 21, with a salary range of $19,300 minimum to $34,000 maximum. The staff manager level covers company pay grades 16 through 21, with a salary range of $14,700 minimum to $34,000 maximum.

Administration of Professional Salaries

Pay decisions regarding professional employees involve some special problems. One concerns the relationship between money and motivation. Although it is certainly not correct to think that money is unimportant to professionals, it can be said that in a large number of cases it is not the main consideration. This is a difficult matter requiring considerably more research, but the following generalizations are probably pertinent.

Except for those who are clearly aiming for the management of professional work and eventually for a general management position, high income expectations are not paramount in the minds of pro-

Table 10. **Professional pay ranges within company salary structure ($ 000).**

Company Overall				*Engineering Structure*				*Staff Structure*			
Level	*Min*	*Mid-point*	*Max*	*Level*	*Title*	*Min*	*Max*	*Level*	*Title*	*Min*	*Max*
25	33.6	42.0	50.4								
24	30.6	38.2	45.8	IV	Scientist	25.5	45.8	III	Staff consultant	25.5	50.4
23	27.8	34.7	41.6								
22	25.5	31.5	37.5								
21	23.2	28.6	34.0								
20	21.1	26.0	30.9	III	Senior engineer	19.3	34.0				
19	19.3	23.6	27.9								
18	17.6	21.5	25.4					II	Staff manager	14.7	34.0
17	16.0	19.5	23.0	II	Engineer	14.7	25.4				
16	14.7	17.7	20.7								
15	13.4	16.1	18.8								
14	12.1	14.6	17.1	I	Associate engineer	11.2	18.8				
13	11.2	13.3	15.4								
12	10.2	12.1	14.0					I	Staff analyst	7.7	18.8
11	9.3	11.0	12.7								
10	8.5	10.0	11.5								
9	7.7	9.1	10.5								

fessionals. Their striving is directed toward producing high-caliber professional work and advancing in their field. However, the professional worker expects pay progress and equitable treatment, and he can, like any employee, become very dissatisfied if he does not receive fair pay treatment. Thus, while high income opportunities may not increase the effectiveness of the professional's work, lack of financial progress or inequitable treatment can contribute to less productiveness.

A second special problem of salary administration for professionals is the need for greater delegation of salary decisions to individual supervisors. This, of course, is because many of the factors involved in pay questions are related to technical matters requiring intimate knowledge of the professional field. Only a lawyer, for instance, can judge the excellence of a legal recommendation.

Frequently, salary administration techniques for professionals are geared to the particular orientations or habits of thought of the professional group. To take an oversimplified example, because engineers tend to be analytical and precise, many salary programs for engineers emphasize charts, scales, and rather sophisticated numerical rankings and weightings. Such techniques should never be used as a substitute for good judgment. But if they assist the supervisor in making pay decisions and in leading his subordinates to greater acceptance of these decisions, they are appropriate.

Methods of salary review can be complicated and administratively burdensome. Some form of salary planning is usually necessary for professional groups. What complicates the process is that typically professionals work on many different projects and activities. Each must be evaluated—frequently by different supervisors. Performance review thus requires multiple ratings by different people. These, in turn, require group dialogue and cross-rating systems.

CAREER DEVELOPMENT

Career development is a part of overall personnel management, or organizational development. In professional jobs, however, it is also an integral part of compensation administration. To a very large extent, career development represents the incentive pay aspect of compensation administration for professional employees.

Pay programs for professionals provide increases essentially as rewards for greater effectiveness—for the ability to handle higher levels of professional work. The various activities which can be employed to motivate and encourage professional development have a direct impact on pay progress. It is in this way that career development is an integral part of compensation administration.

To the professional employee, this aspect of pay administration represents not only an opportunity for higher income but a means of building assets. That is, it enhances the professional's value and esteem among his peers and his value in the marketplace. Moreover, because career development programs can lead to more productive professional work—which represents greater "output"—their cost is really an investment expenditure. The increase in pay resulting from greater effectiveness should be only part of the increased value to the enterprise of the work performed.

INCENTIVE PAY PLANS

Studies of the unique characteristics of successful professional organizations indicate that some form of incentive pay is common among a high percentage of successful professional groups. This suggests that incentive pay plans for professional employees not only are feasible but may be a critical element of successful compensation administration for professionals.

Studies in the pharmaceuticals, chemical, and aerospace industries have identified operating characteristics which are common in successful R&D groups and are generally lacking in ineffective R&D operations. The success elements vary by industry. One which is common to all these industries, however, is the presence of an incentive pay plan for professionals.

Incentive pay plans for professionals are extremely difficult to develop and administer. Experience has shown that there are several unique characteristics.

First, there is the difficulty of articulating performance criteria. Inevitably multiple criteria of performance are inherent in an incentive pay plan for professionals, and their very presence enormously complicates the administration of the incentive system.

Second, under most plans bonus/salary percentage levels are conservative in professional work. This reflects the difficulty of administering these plans, and therefore the tendency to have smaller proportions of total current pay in the form of bonus. But it also reflects the fact that, for professional personnel, there is a higher degree of incentive in career development than in bonus payments.

Third, the time cycles of incentive pay programs for professionals are typically longer than one year.

Fourth, incentive awards are almost always directly related to the accomplishment of individual goals.

Finally, in most plans guidelines are established to restrict the total amount of monies which may be paid. These pay maximums are usually geared to the business value of the work of the professional group.

Special Compensation

There are a number of nonsalary items in professional compensation which may represent real costs to the company and real value to the employee. Many of these items are nonfinancial in nature and relate to the work environment—for example, equipment, facilities, and a management style supportive of high-level professional work. Other items, with cost and/or income value, include:

- Patent recognition.
- Encouragement, support, and compensation for publication in professional journals.
- Special bonuses for inventions, important research, or solutions to major company problems.
- Membership in professional organizations or attendance at professional meetings.
- Encouragement, time off, and financial support for additional education.
- Greater flexibility as to hours of work and location of work.

Although such items complicate pay administration, they are usually vital to proper compensation and motivation of professional employees. All provide important opportunities for better utilization of professional talent within the company.

12

SUPERVISORY, TECHNICAL, AND ADMINISTRATIVE PERSONNEL

SUPERVISORY, TECHNICAL, and administrative jobs, though very different, have one thing in common: they are all intermediate-level positions. Supervisory employees are intermediate between management and nonsupervisory personnel; administrative employees fall between office and top-level staff; and technical employees occupy a place between skilled production workers and professional employees.

Not many years ago there were relatively few positions in this "middle group." As a result, most compensation plans (as well as other personnel activities) for supervisory, technical, and administrative personnel were administered as part of an overall compensation system for operations employees or management employees. Usually there was some modification of practices for this group: either the program for operations employees was extended upward with some modifications or the management compensation program was extended downward with some modifications. Such programs never worked well, because they were not tailored to middle group jobs. They were, however, the only practical solution in view of the small number of employees involved. With the significant growth in the number and diversity of middle group positions, some new approaches and techniques have been necessary.

MANAGEMENT PROBLEMS: THE MIDDLE GROUP

In industrial companies, the middle group represents about 10 percent of employment—and 20 percent of payroll. This amounts to significant enterprise costs. Therefore, effective administration of salaries for middle-level employees, simply from the cost view, is important.

More important, however, is the fact that the effectiveness of employees in the middle group has a significant impact on enterprise results. In fact, within the parameters set by strategic policies and financial commitments by top management, these employees very largely determine business results. For instance, if the given assets for a company have the potential to earn between 5 and 10 percent on assets, the effectiveness of the work of middle-group employees can make a decisive difference in the actual earnings.

Most companies are, in fact, experiencing great difficulty in managing employees in the middle group. These problems have become very apparent to many companies, particularly leadership companies. Other firms will begin to experience problems unless action is taken now.

One basic problem in managing supervisory, technical, and administrative positions is that most of these jobs involve unique technologies. The technologies are not necessarily high level; but they are specific and detailed to the extent that higher management has little understanding of them. Therefore, it is difficult to establish programs which effectively control the work of middle-level employees.

Another problem in managing middle-level workers concerns their productivity. Studies suggest that the productivity of middle-level employees is 25 to 50 percent of what it could be and that these positions are overstaffed by 20 to 30 percent. Thus there is a very major cost savings potential as well as important opportunity for improved operations through better management of the key human resources represented in the middle group.

This basic management problem has many facets. One involves personnel administration generally and, within that context, compensation administration. Effective compensation administration is one step toward more effective management of these key human resources. It is an important subject, because knowledge and experience acquired in recent years make possible significant steps toward tailoring compensation practices to the needs of middle-group positions. To the extent that compensation programs succeed in meeting the needs of these employees, they will assist in producing more effective work—first, by removing disincentives associated with most current practices and, second, by establishing a positive attitude on the part of middle-group employees.

COMPENSATION FRAMEWORK FOR THE MIDDLE GROUP

There are, in fact, a number of distinctly different types of work—and workers—included in the middle group. There are, in most companies, supervisory employees, administrative employees, and technical employees. Further groupings are often made in large companies or when such divisions are desirable from the point of view of compensation administration or personnel administration. The important point is that each of these groups has different job and work characteristics, different labor markets, and distinctly different needs with respect to compensation administration.

On the other hand, of course, all of these employees work together—frequently in the same building, and sometimes in the same work area. Furthermore, many companies find it desirable and occasionally necessary to transfer these employees from one group to another. For example, it would be quite likely for a technical employee to be transferred to administrative work. Thus, from the point of view of simple equity, companies want to make sure that there is reasonable consistency in the treatment of these different groups.

In order to do this, the firm must build a compensation system which provides a framework for consistent treatment of all middle-level employees and which embodies the basic tenets of company compensation policies. Within this framework, compensation techniques and practices can be tailored to the needs of each group of employees. Specific techniques and practices for supervisory, administrative and technical workers will be discussed below.

The exact framework which is suitable for a given enterprise depends on many factors. But in any system at least three elements are essential. First, a single pay structure must be established for all middle-group employees. Such a structure serves not only as a review and control mechanism but as a basic management tool, for it provides, if nothing else, a uniform accounting system of human resources. A single structure is also important because many elements of compensation other than salary are administered on the basis of the employee's pay level.

Second, a survey system must be developed for slotting at least a sample of positions from each group into the salary structure. That is, benchmark jobs must first be selected from the supervisory, administrative, and technical groups and then priced in the relevant labor markets. As will be indicated below, labor markets for these three groups may vary significantly. Benchmark positions are then slotted into the salary structure at that pay grade where the midpoint of the range most closely matches the average market data. This provides the basic means of assuring equal pay for each group.

Finally, methods of pay administration must be similar for all groups. For instance, if a performance increase system is applied to supervisors, the same method of granting increases should be used for all middle-level employees. Thus, if a merit pay budget is used for supervisory employees, it should also be used for technical and administrative employees. Of course, the actual budget percentages will vary depending on the circumstances of each group.

When these requirements are met, management can be assured of two things. First, the basic compensation policies of the firm are being applied to each of these subgroups. Second, resulting pay levels and pay increases, while different, are equitable in the sense that all employees are being treated impartially and that any differences reflect actual market conditions. The supervisor on his part, of course, can be assured that within this framework system detailed compensation practices and methods which generally meet the needs of employees can be evolved and applied.

SUPERVISORY EMPLOYEES

Part of the supervisory job is to explain and administer the salary program of the company to nonsupervisory employees. How supervisors apply the program and how they explain it essentially determine how the rank and file understand it. By the same token, however, salary administration is applied to supervisors. How well they understand what it means to them, and how reasonable they view its provisions concerning their salaries, certainly will influence how they administer and explain the program to their subordinates.

The Supervisory Group

In this section, the term "supervisors" will be used to refer to employees who are organizationally only one or two levels removed from nonsupervisory personnel. These employees do not set policy but carry it out—they get work done through others. Thus supervision is a major part of their responsibilities, and they generally have at least a dozen subordinates over whom they exercise authority in the traditional "hire or fire" sense. They are intimately involved in the assignment of work, the training of personnel, the solution of daily operating problems, and the guidance of subordinates. Finally, they must have, in considerable depth, a technical knowledge of the jobs which they supervise.

These characteristics define the supervisor in the classical sense. Such a definition excludes other employees who also supervise but whose supervisory duties represent only a small part of their overall responsibility. An example is an engineering section leader who has three or four people working for him but whose main value is his professional knowledge and the professional work he performs. The definition also excludes employees who have only limited supervisory responsibility, such as group leaders.

Traditionally, supervisory jobs have been described as the first level of management. These positions are first level in the sense that they represent the interface between managers and operations workers. Supervisors seldom, however, have delegated management authority. Their authority is quite limited by the operations themselves and by policies and procedure. In addition, many of their decisions are very closely reviewed by higher levels of supervisors and lower levels of management. Some parts of the job—such as labor relations, maintenance, and quality control—are frequently the responsibility of others.

Thus it would probably be more accurate to describe supervisors as the front line rather than the first line of management. Because of unique characteristics of supervisory jobs—only summarized here—these positions generally require either special pay practices or important modifications of pay practices and techniques used for other groups.

Use of Job Descriptions

Probably nine out of every ten supervisory jobs are covered by position descriptions. These descriptions have proved quite satisfactory in salary administration for supervisors. The only question is the type of description which is most useful. Many companies have learned from experience that it is usually unwise to merely use office or production job descriptions to cover supervisory employees.

Supervisory position descriptions are not difficult to write. They should, however, not only outline job responsibilities but also cover topics such as these:

- Scope data, including number of employees supervised, asset value of equipment, supplies and equipment utilized, and dollar amounts of budgets.
- Latitude of action or authority possessed by the supervisor. Because of the nature of supervision, it is extremely important to define limitations on authority and to identify those parts of the job of managing people for which others are responsible.
- Additional nonsupervisory relationships required with people both inside and outside the company.
- Climate of the job, including goals and objectives and conditions under which work must be performed.

Importance of Pay Relationships with Subordinates

Because the primary labor markets for supervisory employees are the operations jobs supervised, the key factor in successful salary administration for this group is the creation of reasonable differentials between the pay of supervisors and that of their subordinates. Unless there is a sufficient differential, the company may find it difficult to get the best-qualified operations workers to accept supervisory positions. Also, the attitude and morale of supervisors may suffer.

Companies have devised various rules of thumb to help in judging what constitutes satisfactory differentials between supervisors and subordinates. Usually, no single guide is adequate, and certainly none should be followed without judgment and discretion. Following are five general criteria:

1. The supervisor's pay grade should be at least two levels higher than the grade of the highest-rated job he supervises. In practice, he is usually classified three to five pay levels higher.
2. The supervisor's base salary should be at least 15 percent higher than the straight-time earnings of the highest-paid subordinate.
3. The supervisor's gross pay (including bonuses and any overtime compensation) should be at least 10 percent higher than the gross pay (including overtime) of the highest-paid subordinate.
4. The gross pay of the supervisor should be at least 25 percent more than the average gross pay of all subordinates.

5. The gross pay of the supervisor should be no more than 75 percent higher than the average gross pay of all subordinates.

The process of setting these pay differentials is quite exact, since the "market"—the company's operations jobs—is a 100 percent and thoroughly accurate sample.

This is not to suggest that internal pay relationships are the only factor to be considered in establishing levels for supervisors. Obviously, some supervisory personnel may be recruited from outside the company, and company supervisors may be recruited by other firms. Therefore, a second consideration must be pay levels for similar work in the marketplace. In most areas there is ample information on the pay of supervisors in various categories. Still another important consideration is pay relationships among supervisors within the company. These can be determined by job evaluation techniques.

Thus, in setting pay levels for supervisory personnel, companies must use a multiple-evaluation system, considering (1) pay relationships with subordinates, (2) pay relationships with supervisors doing similar work in other companies, and (3) comparative pay of different supervisors.

Use of Job Evaluation

As noted above, job evaluation can only be one consideration in determining pay levels for supervisors. In most companies it is the least relevant or least important. This is because, from a practical point of view, job evaluation must have less weight than either pay relationships between the supervisor and subordinates or pay relationships of supervisors and pay for comparable work in other companies.

The primary use of job evaluation—if any—is to establish differences between supervisory positions. In addition, when the application of the other two evaluation criteria (pay relationships of subordinates and outside labor market data) suggest that two or three pay levels might be correct, job evaluation can assist companies in determining the appropriate level.

Because of the limited role of job evaluation in setting pay levels for supervisors, it is generally not considered practical to develop an elaborate system for evaluating supervisory positions. Companies are increasingly using a very simple system, such as a ranking system or a modified factor comparison plan that considers only two or three major criteria—for example, scope of the job, latitude of action, and knowledge required.

Pay Increase Practices for Supervisors

Various studies have shown that pay increase amounts and practices for supervisors closely parallel those for office and production employees. Even the procedures and techniques used for administering supervisors' salaries tend to be closer to plant or office procedures than to management or professional methods. These facts again suggest the key role that pay relationships with subordinates play in supervisory salary administration.

Many companies have worked hard at developing a salary administration system for supervisors that gears pay within range to performance on the job. This reflects a general management desire to bring salary administration practices for supervisory workers closer to those used for higher-level staff and line personnel. It also reflects an awareness on the part of management that the absence of some type of performance pay program (particularly if combined with the absence of an incentive pay system) reduces financial motivation for supervisors.

Experience has demonstrated, however, that a performance pay program for supervisors can be successful only if two conditions are met. The first is that supervisory jobs be structured so that individual performance can have a meaningful impact on departmental results. This is essentially a matter of building sufficient authority and scope into the supervisory position.

The second requirement is that there be sufficient differences in pay between supervisors doing acceptable performance and those doing outstanding work. This also involves restructuring the supervisory job so that the pay level for supervisors doing outstanding work is at least 15 percent higher than the pay of supervisors doing acceptable work. The job must be slotted in a pay level where the midpoint is about 30 percent higher than the average pay of the highest-paid subordinate.

Most supervisory jobs do not have sufficient scope and authority to permit these types of differentials. In such cases, a meaningful performance pay system is not practical, and somewhat automatic increases for supervisors are inevitable.

It goes without saying that if greater scope and authority are built into supervisory positions, the company needs to staff the positions with high-caliber personnel who have both the training and the leadership qualities necessary for higher management responsibilities. The key to upgrading and better staffing of supervisory jobs lies in reexamination of the company's method of operation. This is not to suggest that the method of operation of the business and the nature of the supervisory job should be changed for the purpose of introducing a performance pay system. Rather, if upgrading and better staffing are not feasible, the company should not consider a performance pay program.

The Problem of Overtime Compensation

In most companies that do not have or cannot build meaningful differentials between the pay of supervisors and that of their subordinates, the problem of overtime compensation for supervisors is pressing and difficult. When operations employees are required to work a significant amount of overtime during the year, and when the supervisor must work essentially the same amount of time, gross pay inequities are inevitable unless the supervisor's base pay is sufficiently high or unless he receives extra pay for extraordinarily long work hours.

Companies have responded to this problem in various ways. Many firms are reluctant to pay supervisors for overtime for fear that this will lead them to work themselves or their departments unnecessarily long hours in order to get extra pay. Other companies are concerned about the administrative problems which might arise from giving supervisors overtime pay. Still other firms believe that the indirect values in a supervisory job, such as prestige and security, provide sufficient additional income. Finally, a few firms, while they may be reluctant to admit it, are aware of the problem but are convinced that supervisors will accept the situation.

Undoubtedly, the actual cost of paying supervisors for overtime is a key consideration in many companies. It is difficult to conceive of cost as a major problem, however, when the company is already paying overtime to subordinates. The cost of extra compensation for supervisors must be weighed against other factors: the effects of lowered morale, and perhaps lowered efficiency, because of what supervisors may rightly view as pay inequities.

Some companies, of course, do nothing about overtime compensation simply because there is little overtime worked. Others which have intermittent or seasonal overtime work do not pay supervisors overtime because the production workers who receive overtime pay frequently are laid off during the course of the year and therefore have offsetting "undertime" pay. Still other companies handle the situation by giving supervisors compensatory time off when business slows down.

At the other extreme are companies which pay supervisors premium overtime rates for each hour worked beyond the standard work week. This does indeed solve pay and equity problems for supervisors. Unfortunately, it sometimes merely transfers such problems to a higher level. Also, it may encourage supervisors to work themselves and their subordinates longer hours, or at least it may discourage them from tightly controlling overtime work. Finally, such premium payments may lead supervisors to identify more closely with operations workers than the company deems desirable.

An increasing number of companies follow a middle course: they allow some extra compensation, but at less than premium rates and only under prescribed conditions. Many companies, for instance, will not pay supervisors extra compensation for intermittent overtime or for overtime which is not in excess of 45 or 50 hours per week. Many pay straight time for extra hours, and some pay only a part of straight time. Except in extreme cases, these practices preserve reasonable pay differentials while maintaining the supervisor's identity and minimizing the possibility of abuses.

Figure 28 illustrates the effect of four typical extra compensation plans for supervisors in maintaining supervisor-subordinate pay relationships. In each case, the gross pay of the supervisor is assumed to be $10,000 per year, and the average straight-time pay of subordinates almost $8,500.

Bonus Payments for Supervisors

About one in three industrial companies provides some bonus payments for supervisors. In the majority of these cases supervisors do not receive overtime pay. Rather, bonus awards are viewed as a substitute for overtime compensation. Of the bonus plans for supervisors which are in effect, about 20 percent are part of a bonus pay plan for management personnel. That is, the supervisory staff has been included in the management bonus program. About 70 percent of supervisory bonus plans are separate programs which may be described as discretionary award systems. The remaining 10 percent are supervisory incentive compensation systems.

The major problem with paying a supervisor from a general management bonus award program is that the amount of money awarded is not related to the supervisor's performance. The funds available under management award systems are necessarily geared to business results, but supervisory performance is related to departmental or plant results. Consequently, awards for supervisors from these bonus plans are very uncertain. Awards may be very high when

Figure 28. **Pay relationships under various overtime pay provisions for supervisors.**

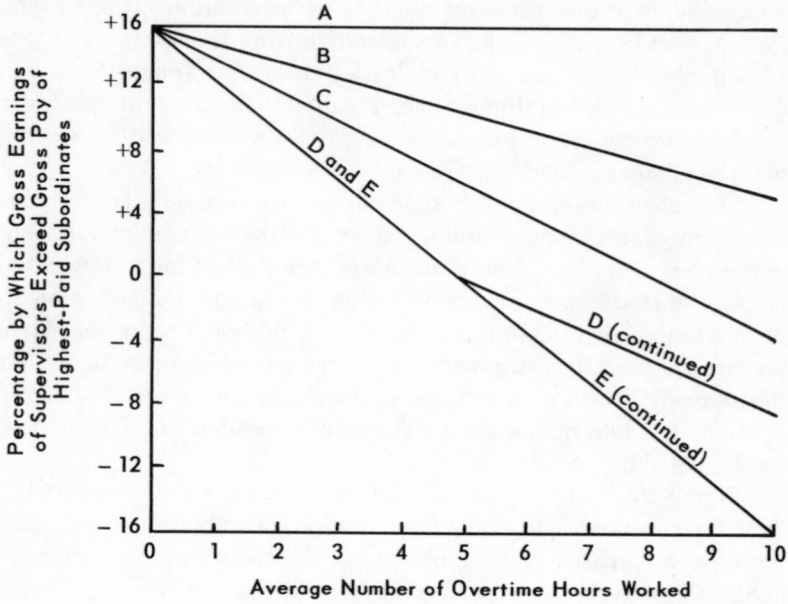

A Time and one-half over 40 hours per week
B Straight time over 40 hours per week
C Half-time over 40 hours per week
D Straight time over 45 hours per week
E No overtime for supervisors

business results are good even though performance in the department or the plant was unsatisfactory; at the other extreme, awards may be very low when business results are poor even though performance in the department or plant was exceptional. Under these conditions, the awards are welcome when received, but they do not represent incentive. In fact, to the extent that the awards are not forthcoming when performance is high, they can represent a disincentive.

Discretionary plans, which represent the bulk of supervisory awards, suggest an arbitrary system. In fact, however, in most discretionary plans management has evolved rather clear criteria for relating award payments to supervisory and plant performance. In many cases the amount of overtime that supervisors have worked is also taken into account. The problem with such plans is that the recipients do not know what the criteria are or how they are weighed. Usually, they do not have a clear idea of what reward to expect for a given level of performance. Thus discretionary plans are not incentive plans because there is no clear relationship between reward and performance.

In the past ten years some leadership companies have developed incentive pay systems for supervisory personnel. Under these plans, performance criteria for each department are established and annual performance targets are set for the supervisory group as a whole and for the individual supervisor. The plans are structured to pay target levels of bonus when performance goals are achieved, to further reward overachievement, and to penalize underachievement.

These plans, therefore, have essentially the same characteristics as management incentive compensation plans, which will be described in detail in the next chapter. The differences are in the nature of the criteria and specific targets.

In order for incentive compensation plans to be practical for supervisory employees, certain elements must be present:

1. Performance criteria must be related to what the supervisor can control and must be tailored to each type of job and each individual supervisor.
2. The plan must be relatively simple in design and administration—not only because of problems of communication but also because of the highly individualized nature of performance criteria.
3. Payout potential under the plan must be compatible both with payout potential under management incentive systems and with payout potential under overtime pay programs for operations employees.
4. Awards must be supplemental; salary alone must be competitive and incentive awards must reflect extra pay for achievement of targets.

Early experience with these supervisory incentive plans has been promising. There seems to be a definite trend toward removing supervisory personnel from eligibility under management bonus plans and putting them in a separate incentive compensation program.

TECHNICAL EMPLOYEES

Technical employees occupy a position between professional workers on the one hand and skilled production workers on the other. These employees perform mechanical duties, administrative work, or other activities in support of professional personnel. Their specific jobs vary greatly with different professional areas. For instance, in economics the technician might be a statistician; in engineering he might be a draftsman.

The labor market for technical employees is quite diverse. Many technical employees are recruited from technical schools. Others are promoted from skilled operations work. Still others acquire the knowledge and ability to perform technical work through years of experience in clerical or administrative positions.

As a result, the labor market for any particular group of technical workers may be entirely or partially internal—like supervisory positions, technical positions are often filled by operations employees. In many cases, however, the labor market is at least in part external—and the narrower the field of work, the more likely that employees are recruited from other companies or technical schools. For example, technical jobs in the financial department would most likely be filled by promotion from senior clerical positions, but EDP programmers would most likely come from technical schools or from other companies.

Under these conditions, an effective salary administration system for technical employees must be built around the market approach. Positions from each major area of technical work must be selected and priced in the marketplace. This slotting of benchmark positions is the starting point in salary administration for technical positions.

Because different types of technical positions must be first related to their real market value, traditional job evaluation systems have limited usefulness in salary administration for this group. The benchmark jobs are priced directly by surveying relevant labor markets. Job evaluation can serve only to assist management in slotting technical jobs which cannot be priced under the benchmark system.

There are a number of specific considerations relevant to technical positions which must be taken into account in designing the salary administration program. These include special problems in evaluating the performance of technical personnel, questions of overtime payments, and problems posed by rapidly changing circumstances in technical labor markets.

Because technical employees have a close working relationship with professionals, and because their own work is subprofessional, a modified form of professional salary administration policies, outlined in Chapter 11, is frequently appropriate for these employees. It is difficult to describe technical work by traditional functional descriptions of tasks performed, methods used, and so on. Therefore, either modified functional descriptions, generic descriptions, or work sample descriptions are appropriate. These descriptions should define specific levels of technical work and should illustrate the types of assignments that are typically given.

In addition, with professional positions, it is important that the position evaluation plan for technical employees gives adequate weighting to knowledge and skill. Some companies have successfully utilized either generic classification systems or career curve methods for technical personnel.

Overtime compensation also can be a special problem with technical employees. Many technicians are clearly within the requirements of the Fair Labor Standards Act and therefore must be paid overtime compensation. Others who are exempt from the act may be at such an income level that they should at least be considered for a modified overtime pay system—both to maintain equity and to preserve the company's internal pay relationships. Here essentially the same principles as those involved in overtime pay for supervisors apply.

With technical personnel, the problem of overtime compensation is one of control. Frequently, technicians work in small groups and are closely involved with the work of professional employees. Professionals may put in long hours, either because of work pressure or because of attachment to their field. Since professionals are not paid overtime, it is often difficult and perhaps unwise to restrict their hours. If it is necessary to have technicians work with them, however, overtime costs for technical personnel are inevitable. Experience suggests that control in this situation must come from day-to-day common sense in administration rather than from any set of rules.

Probably the most difficult problem in salary administration for technical employees, and one which is becoming increasingly prevalent in our technological society, stems from this very relationship to professional workers. To some extent, the technician's role is to do work which the professional could do himself but which would prevent him from concentrating on higher-level activities. The technician can thus conserve the time and increase the productiveness of the professional and thereby make him more effective. Since some of the value of the technician is related to the value of the professional, the technician may be undervalued, if he is appraised only in terms of his prescribed duties. Furthermore, unless compensation administration recognizes the importance of such support, it may actually discourage the technician from performing more effectively in backing up the professional.

A final problem in salary administration for technical employees is the fact that the number and diversity of technicians are growing rapidly. As each new professional discipline and specialized staff position is added to the company payroll, the need for technicians is expanding geometrically. Also, faced with a continuing shortage of professional personnel, alert companies are finding more and more ways in which technicians can assume work that has formerly been done by professionals. This results not only in an increasing number of technicians but in an upgrading of their skills and levels of responsibility.

ADMINISTRATIVE EMPLOYEES

The only characteristic shared by administrative jobs is that they do not fit into management, supervisory, professional, sales, technical, production, or office groups. They usually fall within the top two or three pay levels for nonexempt jobs and within the lowest five to eight pay levels for exempt positions. Except for this, there are more dissimilarities than similarities among administrative positions. Thus there are no guides that fit all the employees who fall into this category; it is best only to describe particular administrative jobs and the special problems associated with each.

Executive secretaries represent one special group of administrative employees. Their relationship to top-level managers is much like that of technicians to professionals, for although they perform various mechanical duties, their primary function is to conserve management time and to help executives perform their jobs better. This suggests that salary treatment of executive secretaries should be similar to that of technicians.

Another special group of administrative employees are the trainees —those who are being groomed for high-level management responsibilities. Here the problem is that the position which a trainee currently holds may have no relation to his real value. Frequently, trainees are rotated in jobs so that they can gain a diversity of experience, and the fact that they are given trainee assignments means that their responsibilities are somewhat limited. By the same token, the long-range value of trainees to the company is great, and the caliber of this group of employees is high. For these few but highly important workers, salary administration policies used for other groups will not be appropriate. They must literally be exempted from the system, and pay scales for trainees must be sufficient both to attract them to the company and to retain them.

At the opposite extreme are the senior clerks—the long-service employees who have come up through operations such as accounting and statistics. Because of their extensive knowledge of the department, they have assumed levels of responsibility beyond the scope and nature of their duties. There are two major problems with this group. First, such employees may have value not easily recorded in position descriptions or evaluated by any system. They may, for example, give advice based on the way a certain event was handled many years ago; they may be the only people who remember where things are or who did what. Or they may have a great store of information on company procedures. Second, such employees frequently are paid a premium unrelated to their jobs, simply as a reward for especially long service. Even without such premiums, they may achieve a salary level which is so high in relation to their duties that additional increases, though granted, are difficult to justify.

These are only a few illustrations of the different types of administrative positions and the special problems in salary administration they pose. A comprehensive list would include dozens of special cases. For the great majority of administrative positions, however, the methods described in the first five chapters are applicable.

13

MANAGEMENT COMPENSATION

As INDICATED in earlier chapters, the unique characteristics of operations jobs, sales jobs, professional jobs, and supervisory, administrative, and technical jobs make somewhat different compensation practices essential for each group. Similarly, the unique nature of management positions calls for special salary practices and forms of compensation for managers.

There are, for instance, a number of forms of compensation which are applicable only to management positions. These include long-term income and supplemental benefits. There are also a number of legal, tax, and financial questions which must be considered in the design of the management compensation program. The starting point in effective compensation for managers, as for any other employee group, is to build a program tailored to the special characteristics of management positions.

THE MANAGEMENT GROUP

While each company has its own definition of management, the term generally refers to those employees whose decisions and judgments have a significant impact on overall company profitability or on the success of organizational units. The management group, on the average, represents about 1 percent of total company employment. This percentage tends to be larger in small or highly decentralized companies. It is also larger in companies with a low capital investment, a rapid growth rate, or a high mix of exempt employees.

There are a number of characteristics of management positions which affect both personnel administration in general and compensation practices specifically. For example, because management decisions have such a significant effect on enterprise results, a high percentage of management pay is usually geared to enterprise performance. For this reason also, management compensation administration is more appropriately focused on *value* or *achievement* rather than on cost. Even though management pay is high, the relative cost of management is not. In most firms management pay could be increased 25 percent without seriously affecting costs. But even small increases in the value of management—in the effectiveness of management performance—have enormous leveraging effect on business results. A 5 percent increase in management performance could, for example, very easily double earnings per share in five years.

There are several other characteristics of the management job which affect the design and administration of management compensation programs:

- Management jobs are not definable in terms of what work is done or how it is done. They must be defined in terms of what is achieved and what managers are expected to accomplish.
- In management the ratio of people to jobs is almost one to one.
- The number of employees in the management group is relatively small, and personnel programs are administered by high-level management employees. This, of course, permits a highly customized and far less structured approach to compensation administration.
- The income expectations of managers are extremely high.
- Managers are highly visible to other companies and, if successful in their duties, are constantly subject to recruitment.
- Management jobs are high-risk positions. Rewards are high when management is successful; the penalty for failure is (or should be) swift and certain—termination or demotion!
- For most managers the time span in top management positions is relatively short. For 90 percent of top managers the period of peak effectiveness does not exceed ten years.
- The content of management jobs varies significantly, even in

positions with the same title. In fact, specific duties and activities can change dramatically in the same position when operating conditions change or when a new incumbent assumes the position. This reflects the degree to which management jobs are shaped by the needs of the business and the capabilities of people.

These characteristics of management positions must be the cornerstone for building effective personnel practices for management positions. They must also be the cornerstone for developing and implementing effective compensation programs for managers.

SALARY ADMINISTRATION FOR MANAGERS

While each of the various forms of compensation is an important part of management income, salary is still the key element. For one thing, salary represents a significant part of the executive's total income. In addition, it is the element of compensation which most directly affects his standard of living. Finally, salary is a basic determinant of the manager's income from other forms of compensation, such as pensions and life insurance.

In recent years significant changes have taken place in salary administration for management positions. Traditional salary practices, described in the first eight chapters, are used by relatively few firms. Most have adapted salary practices to fit the unique characteristics of management jobs. In some companies this has meant modifying traditional techniques. In other companies it has meant adopting a totally new approach—labeled in this chapter the entrepreneurial approach. Both of these approaches are discussed in detail below.

Use of Job Descriptions

Preparation of job descriptions for managers is extremely difficult, costly, and time consuming. Management position descriptions must be constantly rewritten because organizational or operational changes are continually affecting the content of management jobs. Also, there are typically as many management jobs as there are managers. Therefore, the volume of work in preparing and maintaining management position descriptions is considerable.

One of the major problems in writing management position descriptions is that the duties and areas of responsibility of managers are different from those of other employee groups. Figure 29 compares a typical office job description with a management description. The

Figure 29. **Inherent differences in work assignments, management versus nonmanagement positions.**

ANALYSIS OF ASSIGNMENT IN TERMS OF:	TYPICAL OFFICE JOB	TYPICAL MANAGEMENT JOB
Skill	Largely mechanical skills.	Nonmechanical skills such as leadership; organizing ability; ability to coordinate, guide, and control the work of others.
Knowledge	Technical knowledge; knowledge of routine procedures; specific knowledge of "how to do" mechanical or procedural tasks.	Depth and breadth of knowledge of some aspect of company work, field of business, and so on. Understanding as well as know-how.
Responsibility	Responsibility largely for accuracy and technical correctness of own work.	General responsibility for results.
Decision making or judgment	"Task" decisions: Is their work correct or not correct? Should they refer to supervisor or go ahead?	Frequent decisions of a broad nature affecting a section of the business and the work of others.
Planning	Some planning of timing and sequence of own work. Prescribed work procedures restrict areas of planning.	Largely plans own work. Plans directly affect or influence work of others. Planning for new and better methods.
Conditions of work	Concentration; noise, heat, dirt, physical effort; surroundings.	Conditions, as such, not a consideration.
Initiative	Largely specific work assignments; standardized procedures; initiative largely confined to how quickly tasks are performed.	Only broad objectives; high degree of freedom to follow own methods, initiate changes, and so on.
Supervision	None.	A basic aspect of the job.
Influence	Little, aside from suggestions and relationships with other employees working in group.	A basic aspect of the job.

office job is described in traditional terms, as a detailed list of duties and assignments. In contrast, the management position is analyzed in terms of broad functions, areas of responsibility, scope and impact of assignments, degree of accountability, and extent and nature of the supervision and influence involved.

Another problem in writing management position descriptions is the difficulty of separating job duties from individual performance. In theory, job descriptions should be completely impersonal. But in many management positions how well an individual does his job really determines the nature of the job itself. For instance, the personnel manager who motivates others effectively may make quite a different job for himself than the man who merely carries out the mechanical and clerical aspects of the position. Of course, this does not mean that managers assign work to themselves; rather, it means that the able manager who, with the approval of higher management, absorbs greater responsibility has changed the nature of his job.

Management position descriptions must provide more than an outline of duties and responsibilities if they are to serve broad management purposes, salary administration objectives, or management development, staffing, and organizational planning ends. Either the position descriptions themselves or supplemental manuals should supply pertinent information on such aspects of the business as the following:

- Products, operational methods, management practices, distributive systems, and the like.
- Essential characteristics of the company and principal problem areas confronting it.
- Plans and forecasts, such as those represented in five-year plans.
- Organizational charts covering all management levels.
- Nature and extent of competitiveness in various aspects of the business.
- Number, type, and difficulty of decisions made in management positions.
- Technical nature of the business, rate of growth, innovative requirements, and rate of change of products and markets.
- Scope of the functional or operating segments of the enterprise for which the management position is responsible.
- Impact data such as sales, profits, net assets utilized, and number of employees.

In essence, job descriptions for management positions represent descriptions of the *business*. Job descriptions for the chief executive officer are essentially descriptions of the company. For other management positions they are descriptions of that part of the enterprise for which the manager is responsible. Generally, only high-level line or staff employees are qualified to prepare descriptions which meet these specifications. Managers themselves must participate in the process.

Because of the time and cost involved in writing management position descriptions, many companies have concluded that if such descriptions are to be written at all they should be prepared primarily for management purposes. Under this approach, they become basically a management tool used in assigning work, communicating responsibilities, establishing authority limits, setting performance standards, and reviewing the performance of management. Descriptions which are good enough to serve these purposes are more than adequate for use in salary administration. They are also valuable in other areas—for instance, in organizational planning, manpower planning, staffing, and management development.

Classifying Management Positions: Modified Evaluation Plans

When the traditional salary approach is used for managers, methods of job evaluation must be adapted to the unique characteristics of the management job. Some of the factors used to evaluate clerical and production jobs—such as working conditions, physical effort, and visual concentration—have no application at the management level. By contrast, some factors which may not be pertinent to lower-level positions—for example, supervision exercised, relationships, know-how, and responsibility—may measure the essence of relative worth in management positions.

Frequently, too, the same factors have different meanings when applied to management and nonmanagement positions. Responsibility in a lower-level job, for example, may be interpreted primarily in terms of cost of errors. In management positions responsibility is defined more in terms of scope of accountability and impact on the success of the business.

Many techniques have been developed to adapt job evaluation plans to management positions. Two adaptations which have had some success in recent years are modified factor comparison and multiple evaluation.

Modified factor comparison. Application of the factor comparison technique to management jobs requires the following modifications: (1) selection and definition of factors tailored to management jobs in the particular company environment, (2) adaptation of weighting techniques to management jobs, and (3) development of procedures which are geared to measuring management positions.

In some cases selecting appropriate factors for management positions means developing completely new criteria. In other cases it means modifying or giving different emphasis to factor definitions. For example, in management evaluation know-how must be defined in terms of the *types* of things which must be part of a manager's experience rather than, as in the case of office and production jobs, in terms of specific job knowledge.

A modified factor comparison plan for managers should include no fewer than four factors and no more than six. At least four factors are necessary to cover the basic criteria of responsibility, authority, knowledge, and management skills. But if more than six are used, the breakdown of criteria will be much more precise than the knowledge on which judgments are based.

The weighting techniques used in evaluating management positions are somewhat broader and more flexible than those suitable for office and production jobs. It is almost impossible to use predetermined weightings in evaluating management positions, because the various factors differ greatly in importance from company to company. In a sales-oriented firm, for instance, the relationship factor will probably be dominant in determining relative job worth. In an engineering-oriented company relationships may be less important than know-how.

Some companies have found it extremely helpful to use large guide charts to summarize the results of rankings under factor comparison methods. Such a chart helps to focus the evaluator's attention on specific characteristics of management positions and assists the evaluator in gaining an overall view of job worth.

Multiple evaluation. Another technique that is frequently used in classifying management positions is multiple evaluation—that is, evaluation of all jobs at least twice by different plans. Such a technique helps to pinpoint areas in which one evaluation method may be seriously inaccurate. In one type of plan, for instance, all jobs are evaluated three times according to three different definitions of overall job worth: scope and impact of the job, requirements of the job, and difficulty of performing the job. Under each of these plans, factors are utilized. The results of the three evaluations are then compared; if any significant differences come to light, the jobs are rechecked to iron out inconsistencies.

Another multiple-evaluation system calls for using two different evaluation techniques rather than two types of factor comparison plans. The first is a straight factor comparison approach. The second is a system of internal evaluation which requires that each job be analyzed in terms of the relative importance of the factors used. The results of the two approaches, expressed in percentages, are compared. Differences are resolved by reevaluating the job by each method.

Classifying Management Positions: The Entrepreneurial Approach

An alternate approach to management salary administration—the entrepreneurial approach—is made possible by the large amount of information on management pay levels and pay practices which has become available in the past ten years. Under the entrepreneurial approach, the company starts by using market survey data to establish competitive pay levels for a representative number of management positions.

In most cases, at least half of all management positions can be priced directly in the marketplace. Since the market is the ultimate arbiter of appropriate pay levels and equitable pay relationships, this approach assures from the start that the company's management pay levels are appropriate—in the sense that they are proper to attract and retain key personnel and in the sense that they reflect company compensation policy and strategy.

Once jobs which can be priced in the marketplace have been selected, market survey data are used to establish an average pay level for each benchmark position. The result is an "unadjusted benchmark salary" for that position. The data are unadjusted in the sense that they are based only on market data. Various modifications in the data must be made to reflect company policy and strategy.

One important adjustment to market pay data involves what are essentially business considerations. For example, the data must be adjusted to reflect strategic commitments which have been made by the company. For two jobs where the market data are essentially the same, the company may have committed heavy capital and other resources to create growth or change in one of these areas. This strategic commitment must be reflected in actual benchmark salaries if the company is to attract and retain employees capable of achieving its objectives. Another type of adjustment to market pay data considers special roles or values of individual managers. For instance, a manager's counsel may be sought informally on subjects outside his prescribed area of responsibility. Or a manager may have a special value because of customer relationships or great credibility with investors.

These are but a few of the many possible individual circumstances which need to be considered in adjusting market data to the company's needs. Market pay adjustments require the use of factors that are very different from those employed in traditional job evaluation. Furthermore, such factors are generally not definable; nor can job evaluation points be assigned.

The result of these adjustments is an average pay level for each benchmark job which represents, *in the company environment,* the appropriate pay for that position. These jobs are slotted into the salary structure at that point where the benchmark pay most closely matches the structure at midpoint. Other management positions which cannot be set by direct survey are then slotted into the salary structure by comparison with the benchmark positions. Usually, this can be done by a ranking system; more formal methods can be used when business evaluation factors rather than typical job evaluation factors are the criteria for measurement.

Management Salary Structures

Under the entrepreneurial approach, management salary levels are established as an integral part of the benchmark system. Under a modified job evaluation approach, the salary structure is developed after a relative rank order is established. In each case, there are some special considerations relevant to determining an appropriate salary structure. These include questions with respect to sources of information on management income and the proper comparison base and questions relating to technical features of the structure.

Sources of data. During the past ten years a great deal of survey information on management income levels has become available. The most widely used source for such data, based on a poll of members of the American Compensation Association, is that provided by the Executive Compensation Service of American Management Associations. The second most widely used source of data is the Annual Management Compensation Study published by Sibson & Company, Inc., which covers pay levels and practices in over 1,300 companies. A third source of data on management compensation is *Project 777,* which is published cooperatively by a number of large companies. Survey information on top management positions in specific companies can be obtained from proxy statements. Some companies also exchange detailed information on management pay levels, but this is a costly process. Finally, some industry associations publish special surveys of management compensation.

It is usually necessary to use multiple sources of information to set the management salary structure. Some broad-based survey is necessary because of differences in job content—even among jobs with identical titles and similar functions—and because of the great transference among management positions. A second source involves a narrow group of firms, usually selected on the basis of similarity of operating and economic characteristics, for which pay practices as well as pay levels may be determined.

A complicating factor in setting management pay levels is that some management positions have separate labor markets. The competitive market for financial executives may be quite different from that for manufacturing executives. Finally, each of the labor markets for management jobs is a national or at least a regional market.

Technical considerations. Salary structures covering management positions have two unique technical characteristics. First, the within-grade progression is somewhat broader in management structures than in other pay structures. This is because of the greater length of time usually spent in management jobs and because of the greater importance of individual worth over job worth in any management position. This, in turn, indicates the greater opportunity that exists for the individual to contribute on the job. Greater within-grade progression provides significant motivation for management employees to improve their performance. Second, between-grade progressions are greater in management structures than in structures covering other groups of employees. This reflects the greater difficulty of classifying management jobs into levels in the first place. At the same time, greater between-grade progression is necessary when there is greater within-grade progression in order to maintain correct overlapping between grades.

Salary Increase Practices

The fact that job classifications are broader and less precise for management positions than for other positions makes salary increase planning for managers particularly important. The difficulty of separating job worth from individual worth in determining managers' compensation also suggests the importance of individual salary planning.

In planning salary increases, line managers should have basic information on each manager's pay history. They should also have data concerning pay comparisons within the company and some guidelines with respect to pay levels outside the company. Finally, managers who supervise other managers should be given the opportunity to review this information in a systematic manner, and they should have staff personnel or higher-level managers available for counsel and guidance.

Of particular importance in reviewing management pay levels is the fact that salaries for managers have been increasing steadily over the past ten years. Even in years of recession—when the number of management positions declined—80 percent of those still employed received annual increases. The average for all managers (including those who received no increases) has been between 7 and 9 percent. Studies suggest that this trend will continue in the foreseeable future.

There are a number of explanations or hypotheses as to why management salaries have been increasing as described. For those who must decide pay increases for managers, the explanations are less telling than the fact. It means that they must start by planning increases for managers in the 7 to 9 percent range.

Another important consideration in management salary planning is setting appropriate rewards for outstanding contributors. There are —in theory, at least—no marginal or unsatisfactory performers in management positions; there are only satisfactory and outstanding performers. The difference in value between the satisfactory performer and the outstanding performer can be enormous. This suggests, for one thing, a need to establish significant salary differentials for management jobs in which performance and capability are demonstrably superior.

Existing salary practices in most companies are rarely flexible enough to reward the truly outstanding management performers. Is it enough to pay the truly exceptional manager—the individual who is really carrying the burden of leadership, solving major company problems, or building the future of the organization—5, 10, or 15 percent more than the average manager in the group? Would it not be more appropriate to pay him 30, 50, or even 100 percent more? This is one of the most perplexing pay-relationship problems faced by companies.

A final consideration in management salary planning is the fact that management pay structures can be used only as broad guides for decision making. Structures are useful for management positions if for no other reason than that they provide a uniform accounting system. But it is not always appropriate to administer management salaries within the framework provided by a salary structure. For one thing, use of the entire pay range implies that management effectiveness is somehow commensurate with years on the job. A number of studies indicate that there is no correlation between these two factors. No doubt experience matures judgment and in other ways contributes to more effective management. But newness in the job can bring a fresh view, more vigor to the position, and greater dedication to building a record of accomplishment.

Moreover, the midpoint of the salary range is only a guideline to typical or average pay in the marketplace for jobs of a certain type. These "average levels of pay" are representative of relatively few actual cases because of the great dispersion in management pay for any given position.

Finally, the minimum and maximum of the pay range are generally not usable. To put a manager's pay at the bottom of the range is to suggest that he is marginally qualified—or a trainee. There is, of course, no room for trainees in management positions. The top of the pay range has little meaning in selected cases. It is almost impossible to establish a maximum value on a key management position because it is tenuous to assume that there is a maximum level of management effectiveness.

The constraints on management salary levels really involve such things as self-imposed restraint on the part of managers, conservatism on the part of directors, reasonable compensation as defined by the Internal Revenue Service, and considerations of stockholder relations. In practice, therefore, an appropriate salary level is one which is satisfactory to the managers concerned and which at the same time meets these external and internal constraints.

Thus, whether job levels are set by some modified factor evaluation system or by an entrepreneurial approach, pay increases at a given level clearly call for a business or market approach as contrasted to the traditional merit rating approach. The focus should be on relating pay to value.

BONUS PAYMENTS

A second important element of management compensation is bonus payments. "Bonus" is a generic term referring to extra compensation paid periodically—usually once each year. There are a number of different types of bonus plans used for management positions. These include:

Profit-sharing awards—plans in which the amount of money available for bonus is directly related to the profits of the enterprise and all participants share proportionately, usually in relation to salary level.

Discretionary awards—plans in which extra payments are made on the basis of thoughtful consideration of business results and individual contribution to these results but in which the criteria for making these judgments are unknown to the participants.

Incentive awards—plans in which payments are geared directly to the achievement of preset goals and individual contribution to that achievement and in which the participants understand the criteria for bonus award decisions.

About 65 percent of all nongovernment and profit-oriented public corporations have some form of bonus program for managers, and over 65 percent of these are incentive award systems. Therefore, the principal focus of attention in management bonus plans now * is on incentive pay plans for managers.

Features of Incentive Pay Systems

To be effective, a management incentive compensation plan must meet the following requirements:

1. Eligibility for the plan must be restricted to those who by the nature of their work make decisions and judgments which affect business results—either for the corporation as a whole or for a business unit within the corporation. This is not to say that other managers should not have incentive pay, but they should not be eligible for the "management incentive compensation plan" in which the reward systems are geared to overall business unit results.

2. The accumulation of funds for bonus awards must be related to preestablished business goals. The goals, in turn, must reflect significant but attainable management achievement under economic circumstances which prevail in that plan year.

3. The rewards to managers must be significant when these goals are achieved. Just what is significant can be measured in two ways. First, the awards must be competitive with awards received by managers in similar jobs in comparable businesses. In addition, they must be high enough to have a significant impact on the manager's life style.

4. The plan must have some system for rewarding overachievement—achievement beyond established goals—and for penalizing underachievement. Usually, the penalty system includes a threshold of business achievement below which no incentive awards are made.

* It is interesting to note that when the first version of this book was written in 1958, more than one-third of all management bonus plans were profit-sharing plans; more than one-half were discretionary plans; and very few were incentive plans.

5. There must be some system for rewarding the individual from overall funds for his personal contribution to the achievement of the business unit.

6. There can be no "golden handcuffs" provision.

Studies indicate that such plans are feasible for 90 percent of all commercial businesses in the country. They are also feasible for approximately 50 percent of all nonprofit organizations and for a significant number of government agencies and public corporations.

The value of management incentive compensation plans has been amply demonstrated, both by empirical studies and by the experience of individual companies. These sources indicate that management incentive plans contribute to business success. In addition, close observation of management behavior under such plans suggests that incentive formulas have a meaningful motivational impact on managers.

Management incentive compensation plans do not necessarily motivate managers to work harder; nor do they necessarily motivate managers to be more responsible. The overwhelming majority of managers work hard already and are highly responsible. Rather, management incentive compensation plans motivate managers to reorder their priorities and refocus their attention on matters of higher importance in terms of achieving business objectives.

These changes in management behavior may not be great. They may range from a 2 to 5 percent increase in effectiveness for top-level managers to a 10 to 25 percent increase in effectiveness for lower-level managers. Furthermore, changes in effectiveness occur gradually. But even slight improvements in management effectiveness over time can have an enormous impact on the achievement of business objectives; a 5 percent increase in effectiveness could, in ten years, double earnings per share.

Amount of Bonus Payments

Table 11 shows the average bonus payments in industry, expressed as a percentage of base salaries. Note that high-level positions not only get higher bonuses but a higher percentage of bonus to salary. This is a reflection of the basic purpose of incentive compensation plans. Bonuses are designed to reward managers who affect profits by the nature of their positions; thus higher-level positions should have a higher percentage of their total compensation dependent on the success of the enterprise.

Note also that executives in bonus-paying companies receive more total compensation than their counterparts in non-bonus-paying com-

Table 11. **Incentive compensation for general managers: typical industry payments ($000).**

Compensation in Bonus-Paying Companies			
Salary of Manager	*Percentage Bonus to Salary* *	*Total Compensation*	*Compensation in Non-Bonus-Paying Companies*
20	15	23	21
30	25	37	33
40	30	52	47
50	35	67	60
75	40	105	95
100	45	145	125
125	50	187	155
150	60	240	200
175	70	300	250
200	80	360	300

* Percentages are averages only. Actual standards vary greatly depending on industry, compensation strategy, size of firm, type of incentive plan, growth potential of the enterprise, and general economic conditions.

panies. As a general rule, salaries of executives in non-bonus-paying companies are approximately 10 to 20 percent higher; but since bonuses average 25 to 30 percent of salary, total compensation in bonus-paying companies tends to be about 15 percent higher than in firms which do not have bonus plans.

With respect to the form of bonus payments, a company may pay the award all in cash, all in the stock of the company, or some in cash and some in stock. In addition, the company may permit executives to defer their bonus until some future date.

LONG-TERM INCOME PLANS

A third form of management compensation is long-term income plans.* These represent extra compensation paid after a long period of time—usually five to ten years. Typically, the size of award is based at least in part on long-term business results.

* Discussion of long-term income plans is based on the 1973 Annual Management Compensation Study and on tax rules, accounting practices, and other regulations in effect as of September 1973.

The most traditional type of long-term income plan is the stock option. In addition, during the past few years a number of new types of long-term income plans have emerged. This is due in part to less favored treatment of stock options under the Tax Reform Act of 1969, in part to the experience of companies under stock options, and in part to a desire by large leadership firms to develop more competitive plans which would build greater incentive for their key managers to achieve long-term goals.

There are essentially four types of long-term income plans in use today: traditional stock plans, including stock options and phantom stock plans; long-term incentive plans, which are essentially the same as management incentive compensation plans but cover a five-year period; combination plans, where part of the reward is geared to stock price and part to earnings performance; and entrepreneurial plans, which are designed to provide income for managers which simulates the income that owner/managers would receive.

Stock Plans

Approximately two out of every three companies with traded stock have some form of stock option or phantom stock plan for managers. One recent study of 1,300 companies revealed that 80 percent used stock options and half of the rest used some form of phantom stock plan. (About a third of the companies had stockholder approval to use more than one type of plan.)

One type of stock plan is the qualified option. Such a plan must meet rather rigid legal tests. For one thing, the option price must be 100 percent of the market price of the stock when the option was granted. Also, the option must be exercised within five years, and after exercise the executive must hold the stock for at least three years. In addition an option cannot be exercised with capital gains benefits so long as a preexisting option at a higher price is outstanding. Finally, option prices cannot be revalued; nor can a qualified option be issued in tandem with a nonqualified option.

Income from plans which meet these and other requirements are generally taxed at capital gains rates. Capital gains rates are one-half ordinary income rates up to a maximum of 25 percent. However, tax preference treatment under the Tax Reform Act of 1969 can result in tax rates as high as 37 percent.

Another type of stock plan is the nonqualified option, which is simply a plan that does not meet all the requirements for a qualified option. It may, for instance, have an exercise price below market price, although only fourteen companies in the *Fortune* 1000 have plans with this feature. From the company's point of view, payments under nonqualified options are tax-deductible but do not involve a P&L charge.

The number of shares reserved for option plans varies a great deal and depends on the size of the company, capital structure, broadness of stock base, rate of growth, and organization. Typically, a company will reserve 3 to 5 percent of total outstanding stock for purposes of issuing stock options. The amount of stock granted to any individual is normally a function of job level; as in the case of bonus plans, the stock option values are a higher percentage of salary in higher-level jobs.

Table 12 presents a multiple-of-earnings guide for granting stock options. The theory behind this widely used guide is that the price of stock under option multiplied by the number of shares optioned should represent a value which is a multiple of the executive's current salary. Thus in Table 12 the executive making $50,000 would have option grants for stock equal in value to three times this salary;

Table 12. **Stock option plans: typical industry grants and option income ($000).**

Salary of Executive	*Multiple* *	*Percentage of Annual Income* †
20	1.5	15
30	2.0	20
40	2.5	27
50	3.0	35
75	3.5	42
100	4.0	50
125	5.0	60
150	6.0	70
175	7.0	85
200	8.0	100

* Equals price of stock at option multiplied by number of shares optioned divided by salary.

† Equals current price less option price multiplied by number of shares optioned divided by number of years, all expressed as a percentage of salary. Actual value is, of course, a function of trend in the price of company stock.

the executive making $100,000 would have option values equal to four times his salary.

Table 12 also indicates the amount of income which may accrue to executives at various income levels from stock option plans. The study used as a basis for the data was made between 1968 and 1973 and reflects income actually earned by managers from options.* Under these conditions, income from options was about the same as that from incentive compensation plans.

Long-Term Incentive Plans

Long-term incentive plans are similar to one-year management incentive compensation plans except that rewards are geared to long-term targets—usually five years or more. Also long-term income plans may properly have "golden handcuffs" provisions.

The key part of any long-term incentive plan is the appropriateness of the long-term goals which must be achieved in order for managers to receive competitive income awards. If the company's environment makes such forecasting feasible and if reasonable long-term income goals can be established, these plans do have a number of distinct advantages. For one thing, the criteria for management performance under long-term incentive plans can be internalized. Performance can be measured, for example, by improvement in earnings per share, which is a better measure of management performance in a given time span than changes in the price of company stock. Long-term incentive plans make possible the design of long-term programs for each of the subsidiary sections of the company. Therefore, these plans make it possible to create incentive for managers in each of the business units to achieve long-term goals. Finally, the long-term incentive approach enables large, mature companies to develop and implement long-term income plans which are competitive with plans in smaller, more highly leveraged businesses that compete with them for management talent.

There are also problems in long-term incentive plans, other than the obvious one of setting appropriate long-term goals. There is, for instance, the high cost of designing, implementing, and administering the programs, particularly if a separate long-term income plan is designed for each business unit. In this case, a somewhat unique and customized plan must be designed for each and a highly complex

* Data are only for options exercised; zero income from options underwater is excluded.

administrative system must be developed to deal with such likely occurrences as organizational changes and transfers of managers from one business unit to another.

Combination Plans

A number of plans have been developed in the past few years which include elements of the long-term incentive approach, in that achievement of preset goals is part of the reward system, and elements of a stock plan, in that part of the total reward is dependent on the price of the company stock. Two such plans are the performance-share plan and the stock incentive plan.

The performance-share plan has received a great deal of publicity. It has sometimes been billed as the "plan of the future"—to replace options. As a matter of fact, however, after three years of publicity and hard sell only twelve companies in the *Fortune* 1000 have such plans, and at the time of this writing four of these companies expect to drop their programs.

Under a performance-share plan, managers are "awarded" shares of stock in much the same way they would be given option grants. These shares vest—usually 20 percent per year—if certain preset earnings goals are achieved. If vested, the manager receives the full value of the shares at the current market value.

Performance-share plans were designed to give the company certain tax and accounting advantages. Under current regulations, however, the full value of income is chargeable to P&L and they therefore receive unfavorable accounting treatment.* In addition, such plans require the setting of earnings objectives. If these are reasonable, then it would be more logical to use a long-term incentive plan. As matters now exist, performance-share plans combine the worst features of stock plans and long-term incentive programs. This no doubt explains why so few firms have adopted them in spite of the very impressive publicity campaign on their behalf.

Another combination plan is the stock incentive program. Under this plan, managers are given phantom awards equal in value to some multiple of the bonus they receive under an incentive compensation program. Thus the number of units is geared to business unit achievement, but the subsequent value of these units is determined by future trends in the price of the company stock. These plans are quite simple

* First-year income is also fully chargeable under Phase 4 of the Nixon administration's pay stabilization program.

to design and administer. Furthermore, they can be very flexible. For instance, there may be actual reward mechanisms to permit taking advantage of whatever tax and accounting regulations exist without altering the basic concepts of the plan or going back to stockholders to request a new plan.

Entrepreneurial Plans

Quite recently a new type of long-term income plan has emerged which is designed to simulate as closely as possible income (other than salary and benefits) which managers would receive if they were owners of the company. Under such plans, managers are given a one-year incentive award, a five-year incentive award, and special rewards for improvements in stock price, earnings per share, and dividend levels.

SPECIAL COMPENSATION FOR EXECUTIVES

An important form of special compensation for some executives is deferred compensation. Under deferred-income plans, part of the income earned by an executive in a given year is deferred to a future time, usually after retirement. The primary purpose of such plans is to postpone income to a year when the executive is in a lower tax bracket.

Deferred-income plans pose several problems. For one thing, there are strict and complicated tax rules governing deferred-compensation arrangements. Also, complex mathematical formulas are needed to determine whether a deferral is to the advantage of the executive. For instance, calculation of deferred compensation must take into consideration current income of the executive, total retirement income (including pensions and income from savings), likely changes in tax rates, and investment potential from after-tax income. All these factors involve a high degree of uncertainty. Determining the value of current after-tax income, for example, requires judgment as to interest rates and appreciation values from investments.

Because of these uncertainties, deferred-compensation arrangements are prudent only if a considerable safety margin is built into them. As a general rule, executives who are within five years of retirement should earn at least $50,000 in total annual income before deferred-compensation arrangements will be to their advantage; executives who are ten years from retirement should earn well over $100,000 a year in order to make deferred arrangements practical.

There are also a wide variety of special benefits available to executives. For example, many companies have split-dollar insurance programs for their key men. Also, most companies allow longer vacations for executives. In recent years a number of plans have emerged to provide supplemental insurance benefits to managers. Under these programs, managers are equal participants in all company insurance benefits—pensions, life insurance, and so on. In addition, they are eligible for special programs specifically designed to meet the needs of high-paid persons. In some cases several different plans are offered to executives, and the individual may choose those which are best tailored to his needs and circumstances.

Several types of fringe benefits are offered to executives. These are usually not reported and are sometimes difficult either to identify or to assess. For instance, many companies provide periodic physical examinations for executives. Some have special security agreements with executives to protect them against possible discharge because of policy disagreements, changes in the nature of the business, or other factors beyond the control of the individual. Some of these arrangements are formalized in employment contracts; others are informal.

In recent years the government has tightened up considerably on expense account privileges, but there are a variety of legitimate business expense items that represent some value for executives. Management perquisites include size of office, title, type of furniture, and other status symbols. Though these have no dollar value, they can have very real value to the executive.

Estate-building plans are a rapidly developing area of supplemental management compensation. Many companies now offer managers estate-counseling services, in which a firm is hired to analyze the executive's estate, advise him on how he should manage his savings, and assist him in making investments, particularly in tax-sheltered situations. Other estate-building plans include special savings and investment programs designed for managers. These involve low cost to the company, but they can be highly valuable to executives in investing capital and building an estate.

MAINTAINING THE MANAGEMENT COMPENSATION PROGRAM

The management compensation program must be reviewed regularly to make sure it is up to date and appropriate. Changes in salary levels and annual review of salaries are as important for management positions as for other positions. Bonus payments, long-term income awards, and other major pay plans also require constant attention. For instance, under incentive pay plans business unit targets, individual goals, and bonus standards must be reviewed each year.

Management pay programs must also be reviewed to make sure that they conform to existing laws and to regulations of the Accounting Principles Board, the Internal Revenue Service, and other government agencies. At least one significant change in regulations affecting management compensation has occurred every year for the past fifteen years. Company plans must be adjusted to such changes.

New types of programs for managers are emerging all the time. In 1968, for instance, there were essentially only two types of long-term income plans; today there are two dozen. Sometimes a new plan is a "gimmick"—some clever device to take advantage of tax laws or to make executives rich. The "swinging door," nonqualified option, and premium buyout of options are examples. Such gimmicks are invariably short-lived; there are just as many officials in Washington to plug tax loopholes as there are lawyers, accountants, and consultants to invent them. And, of course, such plans really have nothing to do with fair compensation or motivation of management.

High-paid executives are naturally interested in reducing their taxes. There are only two ways to do this with management compensation programs. One is through plans specifically preferenced by act of Congress. For management personnel, this means only qualified options. (Qualified profit-sharing, pension, thrift, and stock purchase plans are also preferenced, but they must be extended to broad groups of employees.) The other way for executives to lower their taxes is through the ownership of property—through the purchase of company stock.

Effective handling of management compensation does not start with tax or accounting questions. It involves the design of programs tailored to the needs and objectives of the firm and its managers. Proper plans reward managers for the jobs they do and for their success in achieving business goals.

14

FRINGE BENEFITS

IN ADDITION TO SALARY, bonus awards, and long-term income, employees receive compensation in the form of fringe benefits. The term refers essentially to all employee income (and hence all company costs incurred directly on behalf of employees) other then direct pay, bonus and long-term income and thus includes:

Insurance benefits
Pay for time not worked
Premium or penalty payments
Legally required payments
Estate-building plans
Employee services
Perquisites

IMPORTANCE OF FRINGE BENEFITS

The term "fringe benefits" is really inadequate to describe the various forms of extra compensation usually extended to employees. Probably, when the term was coined, the amount of these extra payments was so small that they really were fringe items. With the rapid proliferation of benefits and the substantial increase in their costs, they have now become significant. The importance of fringe benefits in terms of overall compensation is illustrated in Figure 30, which shows the breakdown of wage costs for a leading machinery manufacturing company. This company paid 79 percent of its total payroll dollar in the form of wages and salaries and 21 percent in the form of fringe benefits. Of the 79 percent, an estimated 60 percent was base pay; the remaining 19 percent represented extra pay under the firm's incentive compensation plans. Thus employees should recognize that fringe benefits are an important part of their pay, and employers should recognize that they are an important part of the cost of doing business.

Fringe benefits and wage payments complement each other; together they represent employee income and company wage costs. Increases in benefits are not, therefore, supplemental to wage increases; they are granted *in lieu of additional* wage increases. For example, a two-cent improvement in benefits must be regarded not as something granted in addition to, say, a six-cent increase in wages but as an integral part of an eight-cent increase.

There is every indication that companies will continue to emphasize improved fringe benefits as well as additional wage increases in the future. Some of the reasons for this are as follows:

1. *The employer's desire to meet, at least in part, the major economic risks faced by employees.* The principal means of protection offered by the employer are provision for retirement income, insurance against sickness or injury, and some guarantee against loss of income because of layoffs or illness.

2. *The fact that employers can provide for protection against these risks with greater certainty than individual employees.* It would be

Figure 30. **Fringe benefits in the wage dollar.**

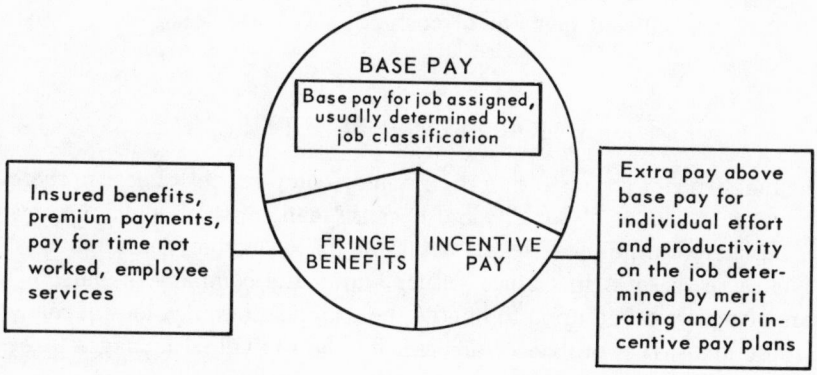

Table 13. **Cost of fringe benefits.**

Benefit Form	*Percentage of Payroll*
Legally required payments	6.3
Pensions, insurance, and other agreed-upon employer payments	10.0
Paid rest periods and similar fringe benefits	3.4
Pay for time not worked	9.2
Other items	1.9
Total	30.8

difficult, if not impossible, for employees—particularly those in lower income brackets—to provide their own protection against all major economic risks. Even those who could do so would not be inclined to invest so heavily in security.

3. *The greater economy with which employers can provide for protection against these risks.* Both the economics of group protection and the provisions of existing tax laws make it much less costly for an employee to obtain protection through his employer than through an individual plan.

4. *The quest for greater leisure.* Employees seek to obtain the benefits of greater productivity in the form of more leisure as well as higher living standards. This is particularly true when living standards continually improve. The quest for more leisure manifests itself in the demand for shorter work hours, longer vacations, more rest periods, more holidays, and earlier retirement.

The cumulative effect of these benefits on a typical company payroll is shown in Table 13. The data are based on the cost of benefits as reported in a U.S. Chamber of Commerce study. Note that each item is a significant element of cost.

MAJOR FRINGE BENEFITS

Fringe benefit administration is extremely complex, both because there are so many kinds of benefits and because many of the benefits involve complicated insurance, legal, actuarial, or economic considerations. For these reasons, specialists—either within the company or outside—are generally called upon to handle the technical ramifications of many fringe items. It is probably sufficient for the individual manager to be familiar with each item in the benefits program and to understand the direct responsibilities he has in administering it. The following checklist identifies the major fringe benefits and their principal provisions.

CHECKLIST OF FRINGE BENEFITS

INSURED BENEFITS: Benefits financed and administered on a group basis and geared to meeting major employee economic risks.

1. PENSION PLANS—formal plans which provide income for the worker after he retires. Key provisions generally include:

   Eligibility. Eligibility may be based on a minimum period of service or may be geared to broad occupational groups.

   Benefit formula. Plans generally aim at giving the retired worker one-third to one-half of his final earnings. Payment may be made in a flat amount, either including or excluding social security benefits. Generally, the amount of payment is geared to years of service or to both age and service. Frequently, a minimum benefit for those who meet the minimum eligibility requirements is prescribed.

   Vesting. Pension benefits typically vest with the employee between ages 40 and 45 with ten to fifteen years of service. Many plans vest at ten years of service without any age requirement. The vested amounts are usually payable to the employee at normal retirement age even if he leaves the company prior to that age.

   Retirement requirements. Generally, plans call for retirement at age 62 to 65, with at least five to ten years of service, but they may permit retirement as early as age 55 at reduced benefits, or postponed retirement up to age 70 with no additional benefits.

   Death provision. Frequently, benefits are provided to survivors in the event that the employee dies before retirement.

   Financing. Typically, employees do not contribute to the cost of the plan, but in some cases they do. Plans may be financed through a bank or insurance company, or they can be administered on a pay-as-you-go basis.

2. HOSPITALIZATION BENEFITS—insurance which provides for various hospital and related expenses. Key provisions include:

   Eligibility. Coverage for employees and dependents usually begins at employment or within one month after.

   Daily hospital payments. Plans include full or partial payment of all charges for hospital room and board for a specified number of days.

   Extra charges. Prescribed payments are made for drugs, X-rays, and so forth.

Dependency coverage. The employee's family is usually covered.

Financing. In most plans the employer pays the employee's premium cost and the employee pays all or part of the cost of coverage for his dependents.

3. SURGICAL BENEFITS—prescribed payments, frequently connected with hospitalization benefits, providing coverage for various types of operations or surgical treatment. Many plans now pay "reasonable and customary" allowances. As in the case of hospitalization plans, coverage begins at employment or within one month's service; dependents are usually covered, and the employee pays part or all of the cost of their coverage.

4. MAJOR MEDICAL BENEFITS—benefits in addition to those provided under basic hospitalization and surgical plans. Key features include:

   Eligibility. Some plans are restricted to certain groups of employees. Typically, employees become eligible within one month of service.

   Corridor provisions. Frequently, an employee must pay $100 in charges over and above other allowances such as hospitalization and surgical benefits before receiving benefits from the major medical plan.

   Percentage payments. Plans usually pay 80 percent of charges over the deductible amount.

   Maximum payments. Most plans specify maximum payments of $20,000 to $25,000 per lifetime per illness, with a trend toward even higher maximums.

   Dependency coverage. Dependents are generally covered.

   Financing. The employer typically pays for the employee's coverage and the employee pays part or all of the cost for his dependents.

5. LIFE INSURANCE—regular or special group life insurance. Key provisions include:

   Eligibility. Usually, one month or less service is required.

   Benefit schedule. Benefits are frequently geared to the annual earnings of the employee.

   Accidental death and dismemberment. Usually, the full face amount of the policy is payable upon accidental death; varying amounts are paid, based on a schedule, for dismemberment.

   Disability provision. Coverage is typically continued until age 65 if the employee becomes disabled before age 60.

   Retirement provision. At retirement, coverage is usually continued in a reduced amount.

   Supplemental benefits. Frequently, supplemental life insurance coverage is available to the employee at his own cost, but at a group rate.

Financing. The employer typically pays the entire cost for basic life insurance coverage.

6. TEMPORARY DISABILITY INSURANCE—insurance benefits paid directly to the employee to offset loss of income due to sickness or accidents. Key provisions include:

   Benefits schedule. As in the case of life insurance, benefits are typically geared to the earnings of the employee.

   Duration of benefits. Usually, benefits last up to 26 weeks.

   Waiting period. There is frequently a waiting period of a week before an employee is eligible to collect benefits for sickness; there is no waiting period in the case of an accident.

   Financing. Typically, the employer pays the cost of coverage.

7. LONG-TERM DISABILITY PLANS—insurance benefits paid for prolonged disability. Key provisions include:

   Benefits schedule. Benefits are typically based on base earnings up to a specified maximum and are reduced by benefits under social security or employer-paid plans.

   Waiting period. Usually, there is a six-month waiting period before benefits begin.

   Maximum benefit period. Typically, benefits continue until recovery or age 65.

8. TRAVEL ACCIDENT INSURANCE—life insurance covering the employee 24 hours a day during business trips. Key provisions include:

   Benefits schedule. Benefits are usually a multiple of salary with stated minimums and maximums. The principal sum is paid at death; varying amounts are paid, based on a schedule, for dismemberment.

   Financing. The employer usually pays the cost of coverage.

PAYMENT FOR TIME NOT WORKED: Various provisions which call for full pay to employees during periods when they are not working.

1. SICK LEAVE—continuation of pay to employees who are absent from work owing to illness. Key provisions include:

   Benefits schedule. Some plans grant full pay. Others pay the difference between full pay and the benefits received from sickness and accident insurance.

   Duration of benefits. Benefits may be limited to one week per year of service or they may continue for an indefinite period, particularly for high-rated executives.

2. VACATIONS—key provisions include:

   Eligibility. Plans specify the length of service required for vacations of one, two, three, four or more weeks.

   Vacation pay. Some programs call for payment of regular base earnings during vacations; others call for payment of average earnings.

   Pay for time worked during vacation. Plans frequently provide for an alternate vacation period, extra straight time, or time and one-half for an employee who works at company request during the regular vacation period.

   Earned right. Many programs provide for accrued vacation pay if an employee leaves.

3. HOLIDAYS—key provisions include:

   Number of paid holidays. This varies a great deal, generally from a minimum of five to as many as thirteen.

   Provision for holidays which fall on a Saturday or Sunday. Frequently, employees are given the following Monday off when a holiday falls on a Sunday and the preceding Friday off when a holiday falls on a Saturday.

   Premium pay for work on regular holiday. Most companies provide some premium payment to the employee who works on a holiday; amounts range from half-time to time and one-half in addition to the regular day's pay.

4. REST PERIODS—formal breaks at specified times during the day or informal time off for personal reasons.

5. SEVERANCE PAY—provisions for payments to employees who are laid off. The amount of the benefit, when specified, is often geared to length of service.

6. SUPPLEMENTAL UNEMPLOYMENT PLANS (also called guaranteed annual wage plans)—partial income payments to employees who are laid off because of lack of work. Frequently, these plans are integrated with the employee's unemployment compensation. Key provisions include:

   Eligibility. Often employees with extremely short service are excluded.

   Duration of benefits. This refers to the number of weeks during a layoff that an employee receives the benefits.

   Financial arrangements. Employers are usually limited in their liability by the amount of money which they have set aside for this purpose.

7. OTHER PAYMENTS—payments for state or national guard duty; jury duty pay (or makeup pay); witness and voting pay allowances; payments for time lost because of death in the family or other personal reasons; paid lunch periods; and paid wash-up, travel, and clothes-change time.

PREMIUM PAYMENTS: Payments, over and above base compensation and premium pay for work on holidays or vacations, which are allowed an employee primarily to make up for undesirable working conditions or for extended periods of work.

1. OVERTIME—premium payments to an employee for work in excess of a prescribed number of hours per week. According to law, an employer must pay covered employees time and one-half for all work in excess of 40 hours per week. In some cases double time is paid for excessive overtime, such as periods of work in excess of 50 hours per week. In addition to the usual provision for payment of overtime, a more generous plan calls for the payment of overtime beyond eight hours per day, or for work on Saturdays and Sundays, regardless of the number of hours which have been worked during the week.

2. SHIFT DIFFERENTIALS—premium payments for each hour of work on night shifts, on either a cents-per-hour or a percentage basis.

3. HAZARD PAY—special extra compensation during periods when the employee is exposed to unusually hazardous conditions.

LEGALLY REQUIRED PAYMENTS: Payments financed in whole or in part by the employer, legally required by a state or federal government, and administered by government agencies.

1. SOCIAL SECURITY—retirement benefits provided to employees at age 65 (reduced benefits at age 62), plus some death benefits and disability provisions. Provisions now cover medical care for the elderly as well.

2. WORKMEN'S COMPENSATION—lump-sum permanent partial disability payments, payments for loss of earnings, and payment of medical expenses or survivor benefits for employees injured or killed on the job. Compensation programs are required by state law.

3. UNEMPLOYMENT COMPENSATION—payments by state agencies to employees during periods of unemployment. The amount and duration of the benefits vary considerably among the states.

ESTATE-BUILDING PLANS: Plans which provide the employee with earnings in addition to regular base pay and premium compensation.

1. PROFIT-SHARING PLANS—plans which call for distribution of part of the company's profits to employees at periodic intervals according to a prescribed formula.

2. SAVINGS PLANS—plans under which the employer contributes cash or company stock to the employee's savings account. Usually, the employer's contribution is directly proportional to the amount the employee puts

into the savings plan. However, the employer's contribution may vary based on profit performance of the company.

3. STOCK PURCHASE PLANS—plans which provide an opportunity for employees to purchase company stock, sometimes below market price. Payment for the stock may be required at purchase or may be permitted over a period of time in installments. Advantages to employees include avoidance of odd-lot charges and savings in brokerage fees resulting from large-scale purchases. If certain conditions are met, employee stock purchase plans may qualify for tax advantages under IRS regulations.

EMPLOYEE SERVICES: Various services, privileges, and activities extended to employees.

1. EMPLOYEE ACTIVITIES—employer-subsidized activities for employees, including sports, social events, and company recreation areas. The cost of these activities can be substantial.

2. CAFETERIA—company-subsidized food catering services provided to workers during lunch and rest periods.

3. DISCOUNT PURCHASE—discount privileges extended to employees in purchasing company products.

4. MEDICAL SERVICES—company dispensaries for emergency medical treatment. Some companies pay for X-rays, polio shots, and other medical services.

EMPLOYEE PERQUISITES: Special allowances, reflections of status, or similar benefits provided to employees.

1. MANAGEMENT PERQUISITES—items such as company cars, maintenance of company cars, company car purchase-leaseback arrangements, meal reimbursements, business and vacation travel, club memberships, executive physicals, financial counseling, group liability insurance, special expense arrangements, office size, furniture, titles, and executive dining rooms.

2. GENERAL EMPLOYEE PERQUISITES—items such as titles, flexible work hours, less stringent timekeeping procedures, salaried versus hourly status, rest areas, day-care programs, employee counseling, housing and moving assistance, loans, parking facilities, and service recognition programs.

DESIGNING FRINGE BENEFIT PROGRAMS

Fringe benefit programs should be designed with extreme care. Only in this way can the company be certain of getting adequate return for what have generally become substantial expenditures.

Of primary importance in designing a fringe benefit plan is the need to customize the program to the organization. Benefit plans, like any other element of a compensation package, should be designed to fit the needs of the company and its employees. Specific items to be considered include the nature of the business, basic company compensation policy, and the employee group profile. For example, do the firm's operations require extremely independent employee activity or highly coordinated activity? What is basic company policy in relation to typical industry practice? Does the company aim to equal or exceed typical practice? Is the employee group generally young or old? Should greater emphasis be given to medical coverage or to pensions?

The plan designer should emphasize employee relations, company policies and plans, employee preferences, and similar matters rather than technical and actuarial concerns. Technical studies should be undertaken only after the plan has been designed and should be aimed primarily at getting legal and tax approvals.

It is also important that the plan designer be thoroughly familiar with the overall benefit situation, including typical coverages, current trends in benefits, and new developments that appear imminent. Finally, during the planning stage, the designer should obtain cost estimates in order to compare the relative value of alternative plans and to estimate their impact.

The following procedures are essential in planning benefit programs:

- A model program should be designed and any elements of the program which are to be adopted or revised should be studied in relation to the model.
- The various aspects of coverage should be considered both in the present and over an extended period of time.
- The effectiveness of various types of benefit plans in achieving overall compensation objectives and management objectives should be considered.
- The desirability of taking full advantage of lower costs resulting from centralized coverages should be considered.
- The ability of the company to pay benefit costs at present and in the future should be assessed.
- Overlapping coverages should normally be avoided.
- Priorities should be set for the adoption of specific elements of the program, based on the urgency of needs and the availability of financial resources.
- Special attention should be paid to employee preferences to make

sure that employees consider the program valuable to them. Such an expression of company interest has a worthwhile employee relations byproduct: it indicates to employees that the company considers their judgments important.

ADMINISTERING FRINGE BENEFIT PROGRAMS

The checklist of fringe benefits presented earlier in this chapter, though only an outline, should help the individual manager analyze the benefits in effect at his own company. Beyond this, he must have a good working knowledge of his company's plans in order to meet his responsibility for administering benefits and for explaining them to employees.

Informing Employees About Benefits

A company should expect to receive certain returns as a result of providing an appropriate benefit program to its employees. A good benefit program may not motivate employees toward superior performance, but it should help to attract and retain good employees and to assure a satisfied work force.

The benefit program cannot perform these functions unless employees fully understand and appreciate the benefits provided for them. Without employee understanding, benefit costs become a company expenditure without return. Effective communication of benefits can be accomplished at low cost—generally an estimated 1 percent of the total cost of the benefit program. Since fringe benefits can amount to 25 or even 30 percent of payroll, it certainly seems wise to spend this additional amount to make sure that employees understand and appreciate their coverages.

Information about the program can be communicated in a number of ways. In most companies booklets describing key items, particularly insurance benefits, are prepared and distributed to employees. These should be written with as little technical jargon as possible. Many companies also give their employees annual individual benefits statements (often prepared by a computer) detailing their specific coverages and the costs involved.

Merely putting such information in writing does not, of course, insure that it is communicated to employees. It provides only a written record for those who choose to read. If the company really wants its employees to understand the fringe benefit program, it must take more affirmative steps. Many companies have personnel or insurance specialists explain various aspects of the program to employees in group meetings; others run special announcements about the program in company publications or post them on bulletin boards. Some companies provide periodic briefings for managers so that they can keep their subordinates informed and have "hot line" telephone numbers which employees can call to get answers to benefit questions. Still other companies have a program through which employees can submit written questions to management, with prompt reply guaranteed.

When specific questions are raised, the supervisor must make sure that the employee understands what provisions are in effect and what their value is to him. For instance, the worker who finds himself with a hospital bill suddenly becomes acutely concerned with the hospitalization benefits provided by the employer. It is at this time that the supervisor has the best opportunity to make sure that the employee understands the program. Similar opportunities occur whenever overtime compensation, vacations, holidays, and other fringe benefits affect individual employees in their day-to-day work.

For some questions, particularly those involving more technical matters, the supervisor will have to refer employees to a personnel specialist or to an insurance counselor. But even here the supervisor can play an important role. He can follow up to make sure that counselors are providing clear and thorough explanations to employees.

Regardless of which methods are used, certain principles should guide the communication of the fringe benefit program:

1. Statements should be honest and sincere so that there is no question in an employee's mind concerning the company's interest in his welfare.
2. Methods of communication should be appropriate to the individuals involved.
3. Every effort should be made to maximize the effectiveness of communication by using direct, simple, and concise wording.
4. Any approach should include two-way communication, so that employees' questions and opinions can be heard and responded to.
5. Communications should be carried out on a continuing basis to insure that employees are apprised of new developments or changes.

6. When possible, communication should be designed to reach the families of employees, since their misunderstandings and dissatisfactions affect the employees.

Handling Controversial Issues

In informing employees about benefits, managers frequently encounter grievances over benefits or become involved in controversial questions relating to them. Probably the most important of these issues is how the company's benefits compare with those of other companies in the area or in the industry. Such comparisons are difficult to make under the best of conditions because of the many kinds of benefits which are available and because of the complexity of some of the provisions.

When a comparison is undertaken, it is essential that the manager avoid the tendency to judge the overall program on the basis of one specific provision. Even an outstanding benefit plan will not have the best to offer in every category. Thus the company with the best overall benefit program in the country may have a less liberal hospitalization plan than some other companies. For this reason, it is extremely important that both employees and managers regard benefits as a "package." The format of benefits, and the provisions on which company and employees place the principal emphasis, may merely reflect collective bargaining demands, industry practices, peculiarities in the company's operations, or employee preferences.

Employees do not always realize the cost of fringe benefits. Some benefits, such as rest periods, tend to be viewed as minor items. As a result, when supervisors enforce the limits on rest periods, employees may consider them guilty of pinchpenny tactics. The fact of the matter is that rest periods can be a large cost item. Furthermore, unless official rest periods are enforced, inconsistent treatment of employees will result. Finally, the number and cost of rest periods may easily become excessive, impairing the company's ability to grant other improvements in wages and benefits. For this reason, the manager should have some idea of the cost of each item in the benefit package and should be able to explain it to employees.

Another controversial issue, which is of particular interest to employees, is why they are required to contribute to the cost of some fringe benefits. A good case can be built up for either the contributory or the noncontributory approach to benefit financing. One of the principal arguments in favor of the contributory approach is that, by taking part in the cost of benefits, employees will have a greater appreciation of their value. While this argument may have validity, it certainly makes little impression on employees. A more compelling argument from the employee's point of view is that the company, at any given time, is able to finance just so much in wages and benefits. By contributing to the cost of the benefits, the employee is, in effect, making broader protection possible.

Preventing Abuses

With a few notable exceptions, employee benefits are applied automatically. That is to say, all employees receive fixed benefits according to predetermined provisions.

Thus benefits as pensions, insurance coverage, vacations, and holidays do not present problems of administration to the supervisor. For these items, the program is essentially self-supervised or is administered by some central office of the company or by an insurance carrier. This is not the case, however, with other benefits, which can become extremely costly to the company.

Sick leave, for example, is easily abused to the point where it becomes merely a supplementary paid vacation for employees, whether or not they are sick. Even the most elaborate system of controls cannot administer it effectively; this is one area which is strictly the responsibility of the individual supervisor. Much the same can be said about rest periods; even minor abuses can result in significant costs over a period of time. Again, only the supervisor is in a position to administer rest period provisions and make sure that employees do not abuse their privileges.

Finally, there is the question of overtime. On many occasions, of course, overtime work is required by operations and is economically justified. However, employees frequently look to overtime merely as a means of increasing their total income. In addition, as they become accustomed to working overtime regularly, they come to regard the extra pay as part of their fixed income and begin to count on it. When overtime becomes a regular practice, it is doubtful whether the company is getting the full amount of additional work which should result from the extra hours. Some studies indicate that employees tend to spread out work to require overtime unless supervisors administer the provisions of overtime work with great care.

15

MANAGEMENT RESPONSIBILITY

RESPONSIBILITY FOR WAGE and salary administration should be fixed carefully so that each person who is associated with the program knows exactly what is expected of him. The question is basically one of determining which responsibilities will be retained by higher-level line management, which will be delegated to the individual supervisor, and which will be assigned to staff personnal.

Limitations by Top Management

There can be little quarrel, of course, with the proposition that the individual line manager must retain the basic authority and responsibility for the pay of his subordinates. To the extent that pay actions serve as instruments of reward, incentive, and discipline, the individual manager must be responsible for them if he is to guide the performance of his subordinates. Furthermore, since he is held accountable for costs in his group, he must have responsibility for the very important element of wages.

In actual practice, the individual manager seldom has complete authority and responsibility for compensation administration. His authority must be limited by higher-level managers for several reasons. First, policy formulation must be retained by top management.

Second, management must limit supervisory authority to insure consistency in administering the program among the different sections of the company. Third, limitations are needed to insure conformity with company policies and proper implementation of those policies. Finally, it is unreasonable to expect all line managers to become experts in the field of compensation administration, which encompasses a considerable body of technical knowledge and skill. Therefore, some duties are properly assigned to staff specialists.

Functions of the Line Manager

Line managers have the basic responsibility for making pay decisions within the framework of policies, practices, and techniques established by the company. The quality of their day-to-day decisions is the key to the success of any pay program.

Frequently, line managers also have a role to play in policy formulation. Even when they do not participate in it on a formal basis, they have an obligation to supply information relating to operating needs to staff or higher-level line management. They should be able to provide constructive ideas for improved compensation administration which they perceive from their operating experiences.

Invariably, the individual manager is involved in policy interpretation and application. Policies represent general statements of intent on the part of the company, and they are established primarily to guide the thinking of management throughout the organization. In applying them, line managers are interpreting what these policies mean. Since each interpretation becomes a precedent which will have a bearing on future interpretations, this function of individual supervisors is a part of policy making.

Consequently, each manager should exercise considerable care in applying policy. Although every problem he faces has unique aspects, he should consider the following questions in relation to each situation:

1. What are company policies on this question?
2. Do I know the important facts and circumstances necessary to answer it?
3. How did I handle a similar problem in the past?
4. Should I discuss the question with staff specialists in order to gain a better understanding of company policy, to benefit from their broader experience, or to see how similar questions have been handled in other sections of the company?
5. Should I consult my immediate supervisor before making a decision?

6. Is the union involved? If so, should I discuss the matter with the union steward or the labor relations staff?
7. Should I tell my other subordinates about the decision?
8. How am I going to explain my decision to the employee or employees who raised the question in the first place?

Ideally, part of the supervisor's job is to gain employee acceptance of the company compensation program. The supervisor is not likely to gain that acceptance unless employees understand company pay policies and practices. Clearly, the basic responsibility for explaining policy rests with him, since he is the one who must deal with the various daily questions and problems that arise. It goes without saying that he cannot explain the program to employees unless he understands it himself.

Functions of the Staff

Staff specialists also have certain areas of responsibility in carrying out the compensation program. While the individual line manager may not be directly concerned with these areas, it is important that he have some knowledge of the staff's role in order to understand his own responsibilities, including what is and what is not expected of him.

Research in compensation administration is a basic staff function. It generally includes such assignments as compensation surveys, preparation of reports, administration of company controls, investigation of programs and techniques used by other companies, analysis of internal wage facts, and development of the data that managers need in order to make logical pay decisions.

This research function is the basis for many other staff responsibilities. Because of the specialized knowledge obtained through research, staff can play a significant role in such areas as recommending salary policies and programs; assisting line managers at all levels in interpreting and applying the programs, and counseling line managers on the various pay problems which may arise.

In some cases staff specialists are also responsible for the design or development of new plans. When the technology of a plan is highly specialized, unusually difficult, or sensitive, companies usually use outside consultants for a large part of the work. In essence, companies are increasingly faced with "make or buy" decisions when it comes to plan design and development. They must evaluate both the capability and relative costs of insiders versus outsiders.

In addition a number of duties are frequently assigned to staff personnel in order to gain efficiency. These are services performed by the staff. A good example is the preparation of job descriptions. Although line supervisors can and often do carry out this function, many companies assign the task to staff analysts in order to speed the process and economize the limited time available to managers.

A final function of the staff lies in the area of control. Top management must establish some means of auditing and controlling the wage and salary actions of managers throughout the company. Staff members are frequently used to provide this control because of their know-how, their participation in policy formulation, and their broad company views.

Auditing the performance of management can, of course, be a highly unpopular undertaking. When the same group which is supposed to advise and constructively influence line supervisors also plays a role in auditing, a delicate situation is created which requires considerable tact and understanding on the part of all concerned. What everyone must realize is that staff is not controlling but merely performing administrative chores so that higher-level management can effectively control the program.

INDEX

accounting, classification systems and, 40
accumulating information and sales, 140
administrative personnel, 174–189
  executive secretaries, 188
  management trainees, 188
  premium payments, 187
  senior clerks, 189
administrative procedures and practices, salary, 24
advertising, as sales support, 154
American Management Associations' Executive Compensation Service, 143
American Telephone and Telegraph Co., 19
annual pay increases, 4
antidiscrimination laws, 121
appraisal systems, supervisory, 99, 100
appraising performance, 86–107
  increasing the effectiveness of, 92
  objectives of, 97
  pay decisions and, 104
  techniques of, 98
automatic pay increases, 78
automotive parts sales, average and total compensation, 145

band position, definition of, 75
base pay versus incentive, 142
base salary, 18
  for salesmen, 144
benchmark jobs, 44, 45, 177
  competing companies and, 109
  professionals and, 169
benefits, 14, 15, 16
  fringe, 24, 212–225
  model program and, 221–222
Black and Decker Inc., 19
bonus plans, 14, 15, 16, 172, 183
  factory workers and, 21
  salary planning worksheets and, 111
  salesmen and, 21, 147, 149

budgetary controls on salary, 112
budgets
  allocated, 75
  merit, 112
  payroll, 112
building materials sales, average and total compensation, 145

cafeterias, 220
career curves, 123
career development for professionals, 171–172
career patterns and compensation (ch.), 123
cars, company, 20, 220
chemicals sales, average and total compensation, 145
classification system, 39–40
collective bargaining, 7, 118, 119
  supervisors and, 120
"combination job," duties of, 48
commission bases, adjustment of, 154
commission sales, 147–148
communication of pay information, 3
  see also pay structure
communications
  about incentive plans, 133–134
  benefits to employees, 222–224
  job descriptions, 33
  job information, 27
  pay information, 12, 24, 125
  salesman compensation plans, 153–154
company environment, 18
  prestige, 19
compensation, elements of, 13–25
  different employee groups and, 21–24
  financial, 14–18, 21
  nonfinancial, 18–21
compensation, forms of (ch.), 16, 17
compensation, planned, for salesmen, 147–149
compensation administration, 1–12
  employee aspirations and, 10
  line manager and, 13
  managers and, 1, 2
  measurement of, 4
  planning and executing, 10
competitive pay levels, determining, 56
computer sales, average and total compensation, 145
computers, 22
consumer-durable goods sales, average and total compensation, 145
container sales, average and total compensation, 145
corporate responsibility, environment and, 121
cost-of-living increases, 11, 60
cost-of-living trends, 113
cross-evaluation systems, 43

day-care programs, 220
deferred-income plans, 209–210
demotions, 82
design goal of pay plans, 7, 8, 9
disability plans, 217
discount purchases, 220
discretionary awards, 201
disincentives and merit increases, 77
downgrading, 49, 82
duties, reorganization of, 111

economic increases, 77
economic worth, 37
education, reimbursements for, 20
electrical equipment sales, average and total compensation, 145
electronics sales, average and total compensation, 145
employee(s)
  activities, 220
  groups, listing of, 22
  groups, pay levels of, 23
  low-paid, 17
  morale, 3–4

pay structure and, 64
perquisites, 220
relations, fringe benefits and, 221
sales, 23
employment process, factors in, 80
estate-building plans, 14, 16, 17, 24, 210, 219
estate-counseling services, 17
ethical pharmaceuticals sales, average and total compensation, 145
evaluation methods, traditional, 163–164
evaluation plans, modified, 195–196
evaluation process, manager's role in, 51–52
evaluation systems, point, 40–41
executives
fringe benefits and, 213
high-paid, 17
taxes and, 211
exit interviews, 9
expense arrangements, 220

fabrics sales, average and total compensation, 145
factor comparison, 39, 41, 42
factory workers, bonus plans for, 21
Fair Labor Standards Act, 1, 21, 187
food sales, average and total compensation, 145
formal wage and salary program, need for, 6
fringe benefits, 212–225
abuses of, 225
cost of (ch.), 214, 224
executives and, 213
importance of, 212
types of, 215–220
fringe benefit programs, designing, 220
administering, 222, 227

General Electric Co., 19
glass sales, average and total compensation, 145
glossary of business terms, 32
goal-setting programs, 101–104
gold-circle situations, 84
government contractors, rates of pay for, 121
government regulations and salary controls, 120, 121
green-circle situations, 84
group incentive systems, 130
guidelines, preset, and pay plans, 8

Halsey gain-share plan, 129
heavy machinery sales, average and total compensation, 145
high school graduates, average annual salary of, 124
hiring, rates of pay, 79
history of employees, pay, 109
holidays, 218, 225
hospitalization benefits, 215
human resources, use of, 115
human resources information system, 104

incentive awards, 202
incentive compensation, trends in, 150
incentive plans
economics of, 137
elements of, 131
installing, 133–135
logic of, 127
long term, 207
types of, 129
incentive versus base pay, 142
income
comparison, 3
financial elements of, 14
long-term, 15–16
nonfinancial elements of, 18, 20
nontaxable, 18, 20
tax-sheltered, 16
increases, pay actions and
general, 67–68
merit, 68–69, 71–76
performance, 76–79

increases, pay action and (Cont.)
promotional, 80–81
within range, 69–71
increases within range, 69–71
automatic approach, 69–70
informal approach, 70–71
merit pay approach, 71
single-rate system, 69
step rates, 69
industrial engineering, classification system and, 40
inequity increases, 83
informal pay increases, 78
instrument sales, average and total compensation, 145
insurance benefits, 15, 16, 215, 216, 217, 225
insurance sales, average and total compensation, 145
Internal Revenue Service and compensation, 211
inventions, compensation for, 173
investment works classification systems and, 40
iron and steel sales, average and total compensation, 145

job(s)
definition of, 28
grouping of, 22
objectives of, 27
requirements, minimum, 48
job analysis, 29
defined, 28
techniques and tools of, 30
job descriptions, 31, 193
format of, 31
former, and job analysis, 30
higher management, 31
management tool, 35
operations level, 31
time and cost of preparing, 33
job evaluation, 24, 37, 41, 46
formula (ch.), 37
grouping and grading, 45
methods of (ch.), 38
ranking system and, 38
job evaluation for professionals
benchmarks, 169
market position classification, 167
salary structures, 168–169
job evaluation plan
judging accuracy of, 49
problems of design in, 47–49
job information, 24, 26, 34
as a basis for appraising employees, 27
communicating job duties, 27
staffing and, 27
job pricing, 24, 66
pay actions and, 66

key jobs, pricing job value and, 57

labor, direct and indirect, 21
labor leaders, salary program and, 119
labor markets, 6, 57
merit increases, 107
pay relationships, 63
law, classification systems and, 40
laws, federal, wage and salary practices and, 120
lawyers, as salesmen, 137
layoffs, 98
legally required payments, 219
life insurance, 216
light machinery sales, average and total compensation, 145
line managers, 7, 9, 13
fringe benefits and, 227
line supervisors
automatic pay increases and, 69
job evaluation and, 51
long-term income, 14, 15, 16, 203

major medical benefits, 216
management
decisions and sales, 140
employees, 22, 23
lowered productivity and, 4

merit increases and, 73
pay problems and, 8–10
perquisites, 220
positions, classifying, 197–198
review systems, 101
"management by objectives" program (MBO), 27, 101
management compensation, 190–211
bonuses, 201–202, 203–204
combination plans, 205, 208
entrepreneurial plans, 205, 208
estate-building plans, 210
fringe benefits, 210
incentive systems, 202, 205, 207–208
position descriptions, 194–195
special plans for, 209–210
traditional stock plans, 205–207
vs. non-management, 193
management decision making, perquisites and, 20–21
management groups
bonus plans for, 201, 203
classifying positions of, 195
definition of, 190–192
salary administration for, 192, 199
management responsibility, 226–229
line manager and, 227
proper work methods and, 135
staff specialists and, 228
top management and, 226
management salary structures, 198–201
increase practices and, 199–201
sources of data and, 198
technical considerations and, 199
management style, work environment and, 19–20
manager, individual, and job analysis, 30
managerial status, average pay rate of, 124
Manhattan Project, 19
manpower control, 98
manpower utilization, 34
manuals, organization, 30
market
approach, 7
area comparisons, 107
characteristics, and sales, 141
evaluation systems, 43, 44
knowledge and sales jobs, 140
survey, 56
worth, 37
meals, subsidies for, 20
measurement, problems of, 48–50
medical services, 220
merit increase(s), 11, 73, 77
allocated budgets and, 75
frequency of, 72, 73
guide for, 76
maximum limitations on, 74
program, 77
merit pay approach, 61, 71, 86
amount of increases, 73
frequency of review, 72
merit rating
budget, 107
purpose of, 97
setting standards for, 94
merit rating plan
appraising performance and, 95
authority of managers and, 96
merit rating techniques, 86–92
checklists, 89, 91
critical-incident method, 92
direct appraisal, 92
graphic rating scales, 89, 90
grouping and ranking, 91
performance factor, 87
problems of, 94–97
merit review, frequency of, 72
metal products-heavy, sales, average and total compensation, 145
middle-level employees, 175
merit increases and, 73
within-grade spread and, 62
minimum wages, 121
minority groups, 121
morale, employee, 3
mutual funds, leveraged, 17

National Labor Relations Act, 118
needs
  attainable objectives and, 10
  identifying company, 9
nontaxable income, 18

observation, direct, and job analysis, 30
office supplies, sales, average and total compensation, 145
operating considerations, merit increases and, 107
operations workers, 21, 22
opinion surveys, 9
opportunity situations, 6
organizational analysis, 27
organizational development, 5
overtime, 21, 120, 219, 225

paper sales, average and total compensation, 145
patent recognition, 173
pay
  adjustments, general, 66–68
  grades, establishment of, 45
  increases, automatic approach, 69–70
  levels, competitive, 3, 56
  programs, 4
  progress, 11, 81
  range, 18
pay actions
  adjustments in, 66–67
  gold-circle situations, 84
  green-circle situations, 84
  hiring rates of pay, 79–80
  increases, general, and, 67–68
  individual, 66–85
  job pricing and, 66
  merit program and, 68–69, 71–76
  performance pay increases, 76–79
  promotional increases, 80–81
  red-circle situations, 83
  silver-circle situations, 85
  within range increases, 69–71
pay administration
  informal approach to, 70, 71
  social pressures and, 121
pay comparisons, employee's criteria for, 11
pay decisions for professionals, 169
pay grade, *see* pay structure
pay problems, 2–12
  management and, 8
pay ranges, maximum, 62–64, 170
pay stabilization, 121
pay structure
  explaining to employees, 64
  pricing the, 54–56, 59–61
  traditional, 61
  see also pay actions
pay surveys, accuracy of, 59
pension plans, 215
performance appraisal
  elements of, 97
  objectives of, 97
performance appraisal techniques
  goal-setting programs, 100–104
  management review, 100
  ratings, 104
  supervisory systems and, 99
performance increase, 76, 77, 78
performance standards, 27, 34
perquisites, 18
  employer, 220
  types of, 20–21
personality traits, rating employees by, 28
personnel
  classification systems and, 40
  decisions, 28
  specialists, 9, 118
  technical, 23
piecework plan, 129
point evaluation system, 40, 41
Polaroid Corp., 19
postal service, classification system and, 40
premium payments, 219
pricing
  high-talent employees, 63

job, 53–66
middle-level positions, 62
pay grades and, 53, 54
pay levels, 64–65
steps in, 53–55
techniques of, 56–59
printing and publishing sales, average and total compensation, 145
procedure studies, 30
productivity, 3, 4
professional employees, lowered productivity and, 4
professional jobs, classification system and, 40
professional organizations, 173
professional personnel, 155–173
career development of, 171
generic descriptions for, 162
incentive pay plans for, 172
job evaluation for, 163
pay progress of, 157
salary administration for, 161, 169
profit-sharing awards, 201
profit-sharing plans, 219
programs, compensation, 10, 101–104
promotional increases, 11, 80
promotions, 63, 98
proprietary drug sales, average and total compensation, 145
Prudential Insurance Co., 19

questionnaire, job, 30
quotas, adjustment of, 154
quota systems for salesmen, 147–148

ranking system, 38
factor-guided technique, 39
paired-comparison (ch.), 39
rates of pay, hiring, 79
ratings
increasing effectiveness of, 92
performance, 104
rating system, *see* classification system
rating techniques, merit, 86–92
recognition, salary planning worksheets and, 111
records, maintenance of, 3
recreational facilities, 20
red-circle situations, 83
reevaluation, 83
relocation problems, salesmen and, 147
remuneration, 14
nonfinancial elements of, 18, 21
total, 17
research, compensation for, 173
research and development laboratories, 159
rest periods, 218
review of performance, 97

salary, 14, 16
levels, minimum, 61
meaning of to employees, 2
programs, union attitudes and, 119
structure, typical (ch.), 62
salary administration programs
functions of, 115
salesmen and, 141
updating of, 124
salary controls, 111, 122
budgetary, 112
outside forces and, 118, 120, 121
personnel audits and, 115
salary planning, 108–111
employees and, 125
techniques of, 109
salary survey, 59
chart, 58
sales by lines, 154
sales districts, allocation of, 141
sales employees, 22
sales incentive program, 151
sales job, described, 139
sales "missionary" work, 140
sales personnel, assignment of, 141
sales supervisors, 154, 155
salesmen
financial risk and, 141

salesmen (Cont.)
functions of, 140
job evaluation of, 146
market evaluation systems and, 44
non-sales work and, 140
salesmen's compensation, 139–154
annual range by industry (ch.), 145
automobiles, 147
base pay vs. incentive pay, 142–144
elements of, 141–142
expense accounts, 147
geographic dispersion and, 142, 147
incentive, 141, 147–150, 151–153
income levels, establishing, 152
levels of, 144
merit pay administration, 146
range by industry (ch.), 145
straight salary and, 147, 148
savings plans, 219
secretarial positions, 49
semiskilled tasks, 22
services sales, average and total compensation, 145
severance pay, 218
shift differentials, 219
shop efficiency, and proper work methods, 135
sick leave, 217, 225
silver-circle situations, 85
skill, highest level of, 48
social pressures, 121
social responsibilities, 16
social security, 219
social worth, 37
soliciting orders, 140
special compensation, 173
specifications, job, 31
staff specialists, job evaluation and, 51
standard hour plan, 129
step rates, 69
stock options, 21
stock purchase plans, 17, 205–207, 220
supervisors, appraisal process and, 99
supervisory personnel, 22, 23, 174, 177
bonus payments for, 183
collective bargaining and, 120
job descriptions of, 178
overtime for, 182
pay increase practices for, 181
surgical benefits, 216
systems of job evaluation, combination, 42

Tax Reform Act of 1969, 205
tax-sheltered, income, 16
Taylor differential piece-rate plan, 129
technical personnel, 22, 174–189
description of, 185, 186
Fair Labor Standards Act and, 187
overtime for, 187
role of, 187
termination, salary planning worksheets and, 111
thrift plans and estate-building, 17
time-study reports, 30
tools and hardware sales, average and total compensation, 145
training needs, determination of, 97
training sessions, 20
transfers, salary planning worksheets and, 111
travel expenses, 20
turnover, pay problems and, 3

unemployment compensation, 218, 219
union attitudes and salary, 119
union leaders, 119
union participation, salary program and, 24
unionized employees, 7

unskilled employees, 22
upgrading, 49, 82

vacations, 218, 225
value-cost concept, 5

wage and salary administration, 24
  cost of, 126
wage and salary controls and government regulations, 120, 121
wage and salary program, formalized, 6–8, 24
  collective bargaining and, 7
  individual bargaining and, 7
  labor leaders and, 119
wage costs, 1, 2
wage incentive plans, 127–138
  characteristics of, 127
  economics of, 137–138
  factory workers and, 127
  fears of employees and, 134
  Halsey gain-share plan and, 129
  installation of, 133
  logic of, 127–128
  manager's role in, 136
  Taylor differential piece-rate plan and, 129
  work standards and, 130, 132
wages, 14
Walsh-Healy Act, 121
within-grade spread, *see* pay structure
women, social pressures and, 121
work environment, 19, 121
work goals, perquisites and, 20–21
work hours, flexible, 220
work sample descriptions, 163
work standards, determining, 130
workmen's compensation, 219
worksheets, salary-planning, 109
  chart, 110
writing skill and job descriptions, 31

Xerox Corp., 19

DATE DUE